Political Parties in the Pacific Islands

Political Parties in the Pacific Islands

EDITED BY ROLAND RICH

with Luke Hambly and Michael G. Morgan

THE AUSTRALIAN NATIONAL UNIVERSITY

E PRESS

ANU

E PRESS

Published by ANU E Press
The Australian National University
Canberra ACT 0200, Australia
Email: anuepress@anu.edu.au
Web: http://epress.anu.edu.au

Previously published by Pandanus Books, Research School of Pacific and Asian Studies

---

Title:	Political parties in the Pacific Islands [electronic resource] / editors, Roland Rich, Luke Hambly, Michael G. Morgan.
ISBN:	9781921313769 (pdf) 9781921313752 (pbk)
Notes:	Includes index. Bibliography.
Subjects:	Political parties--Pacific Area. Pacific Area--Politics and government.

Other Authors/Contributors:
 Rich, Roland.
 Hambly, Luke.
 Morgan, Michael G.

Dewey Number: 324.291823

Cover design by Emily Brissenden, Photography by Bob Cooper

CONTENTS

Figures

Tables

LIST OF CONTRIBUTORS

Alaine Chanter
Division of Communication and Education
University of Canberra

Alumita Durutalo
Pacific and Asian History Division
Research School of Pacific and Asian Studies
The Australian National University

Jon Fraenkel
Pacific Institute of Advanced Studies in Development and Governance
University of the South Pacific

Tarcisius Tara Kabutaulaka
Pacific Islands Development Program
East-West Center, Honolulu, Hawai'i

R. J. May
State, Society and Governance in Melanesia Project
Research School of Pacific and Asian Studies
The Australian National University

Michael G. Morgan
Centre for Democratic Institutions
Research School of Pacific and Asian Studies
The Australian National University

Steven Ratuva
Pacific Institute of Advanced Studies in Development and Governance
University of the South Pacific

Roland Rich
Reagan-Fascell Democracy Fellow
International Forum for Democratic Studies
National Endowment for Democracy, Washington, DC
formerly: Foundation Director
Centre for Democratic Institutions
The Australian National University

Joao M. Saldanha
Timor Institute of Development Studies

Asofou So'o
National University of Sämoa

PREFACE AND ACKNOWLEDGMENTS

ON MARCH 8, 2004, the Consultative Council that advises the Centre for Democratic Institutions (CDI) on the direction of its work met in Parliament House, Canberra. There were some new faces around the table recently appointed by Cabinet. Among them were four senior officials from Australia's major political parties: Brian Loughnane, Federal Director of the Liberal Party of Australia; Andrew Hall, Federal Director of the National Party of Australia; Geoff Walsh, Federal Director of the Australian Labor Party; and Gary Gray, his predecessor. They made their view clear — CDI needed to focus on strengthening political parties in our region of the world. The Australian parliamentarians on the council, the Hon. Chris Gallus, chair of the council, Dr Andrew Southcott and Kevin Rudd, agreed, as did Sir Ninian Stephen, former Governor-General of Australia, Andy Becker, the Australian Electoral Commissioner, and Professor Ian McAllister of The Australian National University (ANU). A consensus had formed and the ball was now in my court.

CDI is Australia's democracy promotion institute funded by the Australian Agency for International Development (AusAID). As part of the Research School of Social Sciences of the ANU, CDI assists the countries in Australia's immediate region to strengthen their key democratic bodies. In its first six years, CDI focused mainly on parliaments and judiciaries. Now a difficult new subject had been placed on our agenda. It seemed to me the first step we needed to take was to gain a better understanding of political parties in the Pacific Islands.

One of the great advantages of being located in the Coombs Building at the ANU is that CDI sits at the crossroads of the leading researchers in the fields of Asia-Pacific studies and political science. So the task boiled down to identifying the leading thinkers in the field, getting them excited about participation in a new research venture, commissioning their chapters and finally putting the book together. Sounds simple ...

My first vote of gratitude must go to the authors: Alaine Chanter of the University of Canberra, Asofou So'o of the National University of Samoa, Jon Fraenkel and Steven Ratuva of the University of the South Pacific in Suva, Tarcisius Kabutaulaka of the East-West Center in Hawai'i, Joao Saldanha of the Timor-Leste Study Group in Dili, and Alumita Durutalo, Ron May and Michael Morgan of the ANU. They stuck to their task diligently, kept to their word limits graciously and eventually met their deadlines grudgingly. I hope they will forgive any intrusiveness on my part.

Several other people played key roles in seeing this publication come to light. Francesca Beddie was of enormous assistance in the editing process. She passed the baton to my colleagues at CDI, Luke Hambly and Michael Morgan, who then ran it to the finish line. As always, our other colleague at CDI, Sally Thompson, provided essential support.

All books must leave their authors' hands and begin a peripatetic new life. But this book will nevertheless remain close to CDI as it will now inform the work we do to strengthen the political parties we have researched and help them play the critical role required of them in the operation of their nations' democracies.

Roland Rich
Canberra
March 2005

ANALYSING AND CATEGORISING POLITICAL PARTIES IN THE PACIFIC ISLANDS

Roland Rich

ACCORDING TO DIAMOND, 'political parties remain an indispensable institutional framework for representation and governance in a democracy.'[1] If so, many Pacific Island nations labour under a political disadvantage in the construction of their democracies because local political parties are generally weak and ineffective.[2] They tend to have little by way of policy platforms and therefore do not discharge the roles of aggregating interests, deliberating on policy or mediating between the policy interests of various social groups. Most political parties in the South-West Pacific lack systematic grassroots organisation and so cannot be expected to be active in civic education or consensus-building. In Melanesia, most political parties are organised around one or more powerful political leaders, with the consequence that personality tends to override policy importance in the decisions of parties. Even the task of getting the vote out on election day is usually delegated to the candidate who must draw on extended kinship or patronage networks for scrutineers, drivers and general cajolers, not to mention ballot-stuffers, intimidators and enforcers. Political parties are therefore a particularly tenuous link in the chain holding together democratic governance in this region.

Comparisons, classifications and coherence

Given that the bulk of our analysis in this collection is fixed squarely on addressing the implications of the lack of established party systems across the Pacific, this chapter seeks to illuminate the underlying assumptions and suppositions behind the importance of coherent and effective parties to overall democratic functioning.

The problem of Pacific Island political parties needs attention and the purpose of this chapter is to help provide the tools for analysis by looking for common themes, hazarding some comparisons with other regions and attempting to apply general taxonomies. In doing so, there is an immediate problem. Even putting to one side half the polities in the Pacific Islands that do not have political parties, as well as several other nations so small that personalisation dominates systematisation,[3] the seven political systems covered in this volume nevertheless are as noteworthy for their differences as for their similarities. The convenience of lumping them together under the heading 'South Pacific' or 'Pacific Islands' should be seen as simply that, a convenient category, not one that necessarily implies wide commonality.

If the colonial model is accepted as broadly influential in the development of systems of governance in post-colonial contexts, then the fact that the seven polities covered in this volume have had at least five and possibly up to seven colonial influences[4] emphasises the reality of distinctiveness. Apart from variations flowing from colonial history, each of the subjects has a unique mix of constitutional and legal regimes, as well as institutional designs and electoral systems, influencing the formal environment in which political parties must operate.

The particular political cultures of the countries under examination in this collection are equally relevant determinants of difference. Arguably, the differences in political styles, behaviour and expectations between highland, coastal, island and urban areas of Papua New Guinea may be greater than differences that exist within any Western nation that has been politically 'homogenised' by civil war, state conquest, industrial revolution or, more recently, national political parties delivering national messages through nationally available media. Among the nations of the Pacific Islands, these differences are further magnified because of linguistic, ethnographic and environmental variations as well as significant differences in leadership cultures.

Regional comparisons

Having accepted the reality of diversity, it is nevertheless necessary to focus on the common aspects of democratic functioning in the region for the purposes of comparison and generalisation. While expansive and diverse, there exists a geographic and ideological Pacific community, derived from an understanding of the island states as linked contiguously by the Pacific Ocean; as 'a sea of islands', to use Epeli Hau'ofa's appealing terminology.[5] One could even argue that a sense of Pacific-ness is growing in the various urban centres of the Pacific Rim. In Los Angeles, Auckland, Sydney or Brisbane, the other-ness of Pacific heritage might promote conceptualisations of a broader Pacific identity, beyond specific national identifications or ethnic classifications of Melanesian-ness or Polynesian-ness.

There is a foreign relations community, formalised in regional architecture such as the Pacific Islands Forum and informally sharing the carriage of Australian influence, as well as alternately bridling at the world's neglect or complaining about the bewildering impacts of globalisation. Built on the principles of self-determination, the establishment of the South Pacific Forum in 1971 was 'the most sophisticated institutional expression of a post-colonial vision of regional community'.[6] Most directly, there is a development community, in which the various countries share aspirations and frustrations, deal with a

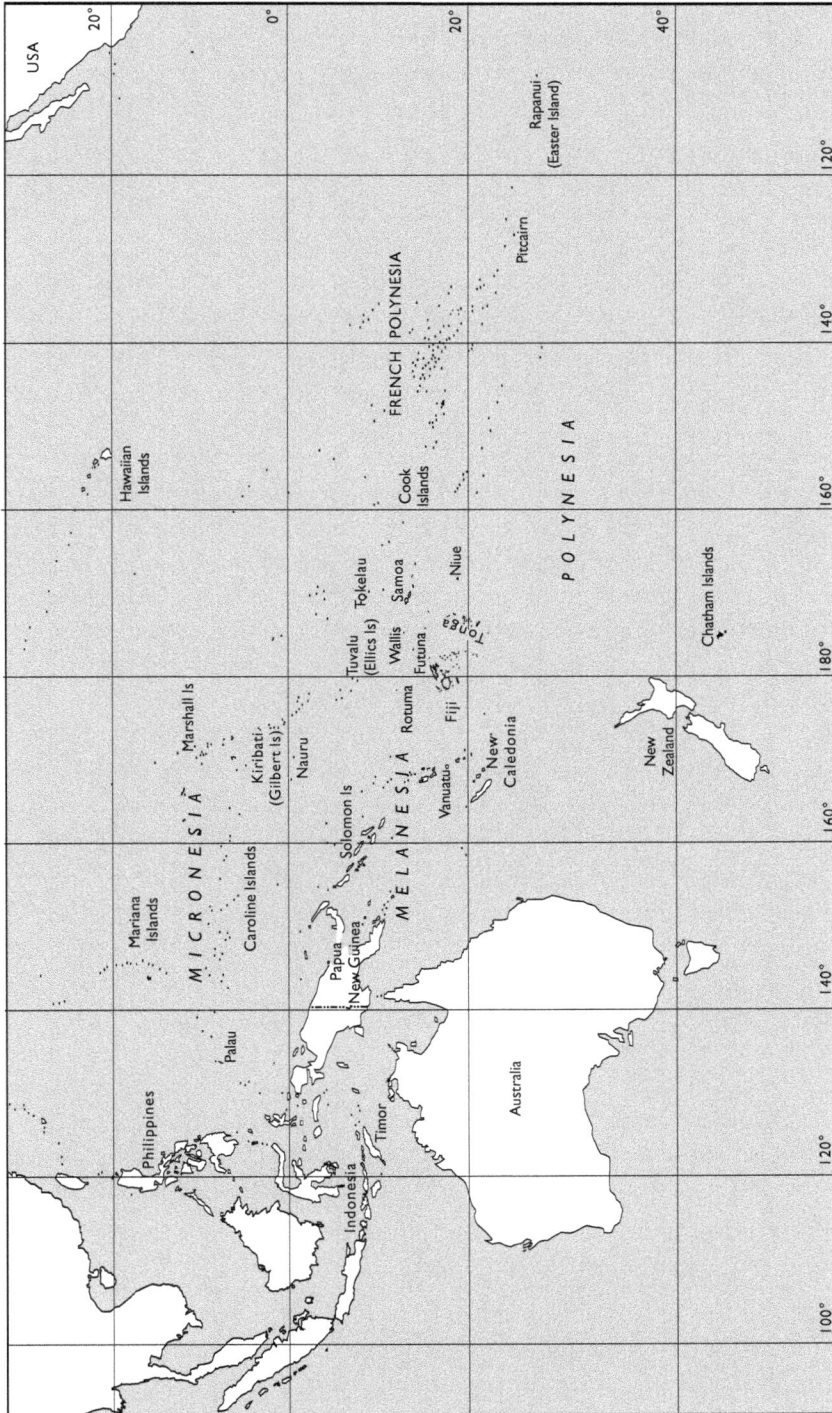

Figure 1.1: Pacific Islands

similar array of donors, merchants and adventurers and face a similar struggle to establish the institutions of governance and free markets. As members of these communities, the leaders follow developments in the other countries assiduously and freely borrow ideas from each other. It is particularly the membership of this imagined policy community that justifies the grouping of these countries for the purposes of this study. Yet even behind the latest iterations of Pacific community are a myriad 'contending visions of regional community, and of community-building', based on pragmatism, alliance, dominance and resistance.[7]

For the purposes of this collection, fault-lines are also in evidence. Clearly, Timor-Leste is an outer planet on the fringes of this system, while New Caledonia is centrally located but tenuously linked within it. Sämoa will often consider itself distinct from the others while many Pacific states tend to put PNG into its own category because of its size and complexity.

The problem of comparing like with like can be resolved partly if those being compared believe they are alike in certain ways and see themselves as unlike the rest of the world in many other ways. Comparisons are thus useful if the group under study is distinct from other groupings. Its own diversity notwithstanding, politics in the Pacific Islands is a distant relation to politics in Europe or Australia. Oral tradition dominates over electronic communications. Personality completely swamps policy in voters' perceptions. Ascriptive allegiances continue to be decisive in the Pacific whereas in European polities voters behave far more as atomised individuals. In the spectrum of political culture and behaviour, Asia, Eastern Europe and Latin America might be slightly closer to the Pacific, but are nevertheless at the opposite end of the spectrum. Perhaps most comparable with the Pacific would be politics in the Caribbean and Africa, though even the latter comparison draws criticism from some Pacificists.[8] Once again, the views of the actors themselves become critical. Michael Morgan points out in his chapter on Vanuatu the influence of the writings of African nationalists Julius Nyerere (Tanzania) and Kwame Nkrumah (Ghana) in shaping the emerging discourse on 'the Melanesian Way'. In his autobiography, Michael Somare recalls that the name given to the Pangu Party was inspired by Kenyan political party names KANU and KADU.[9] And Joao Saldanha notes in his chapter on Timor-Leste the decisive influence of the returned Mozambique expatriates.

Nevertheless, the questions to be asked in relation to regional comparisons need particular care. Common colonial heritage might allow for certain comparisons. Historical intersections might do likewise. Reliance on similar institutional designs might be worthy of study. But in all processes of comparison, generalisation and attempts at cross-regional 'lessons learned', the ultimate reality of distinctiveness remains prominent.

Temporal comparisons

The problem of attempting regional comparison is compounded when temporal calibrations are added. It is certainly not the contention of this chapter that processes of representative democracy follow an inevitable path, well trodden by the early adherents to democracy and slavishly pursued by those who follow. The variation in the design and workings of democratic institutions in established democracies puts paid to any teleological temptation. Choices between presidential or parliamentary systems, unitary or federal states, and unicameral or bicameral assemblies had to be made by Pacific countries just as they were made by long-established democracies. Nor is there anything inevitable about the type of political culture each nation will evolve. Politics in the Pacific Islands is less secular than the politics practised by the former colonial masters, and debate in Pacific parliaments is less robust than is the practice in Australia, the regional power. At the same time, gender problems in Pacific Island politics are even more acute than in neighbouring regions.

While there is no inevitable path, there has nevertheless been a dynamic evolutionary path of institutional development. By tracing the point reached by a Pacific Island country on that path, comparisons are possible with progress made by other polities at similar periods. In most parts of the Pacific Islands, people have now enjoyed an entire generation of institutional representative democracy.[10] Young people voting for the first time in the most recent elections in PNG, Sāmoa or Vanuatu will have known no other system in their lifetimes. There is even a small handful of political parties in the Pacific Islands that came into being at the time of independence and that still exist even though most political parties in this region tend to have a short life span. Comparisons might therefore be attempted with the early period of democratic development in Western countries and with the post-independence period of political development in Africa.

A telling feature of the earliest development of political parties in the United States and the United Kingdom was the tactic of cooperation on certain issues among individual legislators of like mind.[11] Another early development, according to Duverger, was the creation of the 'party of notables'.[12] With the adoption of universal suffrage and the involvement of 'the masses' in elections, mass parties developed in the 19th century from the social and political pressures of the day and evolved to become powerful features of the political landscape in the 20th century.[13] When applying this brief history to the Pacific Islands, it would seem that the point of comparison should be somewhere between the creation of loose clubs of legislators and the early period of outside mobilisation of political passions. We can also find an echo of Duverger's 'parties of notables' in the Pacific context in the creation of parties based on local interests and led by local 'big men'.

When examining key features of post-independence political party development in Africa, two aspects stand out starkly: the emergence of many single-party systems flowing from the results of the national liberation struggle; and the 'primordial loyalties' of adherents to parties in multi-party systems.[14] The relationship between the independence movement and the formation of political parties in the immediate post-independence period in the Pacific Islands will be instructive, as will recognition of the continuing effects of familial, ethnic and kinship relationships.

Classifications of political parties

The next question that presents itself concerns the various methods that have been employed to classify political parties. Mair provides a useful summary of the formative literature by focusing on the principal criteria used in the classifications.[15] Duverger was content in 1954 to simply count the number of parties. By 1966, Dahl had added the important consideration of the competitiveness of the opposition. Blondel in 1968 looked beyond mere numbers of parties and asked questions about their relative size. Rokkan in 1968 also sought a level of analysis beyond mere numbers and included criteria concerning the likelihood of single-party majorities and the distribution of minority party strengths. In 1976, Sartori added an important new criterion concerning the degree of polarisation of the party system through an examination of ideological distance between parties. Measurements can thus be devised to calculate the numbers of parties, their size and strength, their potential to enter into government and the choices they offer the electorate.

The level of sophistication of the measurements has increased commensurate with the levels of complexity of party systems in the world. Sartori transformed the simple counting of numbers into a six-part categorisation:[16]

— Monopoly;
— Hierarchy;
— Unimodal concentration (i.e., prevalence without alternation);
— Bipolar concentration;
— Low fragmentation;
— High fragmentation.

Sartori pointed out, however, that the counting of parties was interesting only insofar as it explained aspects of the mechanics of the party system.[17] His classification establishes a spectrum of systems from monopoly to fragmentation. It is only in the midpoints of that spectrum that one finds party systems that allow for alternation as well as relatively even concentration encouraging system stability. In examining political parties in the polities in the Pacific Islands, a question to be posed is where they fit in this spectrum and whether any are near or approaching the midpoints.

Sartori also introduced another measurement spectrum, the ideology-to-pragmatism continuum.[18] Are political parties motivated by policy outcomes in the interests of their supporters or are they vehicles for politicians to pursue the accumulation of wealth and power? In applying this concept to Pacific Island political parties, it will be useful to distinguish between the two concepts. While pragmatism as an end in itself can be motivated by simple self-interest, it can also be applied in the interests of the group. This aspect will be of particular relevance in Pacific Island political culture in view of the tightness of kinship and *wantok* loyalties and because of the perception of most voters that the role of their representatives is to deliver concrete benefits to their support base.

The ideological classification can be difficult to apply in established democracies and is particularly problematic in the Pacific Islands. Commentators note the current process of ideological convergence in established democracies.[19] But this phenomenon follows a century of cleavage politics with political parties representing fundamental divisions in society. Lipset and Rokkan argue that political parties in Europe established their mass bases from the results of two major social and economic revolutions — the national revolution associated with the emergence of modern nation-states and the industrial revolution leading to urbanisation and the identification of economic classes within society.[20] The class cleavage established the left-right dimension in descriptions of political parties. The national revolutions created regional parties, religious parties and ethnic parties. The task this suggests, for the purposes of this volume, is to identify the Pacific Island social bases for ideological orientations. Ideological comparisons with other polities are possible but problematic: there is clearly no comparison, for example, between the absence of ideological debate in a Pacific Island nation and the convergence of ideological positions in Western democracies.

The most recent, and least Western-centric, typology of political parties comes from Gunther and Diamond, who elaborate a sophisticated matrix with 15 segments.[21] The matrix usefully incorporates time and organisation axes. At one end is the earliest manifestation of political party organisation based on local elites with minimal organisational structure. The matrix evolves through time to mass-based, ethnicity-based and electoralist parties and movements. The matrix also plots the evolution of party structures from thin to thick, beginning with the Duverger's amateurish party of notables all the way to the highly professional Leninist party. Positioning Pacific Island political parties within this graph thus has the advantage of enhancing comparability with other regions and systems. It also adds an element of dynamism to the classification process by providing an indication of where the parties might be headed. Even if the parties discussed in this volume are clumped together in one corner, the Gunther and Diamond chart nevertheless allows them to be situated and thus better understood.

Figure 1.2: Gunther and Diamond: Species of Political Parties

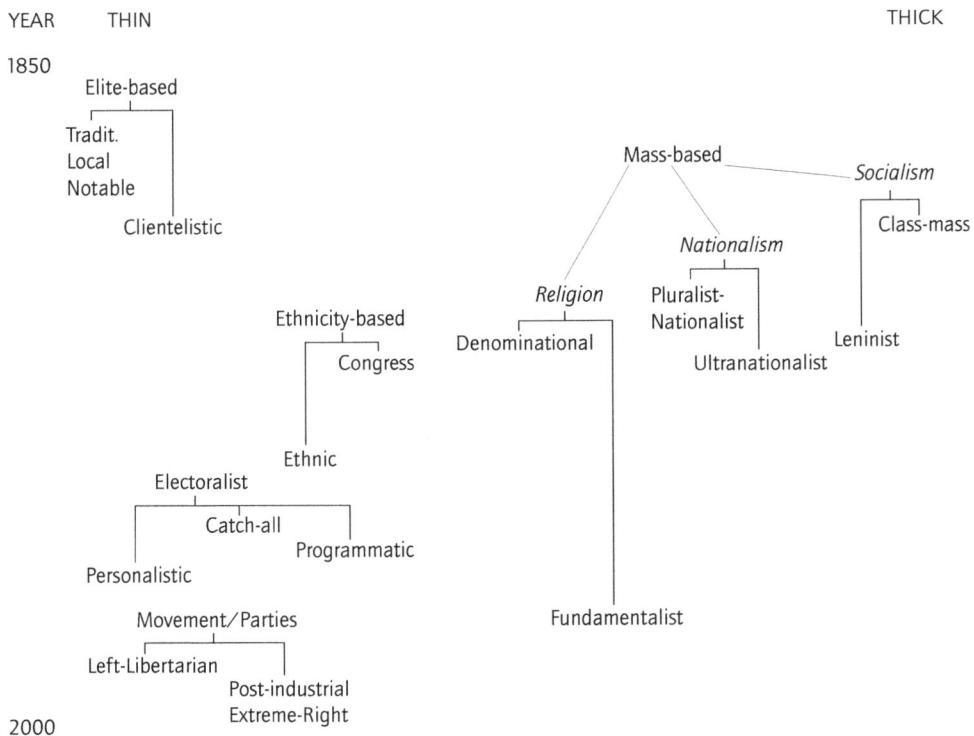

Source: P. 173, Gunther, Richard and Larry Diamond. 2003. 'Species of Political Parties – A New Typology.' *Party Politics*, Vol. 9, No. 2. pp. 167–99.

Institutionalisation of parties and party systems

The final issue of classification requiring application to the Pacific Island context concerns the degree to which the system in which the parties operate has become institutionalised. A necessary corollary to this question is the level of institutionalisation of the parties themselves. The issue was first suggested as critical to democratic practice by Huntington, who identified four dimensions of political party institutionalisation: adaptability and the capacity to survive setbacks; organisational complexity as measured by the number of sub-units; autonomy in relation to other institutions and groups; and, coherence within the party and the ability to resolve differences.[22] In relation to institutionalisation of the party system, Mainwaring and Scully in their study of Latin American systems set out four criteria: regularity of party competition; whether parties have 'stable roots in society'; the extent to which the major players accept election results as 'determining who governs'; and the level of organisation of parties.[23] Clearly, the two processes of institutionalisation are linked and, indeed, it would be expected of one to reinforce the other.

Recent work has been done on applying some of these concepts to Africa. Randall and Svåsand[24] make a number of points that might have some applicability to the Pacific Islands. They point to the origins of the party as a significant factor, focusing in part of the role of the movement or party in the struggle for independence. They argue that the relationship of the party to the leader is critical in the institutionalisation process, with a key test being whether the party can survive the initial leadership transition. They list the overriding advantages of incumbency as possibly destabilising to the process of institutionalisation. They identify clientelism as undermining rules and regularised procedures necessary for institutionalisation to take place. And they note that cleavage in the form of ethnic exclusivity might not be able to serve the same purposes as class cleavage served in the institutionalisation of European political parties.

In relation to party systems, Kuenzi and Lambright[25] applied the methodology utilised in the study of party system institutionalisation in Latin America to the African situation. They found the level of institutionalisation in Africa to be generally lower than in Latin America and that an important factor was the length of time a country has had experience of democracy. Only five of the countries reviewed fell into the institutionalised category. While it is not the intention of this volume to attempt a statistical analysis, a conclusion will be hazarded as to the relation of degree of institutionalisation of Pacific Island party systems in comparison with Africa.

Applying Classifications to the Pacific Islands

Attempts to apply the classic literature on political party taxonomy to the developing world are notoriously difficult. Sartori expressed great caution in applying criteria designed for 'modern political systems' to 'polities whose political process is highly undifferentiated and diffuse, and more particularly to the polities that are in a fluid state, in a highly volatile and initial stage of growth'.[26] Rakner and Svåsand accept that Sartori's typologies might not be applicable to African political parties, but nevertheless argue that criteria concerning party systems may yet be applicable.[27] Even in relation to the large and often strong nations of East and South-East Asia, Sachsenröder argues that Sartori's typologies 'appear rather difficult to apply'.[28] They are even more difficult to apply to the Pacific Islands. There might well be an inverse relationship between the applicability of such criteria and the level of development of the polities in question.

Apart from the development impacts affecting literacy, education and the emergence of a politically engaged middle class, Pacific Island polities are also affected by small size, isolation and poor communications, each of which contributes to placing these polities in Sartori's undifferentiated and diffuse category. Counting the numbers of parties in itself will explain little about the political system other than the likelihood of its fragmented nature. Ideological distance between political parties will rarely be a telling factor in the Pacific Islands because this measure is based on the presumption that the parties are speaking a common language concerning issues of economic growth, trade and service delivery. There might be a common rhetoric under these headings but it could not be dignified with the label of ideology or policy prescriptions. The measurement most applicable in the Pacific Islands in this regard is simply to ask whether a political party has a meaningful policy agenda.

The Gunther and Diamond taxonomy is more useful in relation to developing countries. Its identification of personalistic parties and clientelistic parties is of considerable assistance in gaining a better understanding of the formative motivations of Pacific Island political parties. While there might be some overlap in the classification into categories, and there is also likely to be considerable bunching in the group of parties in early formation with thin organisational capacity, this taxonomy is relevant and useful.

The method that might produce the most interesting results is to ask a series of questions about these political parties, the answers to which will aid in classification and understanding. While some questions might be posed generally in relation to political parties anywhere in the world, others are specific to developing countries and lend themselves in particular to parties in Africa and the Pacific Islands.

Does the party trace its origins to an independence movement?

This question might well point to the most important distinction to be drawn between the political parties under review. Beginning political life as an independence movement is a sure means of obtaining the popular legitimacy and developing the substance, organisation and critical mass to sustain a successful transformation into a ruling political party.[29] Africa is teeming with examples; SWAPO in Namibia, ANC in South Africa, ZANU-PF in Zimbabwe, Frelimo in Mozambique, MPLA in Angola, UNIP in Zambia up to 1991 and KANU in Kenya up to 2002. The independence struggles in Africa also saw the genesis of prominent opposition parties such as Renamo in Mozambique, UNITA in Angola and the Inkatha Freedom Party in South Africa. Decades after independence and, in most cases, after the passing of the independence leader, having been the national liberation movement that took over the reigns of power from the colonial power is probably the most important single factor for success as a political party in Africa.

The transformation from a national liberation movement to a political party presents great difficulties. Baregu describes 10 challenges: the need to set new goals; the change in tactics from radicalisation to consensus-building; eschewing armed conflict; reversing mindsets from that of a destroyer of the system to its defender; the need to cater to voters beyond one's immediate support base; the change from merely making promises to being held accountable for actions in government; the move from secretiveness to openness; the requirement to move to more open internal debate after the habit of suppressing internal dissent; the harmonisation of internal and external wings; and the need to forgo democratic centralism and Leninism in favour of decentralisation and checks and balances.[30] The challenge is thus to carry forward the strengths of the national liberation movement into the self-denying disciplines of multi-party democracy. A lesson from Africa, and southern Africa in particular, has been the preponderance of the old strengths over the new disciplines resulting in single-party or dominant-party systems.

This phenomenon of transformation from national liberation movement to political party repeats itself in the Pacific Islands, though on a more muted and modest scale. As Morgan points out, the Vanua'aku Pati situated itself as the party of independence and had a difficult relationship with the Condominium Administrators. Its reward on being tested in elections was 15 years of government in the first 24 years of independence. As Donald Kalpokas, one of the founders of the party, noted recently, party members were in no doubt about the self-interested nature of the Colonial Administration and refused to enter into pliant compromises, thus strengthening the party's reputation among voters.[31] The party was unable to sustain a predominant role in the Vanuatu party system as it became subject to island politics and conflicting personal ambitions, leading to splits and loss of influence. The end of its predominant role in Vanuatu began in 1991 when its independence leader, Walter Lini, split with the party he helped found.

In Ron May's chapter on PNG, the early success of the Pangu Party is described, as is its slow demise into just another of the fractious political parties in PNG's fragmented party system. Its first leader, Michael Somare,[32] traces the emergence of the party to a small study group including members of the House of Assembly in the 1960s, the 'Bully Beef Club',[33] and their increasing impatience for independence. May notes that once the issue of independence was settled, there was very little by way of policy differentiation between the various PNG political parties.

Similarly, Alaine Chanter's chapter on the politics of New Caledonia situates the FLNKS as the party of independence, describing the difficulties and tactical compromises it had to face over the years as its goal became increasingly difficult to achieve. While FLNKS was able to achieve considerable support among the Melanesian population, it was not able to translate this into incumbency in a society where the Melanesian population is in a minority. FLNKS became subject to the commonplace splits of Melanesian politics.

The independence party of the region most closely resembling the African precedents is Fretilin in Timor-Leste. Joao Saldanha describes Fretilin's dominant position gained through the first post-independence elections and plots Fretilin's path from a revolutionary movement to the main resistance organisation in the struggle against Indonesian occupation to a predominant party holding 55 of the 88 seats in the National Assembly. Fretilin used its reputation as the primary resistance party to reach down to the grassroots level and establish an invincible political position in the formative first elections.[34]

In the three remaining nations dealt with in this volume, the establishment of political parties was not based on the independence process. Asofou So'o in his chapter on Sämoa shows how the first eight years after independence were characterised by a form of consensus politics during which time political parties had not yet been formed. Tarcisius Tara Kabutaulaka notes that parties, in any case of little significance in the first years of the Solomon Islands, did not emerge from the small and scattered independence movements. Alumita Durutalo's chapter on Fiji describes the curious situation in which colonial economic interests and Fijian nativist interests saw a common problem in the growing political demands by the Indo-Fijian community and thus worked together to maintain a large part of the status quo in the immediate post-independence period. The issue for Fiji was not the usual whether and when questions about independence but the more difficult question of how to manage it through democratic institutions without leading to majoritarian results seen as likely eventually to favour the Indo-Fijian community.

A comparison between the African and Pacific Island cases suggests that some conclusions might be drawn from the contrasting experiences. While the transformation of an independence movement into a political party would seem to be the surest path to success in Africa and parts of the Pacific Islands, the differing fates of such parties in the two regions are worth noting. In Africa, many of the parties born from independence movements went on to dominate the political stage in their nations. The popularity and legitimacy gained from the independence struggle facilitated their entry into the electoral process. The strengths and habits built up from resistance days made them reluctant to share power. The result has been a number of single- or dominant-party situations, increasingly the subject of criticism by the international community.

A similar story can be told in some of the Pacific Island states under study in relation to the transformation of independence movements into political parties, but whereas in many of the African cases a position of power has been sustained over several decades, in the Pacific Islands, the political momentum slowed after a decade or so. The reason might flow from the differing experiences in the struggle for independence. Where it took the form of armed struggle, the independence movements had to be organised, disciplined and motivated. They needed leadership, good internal communications and, if possible, national reach. These attributes were put to the test in the sternest manner and thus hardened the fighting independence movements. These are also admirable qualities in a political party. To begin political life with a tried and tested leadership able to communicate with followers who are hierarchically organised throughout the country and exhibit the discipline of a military force is a good recipe for political success. Perhaps the hardest aspect of the transformation is, as Baregu notes, the abandonment of the weapons and techniques of war, both physically and psychologically.

With the exception of some skirmishes in New Caledonia and Vanuatu as well as those problems flowing from the Dutch and Portuguese withdrawals from the region, independence processes in the Pacific were and are political, not military. Leading figures of the local elites, native and expatriate, demanded independence from the colonial rulers. The debates took place in colonial offices and tertiary education colleges. The focus was invariably the capital. Excepting Vanuatu, none of the Pacific Island countries had a national independence movement similar to those in Africa. Almost none had a national organisation, partly for the reason that in some cases the nation was to be forged from an archipelago or from disparate groups only by the flimsy means of a document granting independence and partly because village life remained largely divorced from the urban elites. And so the Pacific Island political parties were not tested in the same way as their African counterparts. They tended to be small groups of committed people with little by way of an organisation to back them up. They benefited from the popularity of having been seen to confront the colonial power, but this tended only to have opened the path to political power in the immediate post-independence period. Thereafter, the Pacific Island parties could not fall back on much by way of organisation, partisans or resources.

Fretilin might eventually challenge this rule. Its struggle for independence was of African proportions but it was directed not at the colonial administration but at the subsequent occupation. Indeed, this struggle might be considered even more daunting than a struggle against British, French or Portuguese colonialism because, having been occupied by a Third World neighbour, the people of Timor-Leste had little by way of support from progressive forces in the colonial capital. A quarter of a century of guerrilla warfare and international agitation against a powerful occupying force might well be the sort of background that helps establish a very strong political party.

Has the party emerged from cleavage politics?

Lipset and Rokkan developed a seminal description of the cleavage basis of many European parties flowing from the nationalist revolutions and the industrial revolution.[35] These events established large identity groups based on unifying factors such as language, culture, religion and class. With the granting of universal suffrage, the basis for mass political parties was established. While not frozen for all time, the cleavage basis of political parties was sufficiently enduring to assure those parties the longevity they required to establish themselves as part of the political bedrock of their societies. Social Democrat, Christian Democrat and regional political parties can be seen as cleavage parties and, in view of their prominent role in European politics, they demonstrate the critical importance of cleavage in politics.

Can we find comparable situations in the Pacific Islands? Fiji provides the starkest example of cleavage politics in the Pacific Islands. Durutalo makes clear the racial basis of party development in Fiji. Beginning with the handover of power to Ratu Sir Kamisese Mara's Alliance Party, Fijian politics has had at its core the issue of how to deal with Indo-Fijian political mobilisation. The first attempt was through the Alliance Party itself, which had Fijian, Indian and general elector wings. This was an attempt to build a Fijian-dominated consociational party along the lines of the Malay-dominated Barisan Nasional of Malaysia.[36] The experiment was to last 17 years before it was cast aside after Alliance lost the 1987 elections. It suggests that consociationalism has a certain logic for a ruling party but not in opposition. It also points to the problems of asymmetrical consociationalism as a basis for enduring national leadership. Malay dominance through UMNO continues to be acceptable to the Chinese and Indian members of the Barisan Nasional because of fears of the Islamist alternative.[37] Fijian domination of the Alliance Party, which is described by Durutalo as 'unbalanced and unequal', ultimately was unable to satisfy any of the cleavage bases of its component parts. The racial, regional and class cleavages of Fijian society eventually demanded expression in parties catering to specific nativist, Indo-Fijian, economic class and regional sentiments. A telling example of the racial basis of Fijian politics can be seen in Yash Ghai's description of the 1995 submissions from the political parties to the Constitutional Review Commission concerning electoral systems.[38] Ghai's analysis confirms the racial basis of the political parties' objectives and concerns.

New Caledonia provides a further example of possible cleavage-based political parties. Chanter describes the basis for such cleavage in the component parts of New Caledonian society: the original Melanesian Kanak people; the early French settlers now dominant economically; the *Broussards*, who, though French, work the land and identify themselves as less privileged than the urban settler elite; the *Metros* who are more recent arrivals from the metropole and who are concerned about their rights and prospects; and the migrant minority communities including Wallisians and Futunians, Polynesians, Indonesians, Vietnamese and ni-Vanuatu. Political parties have been established to respond to the demands of these distinct communities. The FLNKS and its later offshoots represent the Kanak people and agonise over issues of native rights, land owner-ship, independence and autonomy. The RPCR is the party of the establishment and the status quo and as such attracts support from the urban elite and the minority migrant groups concerned about their fate under a future native administration. Insofar as *Broussard* and *Metro* interests do not converge with the establishment, new political parties such as Front Caledonien and the Front National have sprung up to cater to these political needs. As Jon Fraenkel notes in his chapter analysing electoral systems, there might be evidence of an emerging trend in the 2004 election success of Avenir Ensemble of shifting the political agenda away from ethnic issues to common issues of concern such as corruption.

Vanuatu also displays some elements of cleavage politics, though Morgan counsels caution in seeing some of the colonial distinctions as enduring. Geographic distinctive-ness is the most obvious fact of life in the Vanuatu archipelago and it is reflected in the political system. Identification on the basis of the island of origin is probably now the first fact of national life. Political groupings have sprung up in some islands without much ambition of seeking a national audience. The Jon Frum Party from Tanna and Namangki Aute from Malaluka are examples. The next distinction flows from the condo-minium nature of colonial government. British and French influence competed, often pettily, in the New Hebrides and it has left its mark on Vanuatu. The francophone and anglophone distinction was deepened by corresponding Catholic and Protestant allegiances and found political expression in differing views on the pivotal question of independence. In their formative periods, the Vanua'aku Party and the Union of

Moderate Parties, generally speaking, gathered together the nation's opposing political persuasions, the former representing anglophone, Protestant and pro-independence interests, the latter standing up for francophone, Catholic and pro-autonomy views. Thus were the origins of the Vanuatu party system influenced by cleavage. In succeeding decades, however, party splits, leadership ambitions and new ideological questions have weakened the original basis of Vanuatu cleavage politics, leaving personality and island politics as more dominant themes.

PNG sets an analytical dilemma in relation to cleavage politics. As May makes clear, ascriptive allegiance is the dominant theme of PNG politics yet the groups to which the allegiance is owed do not fit within the concept of cleavage as developed by Lipset and Rokkan. Allegiance is owed to a person's *wantok*, those who speak the same language. As there are more than 820 living languages in PNG,[39] the allegiance group tends to be rather small, often no larger than 10,000 people. Though PNG voters continue to vote on the basis of this linguistic affiliation, the diversity of the nation combined with an inappropriate electoral system has not established the conditions for political stability or economic growth.[40] For cleavage politics to influence PNG politics by being reflected in political party formation, voters would need to imagine themselves beyond their *wantoks* as members of wider groups, such as Papuans or New Guineans, or Highlanders, coastal or island people, or people from distinct regions such as the Sepik or Morobe. May notes some hints of this, but, for the moment, PNG politics remains resolutely personalistic and narrowly based on *wantok* loyalty.

Solomon Islands politics follows a similar model. As Kabutaulaka discusses in his chapter, the violence that erupted in the early 1990s in the Solomon Islands had as one of its causes simmering ethnic frustrations and rivalries based on land and resource issues. The frustrations were sufficiently acute to lead to the formation of militias with ethnic names and membership. Yet those same frustrations did not lead to the formation of political parties based on ethnic cleavage. One can only conclude that political parties were seen as an ineffective way of tackling the key problems facing society.

So'o argues in relation to Sämoa that political parties emerged because of differences of opinion among the elected leaders who had begun political life without the benefit of parties. While island and village distinctions remain important in Sämoa, they are not such as to create the sort of cleavages that might lead to the process of forming political parties that respond to their members' needs. Distinctions in Sämoan politics flow from whether one is a *matai*, a family leader or nobleman, from whether one has a foreign education and from issues of opinion, age and friendships. We can conclude that Sämoan political parties have no cleavage basis.

The situation in Timor-Leste is complex. While distinctions exist between localities and between the urban and rural people, these are not sufficiently deep to be the basis for political party formation. There are, however, a number of important dividing lines based on recent history: those who supported Indonesia and those who did not; those who speak Portuguese and those who do not; and among the resistance movement, those who fought from the mountains and those who fought from abroad. Even within the last category, a distinction can be made among the returning Timorese between those returning from Portugal, Mozambique or Australia. Yet Saldanha's description of the political scene puts little emphasis on these historical distinctions. The key to the existence of today's political parties in Timor-Leste lies in the politics of the generation that established these parties in the early 1970s in the confusion of the implosion of the Portuguese Empire. The politics of the 1970s is the guide to why the parties were formed and Fretilin's ability to present itself as the party of victory in the struggle for national independence is the key to its success.

To what degree is the party systematised?

The degree to which a party is systematised is a fundamental determinant of its substance and worth. The mass parties of Europe providing 'cradle-to-grave' services to their members and the Leninist parties of Asia that see themselves as above government, must support their ambitions with vast party structures based on deep membership, rules, congresses and hierarchies. They are quasi-permanent institutions of the political life of the nation, though even the mightiest has succumbed, and others yet might, to revolutionary upheavals. No party under review in the Pacific Islands has such ambitions, and, even if it did, as Fretilin might, it would not have the means to implement them. What needs to be looked at in the Pacific Islands are far more modest structures in keeping with the small village-based societies they represent.

The key distinction is whether the party has some structure beyond the present leadership and its parliamentary support. Is a political party simply a term to describe the livery under which parliamentarians have come together for the immediate purposes of parliamentary business? Is it a type of franchise that candidates must purchase in advance of an election because it is seen as a popular brand? Is the political party synonymous with its leader and, indeed, inseparable from him (it is almost invariably a 'he' in the Pacific Islands)? Or does the party have some manifestation beyond the current crop of parliamentarians sitting under its flag? In this regard, the questions to be asked concern autonomy, membership, branches, congresses, party rules, party officials and party finances, in line with the criteria suggested by Huntington.

One could take as the Melanesian norm the situation in PNG described by former minister Tony Siaguru as follows: 'In Papua New Guinea, we have political parties — plenty of them — but they are creatures of parliament not of the people or country … they form, they grow, regroup, fade and then dissolve all within the context of parliament and with no relevance for what is outside.'[41] The short answer is that the political party with some form of organisation and structure is very much the exception in the Pacific Islands. Neither could one say that the parties are autonomous in the Huntington sense. Either they follow the vacillations of parliament and government or they are in thrall to their leaders. Most political parties are still at the stage of 'parliamentary clubs' akin to the early days of Westminster. Parliamentarians get together usually for the purposes of strength in numbers or sometimes because of a common regional interest. The party is all too often simply livery. There are few party officials, concrete operational party constitutions or separate party accounts. These clubs-cum-parties are often dominated by moneyed individuals or charismatic leaders; the combination of both is rare. These structures seem to be even less coherent than what Duverger imagined might exist in relation to cadre parties. If one were to seek a precedent for this type of party structure it would be in the colonial assemblies in pre-Federation times in Australia. New South Wales and Victoria had populations of only one million each, parties did not exist, politicians were primarily constituency representatives and alliances in parliament were tenuous and transitory.[42]

Among the handful of Pacific Island political parties that can be said to have some degree of systematisation are the Fiji Labour Party (FLP), the Vanua'aku Party, the Human Rights Protection Party of Sämoa, Fretilin and the major parties in New Caledonia, in particular the RPCR and the FLNKS. These parties have, to a greater or lesser extent, established a party structure based on rules, congresses and branches and are run by officials, though most officials have day jobs. For the most part, these are also parties of patronage that rely on incumbency or at least the strong prospect of it for their coherence.

The exceptions to the rule based on the motive of incumbency are the FLP and FLNKS. The unspoken consensus among the Fiji elite is to keep the FLP out of office. When not achieved by electoral means, extra-constitutional methods have been used to that end. Yet, in spite of the coups d'état and the confessionalism introduced into the Fiji electoral system to formalise the Indo-Fijians' permanent opposition status, the FLP continues to function effectively and to insist on its rights under the rules of the game. It could be argued that because of its dim prospect of ever again winning government, the FLP, in its need to benefit its support base, has to compensate by being ever more systematic in its tactics and organised in its approach. Indeed, the need to match the FLP's electoral strategies and parliamentary conduct might be the factor that forces other political parties in Fiji to try to become better organised and more strategically focused. FLNKS has had some experience of provincial government. A moderate line on the issue of independence could, one day, see it share in the spoils of territory government. The reason these parties can succeed beyond the confines of clientelism is that they represent disadvantaged communities and are thus sustained by the logic of cleavage politics.

Does the party have ideology?

Ideology and party platforms are not common currency among Pacific Island political parties. Parties that are clientelist in the narrowest of senses have little use for the encumbrance of policy positions. Parties that are little more than informal clubs of parliamentarians cannot afford to develop firm ideological positions. Candidates who seek support from electorates still influenced by a cargo cult mentality would be wasting their time espousing policy positions when all the voters want to hear are promises of future wealth. Elections in the Pacific Islands are simply not fought over policy positions. Where policies are formulated in the electioneering context, they are more often than not the broadest and crudest form of populism offering unfunded free education or medical care.[43]

Part of the problem lies in the current global confusion over the breadth of the policy spectrum. The left/right distinction had very little echo in the Pacific Islands even at the height of the Cold War. These days, leftist politics has some substance only insofar as the FLP represents sugar-cane and textile workers. Bartholomew Ulufa'alu's National Democratic Party in the Solomon Islands had some links with the trade union movement, as did PNG's Pangu Party in its early days. Perhaps Fretilin is today the closest to its leftist roots in that policy postures were largely frozen during the quarter-century of Indonesian rule. Yet Saldanha points out that the realities of government have forced Fretilin to moderate many positions leading it more in the policy direction of a social democratic party.

It is also difficult to identify much in the way of right-wing politics in the Pacific Islands. The French racist Front National party is represented in New Caledonia, but the Pacific version of the party is quite distinct from its parent. It has adopted a more Pacific way of dealing with issues and its main burden is to secure the positions of those arriving more recently from France. Ironically, its main arguments are based on human rights and non-discrimination in voting rights, a position that would have the effect of increasingly marginalising the Kanak population. A number of parties can be identified as pro-business and pro-status quo. Jacques Lafleur's RPCR is probably the most rigorous of these, though in small societies it can sometimes be difficult to find the dividing line between broad principles and individual interests. The RPCR is certainly the party that protects established nickel interests. Laisenia Qarase's Soqosoqo Duavata ni Lewenivanua (SDL) in Fiji also puts itself forward as pro-business, though it probably should be seen as pro-native business.

To conduct a discussion of policy aspects of Pacific Island politics in terms of left/right distinctions is clearly unsatisfactory as it misses the point. Issues of independence and nation-building dominated the formative stage of Pacific Island politics. Establishing national structures, determining language policy, working out what to do with expatriate experts and learning how to conduct the business of government were the factors dominating the attention of the political leadership in the early years. While it cannot be said that these overriding problems are now resolved, it can be said that the political discourse has gone beyond them. They no longer motivate people the way they did in the first blush of independence.

In many ways, the present political discourse is not policy focused at all. It is about competence and corruption. It is about making government work and having services delivered. Those services, such as roads, schools and clinics, are the issues people worry about and so they become part of the political rhetoric. But it is difficult to describe this discourse in policy terms. The issues being dealt with — teachers and nurses should be paid their salaries, roads should be fixed — are so basic that they defy translation into contested policy positions.

If there is a policy dimension to the public debates in many Pacific Islands countries, it can perhaps be portrayed as being between traditionalists and modernists. As Steven Ratuva makes clear in his chapter, tradition retains considerable rhetorical power in the Pacific. Because tradition has always been an oral and oratorical institution, conceptions of *kastom* (custom) must be recognised as highly fluid and contestable. As Bronwen Douglas noted, one of the paradoxes of nationalism in Melanesia was that despite its diversity the essential ingredients of nationalism were everywhere the same: 'From Papua New Guinea to Fiji, nation makers play particular tunes on the common motifs of custom/tradition and Christianity.'[44] In the context of national parliamentary politics, it has always run the risk of simply becoming a form of sophistry for self-serving politicians. Practices represented as traditional or *kastom* continue to be practiced widely in the region in the form of communal support, circle discussions and status positioning, but they run into difficulty when being applied to the processes of national government. Simultaneously, *kastom* alongside Christianity became central to assertions of nationalism. Tradition tends to be a major part of the political rhetoric of the parties supported by Melanesian Fijians, the Vanua'aku Party and its offspring, and Papua New Guinean and Solomon Islands parties, but it is not much contested by other MPs as virtually all politicians wish to portray themselves as emerging from and supportive of local *kastom*.

Where the rhetoric of *kastom* is strongest is in criticising the disappointments of modernisation. There have been some resounding successes in the Pacific Islands in terms of health improvements, tackling illiteracy and establishing profitable tourist industries in several countries. But, at the very least, the benefits of modernisation have fallen far short of the vast expectations placed on it, thus providing powerful ammunition for politicians' rhetoric. The dominance of foreign companies, the lack of job opportunities for locals, the capricious impacts of globalisation and the politically ever-useful sins of colonialism are standard parts of the traditionalist politician's armoury. Those politicians arguing the merits of 'progress' have the harder case to prove in the popular discourse and it is little wonder that progress soon translates into cargo.

Are there any new policy positions capturing the attention of the voting public? Christianity would have to top this list. Several of the country chapters describe the influence of various Christian churches on the political scene. Yet the issue of Christianity in the Pacific Islands goes beyond the question of influence; it has become part of the policy debate, for example in the many policy proposals to 'Christianise' society. In some ways, Christianity has become the largest segment of tradition in these countries by taking over the role of mediating between individuals and the spiritual world, setting social norms and establishing the means of gaining status. Many Pacific politicians have church backgrounds and many more evoke biblical terminology. When the *Fiji Times* expressed some scepticism about the veracity of a German evangelist faith healer, the then Information Minister, Simione Kaitani, labelled the paper 'anti-Christ.'[45]

Tradition and religion aside, there are few other policy issues that have excited the voting public. While there is a Green Party in Vanuatu, environmental protection issues do not present themselves to Melanesian villagers in the same way as urban Westerners see them. The politics of the environment are entangled with the local patronage politics mentioned above. For example, logging is a keenly contested issue in PNG, Solomon Islands and Vanuatu but the contestants tend to be local politicians making quick deals with foreign logging companies against the donor community, responding primarily to the voters in their home countries. Environmental protection has its champions in the Pacific Islands but it has not gained the momentum to become an issue on which political parties can be built.

Gender equality is another issue that has its champions among Pacific Islanders. Traditional Melanesian society is male-dominated. In the Highlands of PNG a 'big man' will have several wives who will bear his children, tend his gardens and breed his pigs. The PNG Parliament of 109 members currently has one woman member, the widow of the former Chief Justice. The situation is similar in other Pacific Island parliaments, reflecting a traditional view that women are not leaders. Women are becoming better organised and most countries have a formally recognised women's association, though it is difficult to judge at times whether this is an exercise in inclusiveness or tokenism. Women are not sufficiently well organised or committed to elect their own to parliament or to make gender issues politically important. The donor community is a leading proponent for women's rights, often sparring with male leaders extolling the virtues of tradition.

Clientelism generally takes the place of policy or ideology in Pacific Island politics. A candidate who solicits one's vote in PNG and offers nothing concrete in return is considered a 'rubbish man'.[46] Clientelism tends to take a clan dimension in Melanesia, as Tovua notes: 'Loyalty to the wantoks is much greater than loyalty to broader society and it is greater than loyalty to the law, greater than loyalty to the system of democracy.'[47] This inescapable feature of Melanesian society is likely to continue to dominate the policy-setting process.

Is there a party system?

'A party system becomes structured when it contains solidly entrenched mass parties.'[48] Applying Sartori's definition to the Pacific would simply produce a nil return. 'The success of democratization is in part dependent on the existence of institutionalized parties and party systems of government.'[49] Applying Smith's description would lead us to conclude that democratisation has failed in the Pacific Islands. But applying Mainwaring and Scully's four criteria — regularity of party competition; whether parties have 'stable roots in society'; the extent to which the major players accept election results as 'determining who governs'; and, the level of organisation of parties — might allow for a more nuanced result.

In spite of all the turmoil and troubles around election time, PNG has held elections regularly and constitutionally since independence. The elections are hard fought and meaningful in terms of winners and losers. So there is regular competition, but the problem is that it is competition primarily between candidates rather than between political parties. The parties can hardly be said to have stable roots in society and, as noted above, the level of party organisation is low. On the positive side, elections are seen as the key to gaining power in PNG but on the negative side, how the election is won is dependent on what a candidate can get away with. Intimidation, violence, encouraging dummy opponents to split the vote of an opposing *wantok*, ballot-stuffing, curious counting and working courts of disputed returns are all known practices. All this suggests that if there is a party system, it is rudimentary. May describes the various attempts to engineer a party system in PNG culminating in 2001 with the *Organic Law on the Integrity of Political Parties and Candidates* (OLIPPC). The jury is necessarily still out on OLIPPC, but early indications are that it will be no match for the politicians it is trying to police.

Other political processes reviewed in this volume show higher degrees of systematisation. Vanuatu began its national political life with two broad families of political persuasion competing for power. Based as they were on some notions of cleavage, these two groups suggested a political party system in embryo. Since independence, however, the trend has been towards the PNG end of the spectrum with increasing fragmentation, doubts about party longevity and the dominance of personality politics. The Solomon Islands would also need to be situated at the fragmentation end of the spectrum.

Fiji began independence with what looked like a dominant catch-all party committed to the status quo battling a more narrowly based Indo-Fijian party seeking fundamental reform. Again, this had the makings of a party system of some sort. But, if there is a party system in Fiji, it is probably today best described in a series of negative propositions. No Indo-Fijian party will be allowed to have the dominant say in a government. No single party representing the views of native Fijians appears able to gain a dominant position. Personalities and chiefly title, not political party platforms, will continue to play the most influential role. It is a disquieting reflection on the body politic of Fiji that coups have had more impact than constitutions. The ambitious and idealistic Constitution of 1997 has not engineered the results it sought.

New Caledonian politics can give the impression of being systematised along party lines in view of the racial and economic cleavages that underpin the parties. It also has the advantage of being more rules-based than other systems in the Pacific Islands given the applicability and enforcement of French electoral laws. For example, French law requiring an equal number of men and women on the party lists was a contributing factor to a woman leading the Territorial Government. Yet even in New Caledonia, the tendency towards fragmentation is evident. Vote-splitting among Melanesian Kanaks is one reason why they do not have representation commensurate with their voting strength. But the problem exists on the conservative side of politics as well. Chanter traces the various splits that have affected that side of politics in the territory. Thus even where a cleavage basis for party development exists, it seems that fragmentation is nevertheless the direction in which New Caledonia is moving.

While the Melanesian countries have strong electoral competition without necessarily enjoying the benefits of a strong party system, Sämoa and Timor-Leste reflect a different problem. One-party dominance clearly militates against the systematisation of political contestation. It cannot yet be said that the dominance of the Human Rights Protection Party (HRPP) and of Fretilin is immutably entrenched. But the likely cause of any future decline of these parties will not be strong competition from political opponents but rather internal splits. Without a party system that attempts to establish a level playing field, the advantages of incumbency will work to entrench the dominance of the ruling party. Sämoan opposition politicians complain bitterly about the HRPP's dominance of the parliamentary process. The Fretilin Government is already showing ambitions of controlling key aspects of electoral governance.

A persuasive piece of evidence of the lack of party systems in the region is the growing consensus on the need to engineer them. Given the acute nature of the problem in PNG, it is of little surprise that efforts to engineer a party system are most advanced in that country. One feature of OLIPPC is the anti-party-hopping rule intended to reduce the 'horse-trading' that can go on after the election (or after a no-confidence vote in Parliament) by tying elected members to the party that nominated them and with which that member first votes. The tough penalty for crossing the floor is the declaration of a vacancy for that seat and the fighting of a by-election. A sweetener is offered to the parties in the form of a small subsidy from the State to help defray the costs of the organisational requirements of the law. Fiji's 1997 Constitution has a similar anti-party-hopping rule covering not just resignations from the party but expulsion, provided the expulsion was within the rules of a registered political party and does not relate to the parliamentarians' work in a parliamentary committee.[50] The Solomon Islands and Vanuatu are studying these initiatives closely.

Engineering party systems can also be achieved through the voting method employed. Fraenkel points out that Pacific Island nations use a variety of electoral systems and some favour political party systems more than others, though he also notes that the eventual impacts might differ markedly from those intended by the designers. There is no doubt that some institutional designs are less appropriate than others. PNG's first-past-the-post system leading to pluralities in the single digits did much to undermine confidence in the electoral process. It follows that reforms in institutional designs are necessary and beneficial. But the record is not positive in relation to the use of institutional redesign to re-engineer political systems. The more ambitious the intention of the redesign, the less likely it is to succeed. In relation to political parties, neither the Fiji Constitution of 1997 nor OLIPPC have yet borne fruit. The Pacific Islands might prove to be so under-systematised as to be impervious to institutional redesign.

Conclusions

Two caveats need to be placed before attempting to pull some of the threads together. The first has already been alluded to: there is no one-size-fits-all description or analysis applicable to the Pacific Islands. The polities differ in their sizes, economies, histories and politics. The case studies in this volume extend from Timor-Leste to Sämoa, a distance greater than from London to New Delhi, so it is not surprising to find significant political differentiations among them. Having accepted this caveat, it remains that five of the seven case studies are polities with native Melanesian populations. Timor-Leste and Sämoa act as bookends to the Melanesians and share some of the geographic attributes and development challenges. The region therefore lends itself to political generalisations tempered by the need occasionally to take note of exceptions to the rule.

The other caveat concerns the place of political parties in the broader issue of society. Many problems concerning political parties and criticisms of their conduct appear in this and other chapters. This might lead to the erroneous conclusion that political parties are the fundamental problem plaguing Pacific Island societies. If only it were that simple. Village life might well continue at its normal rhythms in many places in the Pacific Islands, economically sustained by fishing and subsistence farming, and spiritually sustained by church and tradition. Some of these villages might be touched by modernisation and globalisation in only the most tangential of ways and thus have little contact with the institutions of modern political life. This is often the South Seas idyll imagined by urbanites in their cold Western cities. But world history and the global economy insist that these polities behave as nations and this is where the problems begin. Establishing, managing and sustaining the governance institutions of a nation in the modern world are tasks that Pacific Island polities are finding particularly difficult to achieve. The reasons for this must be left to other publications in this and other disciplines, but the point to be made is that before we even get to the problems of political parties we must traverse a forest of other national problems; before we arrive at Westminster, we must pass through Westphalia.

If national and industrial revolutions stoke the furnace in which so many political parties are forged, then the Pacific Islands have difficulty in raising the temperature to the required intensity. Generally speaking, the Pacific Island nations are pre-industrial. Village life remains the ideal and while the trend to urbanisation exists, it has not led to the formation of organised working classes. In Fiji, there is something of an exception to the rule in that the FLP is built on the bedrock of Indo-Fijian cane workers and has recruited urban textile workers. The level of development in New Caledonia has also had the effect of a quasi-industrial revolution in its creation of segments of society with common economic perspectives and grievances. But these are timid exceptions when compared with the great workers' parties of the developed world.

The story in relation to national revolutions is more complex and varied. Perhaps it can best begin with the only nation in the Pacific Islands not to be colonised, Tonga. The Kingdom of Tonga was certainly influenced by British colonisers but it remained independent and under the stewardship of its monarchy. Tongans share a common history and see themselves as a people distinct from Maori or Melanesians, but it could not be said that they have had any sort of a national revolution. The struggle in Tonga is that of commoners against nobility and it is played out in polite slow motion. Perhaps one day the nobility's excesses will spur commoners to greater action, but until that time, there are no political parties in Tonga. The Solomon Islands, lightly colonised by the British, comprises a number of islands, including the two most prominent, Guadalcanal and Malaita. Friction between these groups contributed to the violence that ravaged the country. The combatants were militia ostensibly representing the interests of their fellow Islanders. To reiterate a point made earlier, it is noteworthy that the system produced militia to take on these grievances but no political parties to do so.

The closest historical parallel to a national revolution has been the process of gaining independence. As in Africa, the elites leading the independence movements reimagined their lands and islands in accordance with the maps drawn by their colonisers. The debate was not about the return to the pre-national existence of pre-colonialism, but rather the demand to take over the local institutions of colonial governance. The national revolution took place by way of this thought transfer. All at once, disparate peoples became ni-Vanuatu or Solomon Islanders or Papua New Guineans. The problem with this conceptual revolution is that it has been restricted to a small band of urban educated leaders. The majority of the people of these nations think of themselves primarily and perhaps at times exclusively in terms of their village, their island or their *wantok*. The nation suggested by map-makers remains a sparsely imagined construct. Little wonder that we do not see broadly based political parties emerging.

It is the struggle for independence that was the primary force in forging the first political parties. In that sense, the Pacific Islands follow African precedent ahead of European models. The comparison with African examples sheds light on a key difference. Decolonisation in the Pacific Islands was more of a debate than a struggle. To continue the blacksmith's analogy, the fires generated by these debates were sufficient to form political parties but perhaps not to forge them strongly enough to withstand the passing of time and memory. While Fretilin might yet prove to be the exception, the decades since independence have seen the bearers of that mantle fall back to the field. Perhaps the conclusion to be drawn here is that the more intense the independence struggle and the greater the need to form strong, broadly based and disciplined national liberation movements, the greater the likelihood that the emerging political party will have the longevity and organisational ability to make a prominent if not dominant place for itself in the newly independent state.

The first generation of leaders has passed or they are on their last political legs in the Pacific Islands. Ratu Sir Kamisese Mara, Walter Lini, Matä'afa Fiamë Faumuinä Mulinu'ü and Jean-Marie Djibaou have all died. Michael Somare has been politically resurrected in PNG. Peter Kenilorea is the non-elected non-partisan Speaker in Solomon Islands. Mari Alkatiri in Timor-Leste is the exception in that he probably sees himself as the long-term leader of his country. They are all better known than the parties they led, again with the exception of Alkitiri's Fretilin. Ratu Mara's once formidable Alliance Party has disappeared. Matä'afa in Sämoa always saw himself as above parties anyway. Walter Lini and Michael Somare abandoned the parties they helped form. This is a rather sorry record from the point of view of political parties and suggests that leaders are the more prominent political institution.

The conclusion to be drawn is that personalisation of politics is a more enduring feature of the Pacific Islands than its systematisation. The regrettable corollary is that opportunism generally wins out over policy in such a system. One highly visible manifestation of this situation is the prevalence of party splits, walkouts, revolts and abandonments. Fretilin has so far been spared but its prominence is in part due to the dismemberment of the CNRT, of which it had been a leading member. Virtually all the major Melanesian political parties have been subject to this fissiparous phenomenon. Gelu provides a striking example in cataloguing the splits in the Pangu Pati, starting with the first split in 1985 followed by further splits in 1986, 1988, 1992, 1994 and two in 1997.[51] Melanesian 'big man' concepts seem to militate in favour of rugged individualism and personal ambitions over disciplined membership of a group and broad societal ambitions. There does not appear to be an imminent circuit-breaker for this cycle of splits. Melanesian politics therefore appears to have an almost inevitable trend towards high fragmentation. It is a fragmentation not based on representing the spectrum of policy positions but generated by personal ambitions and narrow small-group interests. This clearly does not augur well for the systematisation of the party system, or for stability in politics. The Pacific Islands region is therefore probably behind Africa in terms of the systemisation of political parties.

Perhaps the most positive comment open is that Pacific Island electoral politics is in its early years and might well mature into a more stable and cohesive framework in which political parties play the role foreseen by the theorists. This could support an argument situating many of the parties in Duverger's description of the party of notables. This is an early manifestation of the political party with narrow membership and thin organisation. Gunther and Diamond begin their typology at the same spot and this would be the closest point at which Pacific Island parties could be accommodated. But there are hints of other typologies as well. Staying with Gunther and Diamond, the notables or big men have certainly adopted clientelist features into their political philosophy, though the parliamentarian himself is all too often the principal client. There are some suggestions of ethnic parties, especially in Fiji and New Caledonia, but not within the predominantly uni-racial nations. There might well be a trend towards denominational parties with the increasing prominence of the churches in politics. Personalist parties are common but not strong. And there is a hint of a party with Leninist dispositions in Timor-Leste. These classifications are helpful for analysis and comparisons but there is an inevitable degree of artificiality in applying them to a system with such weak party systems.

The comparison with the early parliamentary periods in other polities might be more to the point. Political parties at this point of political development resemble clubs more than disciplined organisations. There might be a concept of club membership and livery but it tends to be loose to the point of interchangeability. The members of these clubs are primarily constituent representatives and ambitious individuals with quite narrow goals and often consumed with the reality that they might have only one parliamentary term in which to achieve them. Eventually, changes in the demands of society, the rules of parliament and the stability and longevity of the political system would lead these clubs to the path of parties. This might be the path down which the Pacific Island polities are currently meandering.

Footnotes

1   Diamond, Larry. 1999. *Developing Democracy: Toward Consolidation.* Baltimore: The Johns Hopkins University Press. p. 96.

2   Rich, Roland. In press. 'Reviewing Democracy in the Pacific: Participation and Deliberation.' In Steven Ratuva (ed.), *A Kind of Civility: Civil Society, Development and Governance in the Pacific.*

3   Steven Ratuva in his chapter in this volume lists seven (Micronesia, Niue, Nauru, Palau, Tokelau, Tonga and Tuvalu) of 15 polities as having no political parties, while Cook Islands (three), Kiribati (two) and Marshall Islands (one) might have political parties but have very small populations and thus tend to be difficult to analyse on the assumption of systemisation. Anckar and Anckar in their study of the Pacific Island states without political parties accept that diminutive size is a reason but also point to 'cultural resistance' in the form of tradition, which obstructs political party formation: Anckar, Dag and Carsten Anckar. 2000. 'Democracies Without Parties.' *Comparative Political Studies,* Vol. 33, March. pp. 225–47. The problem with this argument is that cultural resistance in similar Pacific polities has not stopped political parties from being formed, leaving diminutive size as the dominant reason.

4   Australia, France, New Zealand, Portugal and the UK plus pre-World War I German colonisation of New Guinea and Sämoa, and Indonesian colonisation of East Timor.

5   Hau'ofa, Epeli. 1994. 'Our sea of islands', *The Contemporary Pacific*, Vol. 6, No. 1. pp. 148–61, at p. 160.

6   Fry, Greg. 2004. 'Whose Oceania? Contending visions of community in Pacific region-building.' *Research School of Pacific and Asian Studies, Department of International Relations Working Paper*, 2004/03. pp. 6–7; See Fry, Greg. 1994. 'International cooperation in the South Pacific: From regional integration to collective diplomacy.' In W. Andrew Axline (ed.), *The political economy of regional cooperation*. London: Pinter Press.

7   Fry, 1994, ibid.

8   Fraenkel, Jon. 2004. 'The Coming Anarchy in Oceania? A Critique of the "Africanisation of the South Pacific" Thesis., *Commonwealth and Comparative Politics*, Vol. 42, No. 1. pp. 1–34.

9   Somare, Michael. 1975. *Sana — An Autobiography of Michael Somare*. Port Moresby: Niugini Press. p. 51.

10 Rich, Roland. 2003. "The Quality of Democracy in the Pacific", *New Zealand International Review*, Vol. 27, No. 6. pp. 10–15.

11 Strom, Kaare. 1995. 'Political Parties.' In Seymour Martin Lipset (Editor in Chief), *The Encyclopaedia of Democracy*, Vol. III, London: Routledge. p. 923.

12 Duverger, Maurice. 1954. *Political Parties: Their Organisation and Activity in the Modern State*. London: Methuen.

13 Strom. op. cit.

14 Sartori, Giovanni. 1976. *Parties and Party Systems — a Framework for Analysis*, Vol. 1. Cambridge: Cambridge University Press. pp. 248–54.

15 Mair, Peter. 1996. 'Party Systems and Structures of Competition.' In Lawrence LeDuc, Richard G. Niemi and Pippa Norris (eds), *Comparing Democracies: Elections and Voting in Global Perspective*, Thousand Oaks, California: Sage Publications.

16 Sartori, op. cit. p. 128.

17 Ibid.

18 Ibid. p. 78.

19 Webb, Paul. 2002. 'Political Parties and Democratic Control in Advanced Western Societies.' In Paul Webb, David Farrell and Ian Holliday (eds), *Political Parties in Advanced Industrial Democracies*, Oxford: Oxford University Press. p. 438.

20 Seymour, Martin Lipset and Stein Rokkan (eds). 1967. *Party Systems and Voter Alignments*. New York: Free Press.

21 Gunther, Richard and Larry Diamond. 2003. 'Species of Political Parties — A New Typology.' *Party Politics*, Vol. 9, No. 2. pp. 167–99.

22 Huntington, Samuel. 1968. *Political Order in Changing Societies*. New Haven: Yale University Press.

23 Mainwaring, Scott and Timothy Scully. 1995. *Building Democratic Institutions: Party Systems in Latin America*. Stanford: Stanford University Press.

24 Randall, Vicky and Lars Svåsand. 2002. 'Party Institutionalization in New Democracies.' *Party Politics*, Vol. 8, No. 1, pp. 5–29.

25 Kuenzi, Michelle and Gina Lambright. 2001. 'Party System Institutionalization in 30 African Countries.' *Party Politics*, Vol. 7, No. 4. pp. 437–68.

26 Sartori, op. cit., p. 244.

27 Rakner, Lise and Lars Svåsand. 2004. 'From Dominant to Competitive Party System — The Zambian Experience 1991–2001.' *Party Politics*, Vol. 10, No 1. pp. 49–68. p. 51.

28 Sachsenröder, Wolfgang. 1998. 'Party Politics and Democratic Development in East and Southeast Asia — a Comparative View.' In Wolfgang Sachsenröder and Ulrike Frings (eds), *Political Party Systems and Democratic Development in East and Southeast Asia — Volume I: Southeast Asia*, Aldershot: Ashgate Publishing. p. 12.

29 Smith, B. C. 2003. *Understanding Third World Politics — Theories of Political Change and Development*. Hampshire, UK: Palgrave MacMillan. p. 143.

30 Baregu, Mwesiga. 2004. 'From liberation movement to ruling parties in southern Africa.' In Chris Landsberg and Shaun Mackay (eds), *Southern Africa Post-Apartheid? The Search for Democratic Governance*, Cape Town: IDASA. pp. 97–8.

31   Kalpokas, Donald. 2005. 'The Vanua'aku Party and Vanuatu Democracy.' *2005 Annual Address of the Centre for Democratic Institutions*, Parliament House Canberra, February 16, available at http://www.cdi.anu.edu.au/activities/activity_AnnualAddress_Kalpokas_16.2.05.htm

32   Somare, op. cit. p. 50.

33   Fortune, Kate. 2000. 'Pangu Pati.' In Brij V. Lal and Kate Fortune (eds), *The Pacific Islands — An Encyclopedia*. Hawai'i: University of Hawai'i Press. p. 310.

34   Hohe, Tanja. 2004. 'Delivering Feudal Democracy in East Timor.' In Edward Newman and Roland Rich (eds), *The UN Role in Promoting Democracy — Between Ideals and Reality*. Tokyo: United Nations University Press. pp. 302–19, at p. 308.

35   *Party Systems and Voter Alignments*. New York: Free Press.

36   Loh, Francis Kok Wah and Khoo Boo Teik. 2002. 'Introduction.' In Francis Loh Kok Wah and Khoo Boo Teik (eds), *Democracy in Malaysia — Discourses and Practices*, Richmond, Surrey: Curzon Press. p. 4.

37   Hussein, Syed Ahman. 2002. 'Muslim Politics and the Discourse on Democracy.' In Francis Loh Kok Wah and Khoo Boo Teik, ibid., p. 82.

38   Ghai, Yash. 1997. 'The recommendations on the electoral system: the contribution of the Fiji Constitution review.' In Brij V. Lal and Peter Larmour (eds), *Electoral Systems in Divided Societies: The Fiji Constitution Review*, Canberra: National Centre for Development Studies. pp. 147–59.

39   *The Ethnologue: Languages of the World*, published by SIL Inc., lists 823 living languages for PNG. See http://www.ethnologue.com/show_country.asp?name=Papua+New+Guinea

40   Reilly, Benjamin. 2002. 'Political Engineering and Party Politics in Papua New Guinea.' *Party Politics*, Vol. 8, No. 6. pp. 701-18.

41   Siaguru, Anthony. 2001. *In-House in Papua New Guinea with Anthony Siaguru — The Great Game in PNG*. Canberra: Asia Pacific Press, pp. 126–27.

42   Loveday, P. and A. W. Martin. 1977. 'Colonial Politics Before 1890.' In P. Loveday, A. W. Martin and R. S. Parker (eds), *The Emergence of the Australian Party System*, Sydney: Hale and Iremonger. pp. 26–33.

43   Kavanamur, David. 1998. 'The politics of structural adjustment in Papua New Guinea: some policy lessons.' In Peter Larmour (ed.), *Governance and Reform in the South Pacific*, Canberra: National Centre for Development Studies. p. 117.

44   Douglas, Bronwen. 2000. 'Weak States and Other Nationalisms? Emerging Melanesian Paradigms.' *State, Society and Governance in Melanesia Project Discussion Paper*, No. 03. p. 4.

45   *ClariNews*, Special Edition, Suva, September 27, 2003.

46   Siaguru, op. cit., p. 130.

47   Tovua, Paul. 2004. 'Rescuing Democracy in the Solomon Islands.' *Annual Address of the Centre for Democratic Institutions*, Parliament House, Canberra, March 8, available at http://www.cdi.anu.edu.au/CDIwebsite_1998-2004/annual_address/aa_downloads/Paul_Tovua_speech.pdf

48   Sartori, op. cit., p. 244.

49   Smith, op. cit., p. 148.

50   Section 71(1).

51   Gelu, Alphonse. 2003. 'A Democratic Audit for Papua New Guinea.' In David Kavanamur, Charles Yala and Quinton Clements (eds), Building a Nation in Papua New Guinea — Views of the Post-Independence Generation, Canberra: Pandanus Books. p. 37.

PRIMORDIAL POLITICS?
POLITICAL PARTIES AND
TRADITION IN MELANESIA

Dr Steven Ratuva

Introduction

This chapter is concerned with the role of cultural tradition in political parties in the Pacific. Specifically, it explores how 'tradition' is deployed as an organising and mobilising schema, how it is transformed into a political ideology and how traditional institutions and leadership systems are used to facilitate party interests. The chapter argues that tradition plays a significant role in shaping the form and dynamics of political parties in the Pacific, with parties embracing tradition as an instrument of mobilisation and legitimisation. As a consequence political parties also become agents of political and cultural transformation and reproduction.

Political parties are relatively recent innovations in Pacific Island polities and are still in various stages of formation and transition. There are presently about 57 political parties registered throughout the Pacific that follow various organisational and political ideals, and many more social organisations that seek political power but which fail to fulfil the respective requirements of party registration.[1] At one end of the continuum are those political parties (as in the case of Fiji) that are established and institutionalised with a structure and ideological framework. At the other extreme are political groups held together loosely under various labels by individuals or self-centred political interests. Party names are often symbolic of the party's identity, interests or principles, but sometimes they might be largely rhetorical (such as when they incorporate 'democratic', 'unity', 'people's', 'national', 'alliance'), chosen to articulate certain broadly recognised principles. This is true of many political parties in PNG (United Democratic Party), Fiji (National Alliance Party), Solomon Islands (Peoples Alliance Party) and Vanuatu

(Melanesian Progressive Party). In between the two extremes are groupings that encompass varying degrees of coherence in organisation and principle. Increasingly, ideological parties have emerged in urban areas — Fiji, Vanuatu, Solomon Islands and PNG each have Labour Party — but most political parties in the Pacific Islands represent specific local, tribal or ethnic interests.

Globally, the major forces in the spawning of political parties were the waves of decolonisation that swept the globe from the 1940s to the 1980s and the collapse of the Soviet Empire and demise of one-party Marxist regimes in the 1990s. Most political parties in the Pacific emerged after independence. While colonial hegemony was highly centralised under the colonial state, independence saw a period of transition towards more local control and democratisation. The new mode of post-colonial leadership was organised around political parties and signalled a new era of democratisation, while also manifesting the complex relationship between tradition and modernity.

In this chapter, I define the term 'tradition' rather loosely to refer to practices, values, institutions and belief systems that were inherited from the past. This notion of "past" is quite complex because history consists of a continuity of events that are constantly changed, reshaped and redirected by internal forces (such as warfare and political struggle) or external forces (such as globalisation). In Pacific states, as in other post-colonial states, what is usually considered 'tradition' is a combination of surviving pre-colonial practices, colonially reshaped institutions and practices and even some new post-colonial values repackaged as 'traditional'.[2]

I use the words 'tradition' and 'modernity' here not in a dichotomous sense but as dynamic concepts with highly adaptive and interchangeable characteristics. For instance, tradition does not necessarily imply only primordial features but can be reinvented, repackaged and rearticulated as something to suit emerging circumstances. On the other hand, modernity is not a fixed state since it embodies a range of characteristics, some of which are 'old' and some of which are 'new'. Within the dynamics of cultural transformation tradition and modernity not only define each other, they oscillate between each other to the extent that sometimes it is difficult to distinguish one from the other.

This chapter is divided into four main parts. The first provides an overview of political parties in the Pacific and the basic principles on which they operate. This is important to gauge the extent to which political parties use various modes of traditional organisation such as kinship for purposes of mobilisation and legitimisation. Secondly, it provides a broad framework within which we can understand the dynamic and utilitarian nature of tradition and how it is deployed readily as an instrument of politics. Thirdly, it discusses some of the dynamic relationships between political parties and tradition and how one uses and modifies the other; and, lastly, the chapter looks briefly at the continuing dilemma between tradition and democracy as a 'foreign flower'.

Political parties in the Pacific: an overview

It is difficult to make generalisations about political parties in the Pacific because of their diversity. At one extreme are political parties with cohesive organisations and coherent ideologies and at the other are those that are much looser and less coherent. The oldest political parties in the Pacific were formed in the 1950s and '60s, although there have been political protest groups in existence since the 1800s. The average life expectancy of political parties in the Pacific is relatively short. In the case of the Solomon Islands, some political parties emerge in a few days and disappear, some live for a month or two and, if lucky, some might exist for more than one year. There is usually a proliferation of parties during the elections and many die out after that.

Although there are a lot of differences between political parties in the Pacific, there are also similarities that are worth generalising. First, many are small and elitist in nature, without mass party membership as in many Western liberal democracies or even socialist regimes. Often the leaders of parties are also the only members. Secondly, many political parties are very unstable and often break up into different parts as a result of power struggles, differences of opinion or defections to greener pastures. Thirdly, many lack coherent political ideologies and are driven by specific local interests rather than the national interest. Hence, many parties are held together by kinship ties or networks of patronage, making them more accountable to the local community than to a national constituency. This makes political parties organisations that are embedded in community rather than national institutions. Fifthly, tradition is used as a mobilising and legitimising tool; and, lastly, churches exert a strong influence in the party membership and leadership (see Table 2.1).

Table 2.1 represents political parties registered officially under their country's respective electoral laws, irrespective of their representation in parliament. It shows that some states, especially the Melanesian ones, have significantly larger numbers of political parties than the smaller Micronesian and Polynesian states. The only Polynesian states with formal political parties are Sämoa and Cook Islands. A large number of states, such as Kiribati, Tuvalu, Tokelau, Tonga, Federated States of Micronesia (FSM), Niue, Palau and Nauru, do not have political parties, while Marshall Islands has only one. For these states, elections revolve around personalities, kinship and loose associations of individuals rather than formally constituted parties.[3]

In recent years, PNG, Solomon Islands and Vanuatu have witnessed a proliferation of political parties before national elections. Small political parties that fail to win elections tend to dissipate quickly, although they might resurrect themselves using the same name and form to contest future national elections.

Many political parties articulate socioeconomic and political issues as platforms for their debates; however, the principles on which they exist and mobilize support and membership are still strongly linked to kinship and local loyalty. Some parties do not even articulate national issues since their focus is largely local. There is a complex interaction between issues of personality, kinship, tribal-regional loyalty and ethnicity. Ideological differences in terms of adherence to standard political principles as in Western liberal democracies or in terms of religious or cultural ideologies rarely exist.[4] In Fiji, these ideological differences find expression through the platforms of the major parties. For example, some Fijian political parties are based on conservative nationalist principles (such as the Matanitu Vanua), with others being more moderate and multiracial (such as the Fiji Democratic Party). The Fiji Labour Party (FLP), which was founded in 1985 on social democratic principles, later evolved into an ethnic party (for Indo-

Table 2.1: Number of Pacific Island Political Parties and their Political Principles as at October 2004.

Country	No. of political parties	Major principles of party organisation, support and membership
Cook Islands	3	Kinship, business connections, locality, religion
Fiji	11	Ethnicity, political ideology, regional loyalty, religion
Kiribati	2	Personality, kinship, religion
Marshall Islands	1	Personality, kinship
Federated States of Micronesia	0	–
Nauru	0	–
Niue	0	–
Palau	0	–
Papua New Guinea	24	Personality, kinship, regional/tribal loyalty, religion
Sämoa	7	Personality, kinship, religion, locality
Solomon Islands*	2	Personality, kinship, regional/tribal loyalty, religion
Tokelau	0	–
Tonga**	1	Democratic Participation of commoners in the affairs of state
Tuvalu	0	–
Vanuatu	7	Personality, kinship, regional/tribal loyalty, language
Total	**57**	

*In the Solomon Islands, although there are two major political parties, there are numerous groupings and parties that comprise these.
**The Human Rights and Democracy movement in Tonga is technically not a political party, although it campaigns for elections and fights for issues just like normal political parties.

Fijians) after the leading leftist intellectuals quit the party in response to Mahendra Chaudhry's autocratic and conservative style of leadership.

Issues of personality, kinship and regional-tribal loyalty are closely associated with cultural traditions. In fact, these are some of the social mechanisms within which tradition is defined, articulated and reproduced. The fact that they feature prominently in the dynamics of political party formation and function shows the significance of tradition in the political process. Before we discuss the relationship between political parties and tradition, we need to consider the broader issues relating to tradition and politics.

Contextualising political parties: the politics of tradition debate

Political parties in Melanesia engage in a dynamic process of identity creation. On one hand is the appeal to tradition and on the other is the accommodation of modernity. To understand the relationship between political parties and tradition it is important to contextualise our analysis within the broader debate relating to politics and tradition and how this informs our empirical study.

The dynamic relationship between tradition and politics often involves reinventing certain assumed primordial aspects to serve practical purposes in given situations, usually for the benefit of dominant groups, political parties or elites. The notion of 'inventing tradition', especially in relation to the encapsulation of presumed past practices to exert new identities, has been the subject of analysis by people such as Hobsbawm and Ranger.[5] Others, such as Shils, Clifford, Keesing and Lawson, have explored the theoretical issues of representing and evoking traditional identity using new norms in post-colonial societies.[6]

Keesing described the trend in the Pacific thus:

> Across the Pacific, from Hawai'i to New Zealand, in New Caledonia, Aboriginal Australia, Vanuatu, the Solomon Islands, and Papua New Guinea, Pacific peoples are creating pasts, myths of ancestral ways of life that serve as powerful political symbols. In the rhetoric of post-colonial nationalism (and sometimes separatism) and the struggle of indigenous Fourth World peoples, now minorities in their own homelands, visions of the past are being created and evoked.[7]

The links between 'creating pasts, myths of ancestral ways of life' and 'political symbols' is part of a complex historical process emanating from contact between Europeans and indigenous people. Some of these were defensive reactions to colonialism and cultural encroachment while some were to facilitate change. For instance, recreation and articulation of 'new' identity by Aboriginal Australians or New Zealand Maori were part of resistance to colonial dispossession as well as adaptation to the new society. The same could be said of the Tahitian and Kanaky colonial situation, where political resistance meant creating new identities to consolidate an anti-colonial front. However constructed, these identities provided an important ideological reference framework with which they could redefine their position in the changing world.

The politics of resistance involves invoking traditional identities, whether based on assumed primordial links or recently created discourses, which act as powerful political symbols. In the case of Fiji, tradition as a basis for identity construction has in the past been used for the purpose of colonial resistance (as in the case of the semi-religious Luveniwai Movement) and, more recently has been deployed to maintain chiefly authority and communal hegemony and as an ethnic leverage against Indo-Fijians.[8]

Keesing's basic argument is that there is a fundamental contradiction in the process of political and traditional identity creation in the Pacific in the sense that 'the temporary discourse of cultural identity derives from Western discourses'.[9] In other words, many things that have been presented as being authentically traditional have often been based on colonial practices and discourses and have been accepted as immemorial. France makes the same observation about the land-ownership system in Fiji, arguing that what is now assumed to be the traditional Fijian landowning system was in fact a codified system recommended by a colonial Lands Commission in the early 1900s.[10]

In her study of the political systems of Fiji, Tonga and Sämoa, Lawson observed two interrelated processes taking place with respect to traditionalism and cultural revival.[11] The first pertains to the transformation of the notion of tradition into a political ideology and how this is deployed by political elites to serve specific purposes. The second deals with constructing a dichotomy as a way of invoking an oppositional image and providing justification for the ideology of traditionalism. An example is the use of the term 'Pacific Way' in the Pacific to mobilise opinion against what are seen to be 'Western' or 'foreign' ways.

The terms 'Melanesian Way' or '*wantokism*' have also been coined to serve the same political purpose. This refers to attempts to rediscover some primordial cultural or *kastom* (custom) links between the people of 'Melanesian' background as the means of political and cultural unity.[12] In a country as large as PNG, with more than 820 languages,[13] the notion of *wantok* would have various levels of contextualisation. At one level, it would refer to identification according to the same language and at another level it might refer to identification in relation to the same province or region.

Institutionalisation and deployment of tradition can take place in two forms. First, it might be used as an anti-foreigner ideology, as studies in Africa have shown.[14] To some extent, this has also been true in the Pacific, where appeal to traditional culture has been a reference point for anti-foreign articulations such as 'democracy is a foreign flower'.[15] Secondly, tradition can be deployed as a means of reinforcing the political status and power of traditional and 'modern' elites and political parties. The deployment of tradition as a legitimising tool in politics takes place in 'Western' and 'non-Western' societies. It has been observed that the preoccupation with genealogy by the European ruling classes was a way of legitimising their contemporary dominance and perpetual exclusion and subordination of the lower class. For example, Melman argues that various desirable aspects of the Anglo-Saxon traditions have been fabricated to maintain exclusivity of membership for the group.[16]

In Fiji, the development of tradition for political ends has always been linked to conservative and racial politics. Political practices and institutions, considered by many Fijians to be immemorial, were colonial constructions — formally codified and universalised practices deemed appropriate to colonial rule. For example, the Great Council of Chiefs and Fiji's land-ownership system were created as institutions of colonial dominance, but came to be thought of as 'traditional' over time. These were imbued with divine authority thus strengthening their normative force and authenticity. In this sense, elite indigenous interests dovetailed with British colonial agendas.

The close (and often inseparable) links between the church and the indigenous Fijian socio-cultural system and traditional hierarchy provided the framework for the unquestioned divinity and reification of tradition. Local practices that served the purposes of the local elites and colonial states were codified and became timeless tradition to be observed. Hobsbawm and Ranger summarised this tendency thus:

> Codified tradition inevitably hardened in a way that disadvantaged the vested interests in possession at the time of its codification. Codified and reified custom was manipulated by such vested interests as a means of asserting or increasing control ... Paramount chiefs and ruling aristocracies ... appealed to 'traditions' in order to maintain or extend their control over the subjects.[17]

During the post-colonial period in the Pacific, political parties became important vehicles for local political rule as well as for redefining and reproducing tradition whether codified or practised. This was especially so since many Pacific political parties emerged from community organisations and were spawned by the new era of decolonisation and self-expression. Their survival and legitimacy depended on how well they used and articulated tradition, whether invented or authentic. The importance of the distinction between authenticity and invented tradition deteriorated in the minds of political leaders because the issue was no longer to do with understanding and analysing the contents and dynamics of tradition but how tradition could be used for practical political purposes. Tradition thus became a political ideology in itself, which was subject to modification and manipulation by political parties. We examine this in more detail next.

Political parties and tradition: the dialectical relationship

Pacific political parties engage dialectically with tradition in various ways. These include political parties transforming traditional values into political party ideology and using them to mobilise support; traditional socio-cultural networks and kinship systems can be invoked to extend and consolidate influence; traditional modes of leadership can be used to consolidate support and legitimacy; and political parties often use revival of tradition as a party policy to win acceptance by the community. These processes often have a two-way dynamic between political parties and community: the political parties might make use of the community for purposes of mobilisation and legitimacy and likewise the community (or various sections of the community for that matter) might make use of political parties to serve their own interests. As the epitome of political organisation and articulation of political issues, political parties represent the link between the political community (defined narrowly here as politicians and the State political hierarchy) and the civil society at large. In the Pacific, this takes place in a complex way because of the influence of tradition through kinship, regional and tribal loyalty.

Traditional values as political party ideology

Traditional values have often been used as a basis for creating political ideology to invoke a sense of continuity, immemoriality and mythology to ensure political legitimisation and a sense of permanence. Political ideology is defined here in a general sociological sense to refer to a body of values and ideals, which is used as the basis for political action.[18]

This has especially been the case in Melanesian societies, where the use of traditional cosmology, whether in its symbolic or practical forms, by political parties to bolster ideological appeal is common practice. Because of its mystical nature, traditional cosmology can be translated easily into political ideology. The will of the ancestors and the power of the land can be invoked to maximum effect by political parties to project themselves as the anointed ones. Parties in the Solomon Islands, PNG and Vanuatu use local traditional cosmological discourses as their basis for consolidating legitimacy. Moreover, the dynamics of politics is often based on a reciprocal relationship where politicians are supposed to provide something tangible for the people in return for votes.

To consolidate their local popularity and legitimacy, politicians invoke traditional cosmological discourses. Ancestral spirits are often called on in ceremonies for their intervention to make a politician win an election and thus bring prosperity to his community. An election loss is sometimes blamed on sorcery by opponents. The use of sorcery is an effective political tool for 'weakening' and defeating adversaries in elections. Traditional symbols with deep cosmological significance might be used as party symbols. A case in point is the use of whale tooth (*tabua*), a symbol of peace and wealth, by the Fijian National Party (FNP).

One of the common tendencies is to invoke the traditional cosmological order to provide spiritual and psychological appeal. In Fiji, the Alliance Party, which ruled Fiji for 13 years before being ousted in a general election in 1987 by the FLP, used the appeal to the mythical *mana* of the *vanua* effectively as a means of mobilising support among indigenous Fijians. The notion of *vanua* in Fijian communal thinking exists at three levels. The first refers to land as an entity for subsistence living; the second to the totality of socio-cultural relationships and individual roles within these; and the third to the cosmological dimension — the ancestral and spiritual worlds.

As the only Fijian political party in the first seven years after independence, the Alliance Party had the monopoly over the appeal to Fijian cosmology. The political logic was that Fijians were bound by their *vanua* and therefore their political loyalty should be directed to the Alliance Party as the ancestrally ordained *soqosoqo vakapolitiki ni vanua* (party of the *vanua*). Those who did not support the *soqosoqo vakapolitiki ni vanua* were exhibiting un-Fijian characteristics and would be punished by the jealous ancestors. While this synergy between tradition and ideology was taking place at one level, the Alliance Party was articulating a multiracialist discourse at another in order to appeal to other ethnic groups and win national and international legitimacy.

Other Fijian political parties subsequently used the same cosmological appeal, provoking competition over who was the legitimate guardian of the Fijian cosmology. Winning the election was a way of exerting one's claim. Sometimes, debates about economic and political issues between Fijian political parties would degenerate into competition about who best represented the *vanua* and Fijian-ness and thus who best represented the Fijian cosmology. This was most evident in the formation of the Kudru na Vanua (Grumble of the Land) Party, headed by a defrocked Catholic priest, which has failed ever to win a parliamentary seat. The leader claimed that his party was the only one to have the blessing of the ancestral spirits of Fiji and that he was a *kalou vu* (ancestral god), who in cosmological ranking was higher than everyone else in Fiji, including the high chiefs.

In Vanuatu, political party issues revolve largely around the notion of land. Land is the embodiment of culture and tradition, the link to ancestral cosmology. The name Vanuatu literally means 'our land' and the ruling party after independence, the Vanua'aku Party (party of 'our land'), adopted a policy that supported ownership of land 'according to custom' and the 'reservation and protection of important *tambu* [taboo] places'.[19] Indeed, such policies are common reference points in Vanuatu's political culture. Perhaps the most prominent party advocating the protection of *tambu* places is the Jon Frum Party, which started as a cargo-cult type movement in 1940, but which remains a powerful political force on the island of Tanna. In these instances, *kastom* represented a remedial strategy to Western advance. Indeed, one of Vanuatu's most prominent *kastom* groups, Nagriamel, advanced the theory that returning to *kastom* was the best way to protect community land from encroaching European ranchers. Their policy perhaps summarised what most Vanuatu political parties believe: 'Land is the basis, the essence of everything. Restore KUSTOM.'[20]

Use of traditional socio-cultural and kinship networks

Throughout Melanesia, parties usually consist of loose associations of individuals and groups whose political orientations are locally based, with community-oriented land policies being prominent in party platforms. Thus, utilising kinship systems is a common political strategy for political mobilisation by parties and candidates. These systems constitute an important mechanism for reproducing traditional culture in the Pacific. Kinship is the major means for socialisation and cultural reproduction and ensures the survival of a community. Kinship is a system and a process and has complex links to land and to the cosmological world of the ancestors.

Kinship is often a powerful centripetal force around which political party loyalty revolves. Because many politicians have localised interests, kinship is a means by which they can access the community to carry out campaigns and also the means whereby the local communities demand 'payback' in terms of money and services. This is where the dilemma between kinship responsibility and public accountability becomes obvious. For the politician, using public money to satisfy his or her kinspeople's wishes could be labelled 'corruption'; on the other hand, being seen not to be giving generously to his or her people would be political suicide.

There are two types of kinship: biological kinship and social kinship. Biological kinship is where there are identifiable blood ties. Social kinship has to do with links that are based on claims to common origin, history or experiences. Blood ties also have social obligations and relationships to make them legitimate and social kinship is sometimes assumed to also involve primordial relations with common biological origins at some point in the past. In Melanesia, the notion of *wantok* represents biological and social kinship existing at different levels. There are circles of *wantoks* starting at the nuclear family and extending outwards. The external boundary extends as far as one can identify (in many cases assume) a common feature of identification. Thus, the external boundary could be just a nuclear family or extended family, a tribe, a region, a town, a country or even all speakers of Melanesian pidgin.

Political party mobilisation usually takes place at the most immediate boundary, usually at the nuclear family, extended family and tribal levels. This is not only because of the closeness of the social links and the existence of the traditional obligations that bind people together, but because closer kinship groups are considered the most politically trustworthy. Close kinspeople tend to see the political success and associated privileges of their relatives as their own.

For political parties in Melanesia, the use of kinship provides the easiest, cheapest and most effective way of mobilisation, extending influence and winning legitimacy.

Over the years, many political parties in Fiji had developed extensive links and networks based on kinship. The Alliance Party used these networks extremely successfully after independence in 1970. Whole families were recruited by relatives to join the party and all the leading Alliance politicians in the 1970s, namely Ratu Sir Kamisese Mara (the Prime Minister), Ratu Sir Penaia Ganilau (Deputy Prime Minister and later Governor-General and President), Ratu Sir George Cakobau (former Governor-General), were all related by blood. There were lower levels of chiefs who were also related to these 'big three'. The hierarchy reached down to the village level where various levels of kinship were linked together through their links to the Alliance Party. The Alliance Party was not only 'the' Fijian party — it was also 'the' family party. Any member of the family who did not vote for or support the Alliance was considered a *dau vakau nona* — a political 'deviant'.

A number of political parties that were formed in the 1980s and 1990s used kinship in subtle and obvious ways. For instance, a number of parties, such as the Party of National Unity, Tako Lavo and the Bai kei Viti (literally, fortress of Fiji), both formed in the 1990s, revolved around tribal and kinship linkages. The Matanitu Vanua, formed by supporters of coup-maker George Speight, had a significant kinship base in the Tailevu Province.

Traditional leadership and political legitimacy

Closely associated with the use of kinship is the use of traditional leadership. Notions of 'traditional' leadership in the Pacific have evolved in various ways over the years, some reinvented and some retaining certain aspects that were presumably pre-colonial in nature. By and large, the two most significant determinants of 'traditional' leadership are inheritance and achievement. On the 'hereditary' extreme is Tonga, where monarchical or noble status is purely through birth, while on the other 'achievement' extreme are some Melanesian communities that do not have chiefs as such but 'big men', who gain social prestige through the accumulation of cultural capital such as leadership skills, personal and social wealth. In between these two extremes, however, are shades of hereditary and achievement and often a coexistence of these two modes of traditional leadership.

In Fiji, there is a complex interplay between hereditary and achieved leadership. Through their Native Policy, the British restructured the chiefly system to facilitate indirect rule. The previously isolated chiefdoms were centralised under the Fijian Administration. New chiefly titles were created and made to fit into the new hierarchy. The inherited and highly stratified system of leadership that was prevalent mostly in the eastern parts of Fiji was universalised as traditional, although many parts of Fiji possessed more egalitarian Melanesian modes of leadership. Today, because of the complex interplay between the inheritance and achievement leadership modes and the lack of clear guidelines regarding inheritance, there is constant competition for chiefly positions. Given the complexity of what now constitutes traditional leadership after recent reconceptualisation and restructuring, this chapter will define it specifically in terms of localised modes of leadership in community settings such as villages and clans, which are recognised as 'traditional' by the communities concerned.

Political parties in Melanesia have used traditional leadership as a means of mobilisation and legitimisation. Often traditional leaders have deliberately been made party leaders, leaders of local party branches, campaign managers and party stalwarts, or election candidates, as a way of consolidating party discipline and authority as well as to project images of respectability and coherence to the public.

In Fiji, Mara, the first leader of the Alliance Party and first Prime Minister, had three very high chiefly titles as well as having read economics at the London School of Economics and being an MA graduate from Oxford. In his lifetime, he was awarded two knighthoods and a host of other decorations, including honorary doctorates and fellowships from universities around the world. Mara's standing as a regional and Commonwealth statesman no doubt contributed to his heightened *mana*. His case was a classic example of a situation of synthesis between inheritance and achievement, but still needs to be put in proper historical context. For instance, Mara's education was driven largely by the colonial policy of deliberately educating chiefs to prepare them for future leadership. He was no doubt a brilliant scholar — being chosen from the rank of potential Fijian chiefs — but he was also advantaged by the 'accident of birth'.[21]

The political organisation and structure of the Alliance Party revolved around Mara's skilful political strategising, as well as his chiefly *mana*.[22] Interestingly, his closest friends were Indo-Fijian businessmen and politicians, not Fijians, because Fijians were restricted by socio-cultural protocol compared with Indo-Fijians, who were not bounded by the traditional Fijian hierarchy.

In Vanuatu, chiefly titles are either hereditary or achieved. Both are linked to party politics in dynamic ways. For instance, one's chiefly background could provide an important fulcrum for political party leadership. The first leader of the Vanua'aku Party and first Prime Minister of Vanuatu, Father Walter Lini, was a hereditary chief (from the maternal and paternal sides) from the island of Pentecost, with the bestowed title of *Molbwango*. His chiefly status boosted his political career.[23]

Some, such as the controversial politician, Barak Sope, managed to accumulate a number of traditional titles as a result of their national political status. In turn, they used the socio-cultural status of these titles to mobilise political support. This is also the case in the Solomon Islands and PNG, where national political status is gained largely through one's success in politics. Later, this success is often used to build up 'traditional' status within the community. Consequently, this newfound status is later used to reinforce national political status further. A consequence of this is the development of a mutually reinforcing relationship between traditional status and political party interest.

To ensure acceptance by the community, it is common in Melanesia to use traditional chiefs as a medium for party campaigns at the local level. In cases where traditional leadership is hereditary it is usually easy to identity who the chiefs are, but in cases where there is open competition for chiefly positions, there are competing claims that can cause conflict. In such cases, links with political parties might provoke further tension. Political parties are usually wary of individuals who make arbitrary claims to the 'big man' title since they might turn out to be political liabilities.

There are, however, times when chiefs are not used directly as instruments for political mobilisation within a local community. This is because of sensitivity about potential tension due to allegations of political bias, with some chiefs wary of losing their traditional status in the event of conflict. In these circumstances, political parties rope in relatives of chiefs (usually through the secret blessing of chiefs) as tactical manoeuvres to avoid any publicly visible connection that might prove politically fatal for the chief.[24]

Tradition as party policy

Tradition is often the subject of political campaigns. This involves tradition or particular interpretations of it being used as a subject of debate by political parties in order to legitimate their projects and policies. In Fiji, PNG, Vanuatu and Solomon Islands, almost all indigenous political parties refer to preservation of tradition as one of their aims. Although it is usually somewhat unclear how this is to be done, the political purpose is apparent — the ideological undertones sound positive and are comforting to voters who feel that tradition and cultural identity are synonymous and need protection.

Most Melanesian political parties have not really articulated the 'tradition as policy' argument nor put in place practical frameworks to preserve culture.[25] In Fiji, tradition has often been invoked as a means of 'saving' Fijian culture and a tool of ethnic mobilisation to arouse fear of Indian domination, and in Solomon Islands and PNG it has been a utilitarian tool for party unity and attracting votes. Perhaps the only country where this has happened successfully is Vanuatu, where, in the early days of independence, the policies of the Vanua'aku Party attempted to unite the country through preservation of traditional culture. This found expression in the Vanuatu Cultural Centre (VCC). The VCC was formed before independence but was nurtured and given inspiration by a succession of ruling parties.[26]

In Fiji, traditional institutions that are meant to protect Fijian culture, such as the Fijian Affairs Board, Native Land Trust Board and Ministry of Fijian Affairs, are theoretically outside the ambit of party politics. Nevertheless, over the years all the major Fijian political parties, such as the Alliance Party, Soqosoqo ni Vakavulewa ni Taukei (SVT) and the currently ruling Soqosoqo Duavata ni Lewe ni Vanua (SDL), have used these institutions to serve their political ends. Moreover, because Fijian tradition is assumed to be alive and well through these institutions it is not deemed necessary to do anything further to revive it.

The dilemma of party identity: 'foreign flower' versus tradition

As we have seen, most indigenous political parties in Melanesia use tradition extensively to consolidate their identity. So while political parties are at one level organisational manifestations of modern democracy, they have also been 'traditionalised', often as a reflection of sentimental opposition to foreign influence. In countries such as Fiji, the notion of democracy as a 'foreign flower' has been part of the nationalist vocabulary since the military coups in 1987. In other Melanesian societies, there is sometimes an inherent disdain of the 'foreign' and love for the traditional. The flawed logic behind this is that democracy has destroyed traditional institutions and thus democratic ideals and influences need to be minimised in favour of retaining traditional systems.

This presents an interesting set of contradictions. Much of what is being referred to here as traditional is in fact quite recent in origin and is often a product of the colonial era. Furthermore, in many cases, those who articulate for the anti-foreigner and pro-tradition stance are some of the greatest beneficiaries of modern education and modern life. Theirs becomes an ideological construction to look for scapegoats (often foreigners) as well as a mobilising tool for local political support, especially from more conservative members of the electorate.

This was particularly evident in Fiji, where the utility of the concept of 'the foreign flower' grew in parallel with the waning fortunes of the Alliance Party. Invoking tradition was used as an anti-Indian rallying call by supporters of the Alliance Party, which lost the 1987 election to the FLP, a month before the May coup.[27] The rhetoric was that the foreign flower benefited only foreigners and undermined the political aspirations of the indigenous people. While the Alliance Party was winning elections between 1965 (when Fijians were first allowed to vote) and 1987, the foreign flower concept was never heard of. Indeed, it was only after the Alliance lost the election that democracy came to be demonised.

Because of their dynamic roles, political parties will continue to face the dilemma of multiple identities — being a vanguard of tradition one minute and an agent of modernisation the next. This process of identity flux continues to define the ideological and political characteristics of Pacific political parties.

Conclusion

Tradition still plays an important role in the broader dynamics and configuration of politics in the Pacific. Articulations of tradition by politicians are reinvented to suit particular circumstances and interests, just as politics can be used to reinforce certain traditional modes of organisation. Political parties need to be understood in the context of this broad schema.

The relationship between political parties and tradition can be understood in four key ways. First, tradition can be used as the basis for formulating political ideology as a means of mobilisation and legitimisation. In this way, political parties invoke traditional socio-cultural mythology and cosmology to provide convincing arguments based on ancestral and divine intervention. Second, the use of socio-cultural and kinship structures and linkages expands party influence and consolidates community support. One's own kinspeople provide visible avenues for electoral support. Traditional socio-cultural systems based on reciprocity also come into play in a dynamic and functional way. Third, the tendency of traditional leaders to become party leaders, candidates for election or party stalwarts involved in community party organisation is commonplace. Last, there is the use of tradition as a policy framework in itself; that is, the preservation of tradition as a policy for cementing community support.

Political parties in Melanesia range from very loose associations of individuals and groups to more organisationally coherent groups. Some are relatively stable while others are constituted opportunistically to contest national elections. While what qualifies for a political party is generally determined by the respective laws of the Pacific Island countries, their operation on the ground is guided by broader political and socio-cultural forces. Tradition constitutes one of those forces and will continue to be a defining factor for Melanesian political parties for years to come. Tradition is embedded in people's communal psyche and, as such, becomes a powerful political force for mobilisation and legitimisation. Its utilitarian characteristics make it readily deployable by political parties for various purposes — all the more so because tradition is highly adaptable and subject to constant transformation.

Footnotes

1   See chapters on political parties in Fiji, Solomon Islands, Vanuatu, Tonga, Sämoa, Tuvalu, Kiribati, Nauru, Marshall Islands and Federated States of Micronesia by Steven Ratuva in Alan J. Day and Henry W. Degenhardt (eds) 2004, *Political Parties of the World*. London: John Harper Publications. There are now more than 2,550 political parties across the globe. See Day. 2004. 'Introduction.' In Day and Degenhardt (eds), ibid. p. vii.

2   See Lawson, Stephanie. 1997. *Cultural Tradition and Identity Politics: Some Implications for Democratic Governance in Asia and the Pacific.* Canberra: ANU Publishers.

3   See Ratuva, 2004, op. cit.

4   It must be stated here that ideological differences between political parties are decreasing the world over. For instance, the differences between the once left-wing British Labour Party and the conservative Tory Party are no longer as obvious as before.

5   See Hobsbawn, E. and T. Rangers (eds). 1983. *The Invention of Tradition.* Cambridge: Cambridge University Press.

6   See Shils, E. 1981. *Tradition.* London: Faber and Faber; Clifford, J. 1988. *The Predicament of Culture: Twentieth Century Ethnology, Literature and Art.* Cambridge (Mass): University of Hawai'i Press; Keesing, R. 1989. 'Creating the Past: Custom and Identity in the Contemporary Pacific.' In *Contemporary Pacific*, Vol. 1, pp. 19–42; and Lawson, Stephanie. 1996. *Tradition Versus Democracy in the South Pacific: Fiji, Tonga and Western Samoa.* Canberra: ANU Press.

7   Keesing, ibid. p. 19. See also Keesing, Roger and Robert Tonkinson (eds). 1982. *Reinventing Traditional Culture: The Politics of Kastom in Island Melanesia. Special Issue Mankind*, Vol. 13, No. 4.

8   See Ratuva, Steven. 1999. 'Ethnic Politics, Communalism and Affirmative Action in Fiji: A Critical and Comparative Study.' PhD Thesis, University of Sussex.

9   Keesing, 1989, op. cit., p. 19.

10   See France, Peter. 1969. *The Charter of the Land: Custom and Colonization in Fiji.* Melbourne: Oxford University Press.

11   Lawson, 1996, op. cit.

12   Narokobi, Bernard. 1983. *The Melanesian Way.* Port Moresby: Institute of Pacific Studies.

13   *The Ethnologue: Languages of the World*, published by SIL Inc., lists 823 living languages for PNG. See http://www.ethnologue.com/show_country.asp?name=Papua+New+Guinea

14   See Hobsbawm and Ranger, op. cit.

15   The term was first used after the coups of 1987 as the tide of Fijian ethno-nationalism swept Fiji. One of the most vocal nationalist politicians, Finau Tabukaucoro, first introduced the term in a public speech in Suva in May 1987. See also Larmour, Peter. 2005. *Foreign Flowers: institutional transfer and good governance in the Pacific Islands.* Honolulu: University of Hawai'i Press.

16   See Melman, B. 1991. 'Claiming the Nation's Past: The Invention of an Anglo-Saxon Tradition.' *Journal of Contemporary History*, Vol. 26, No. 3l. pp. 575–95.

17   Hobsbawm and Ranger (eds), op. cit., p. 254.

18   See Day, op. cit. For most of the modern political discourse, especially in the 20th century, political parties in western states were identified in relation to either 'left', 'right' or 'centre' and variants in between ('centre-left', etc.). There are also those with non-secular ideology, based on religion and other mythical beliefs.

19   Lini, Walter. 1980. *Beyond Pandemonium: From the New Hebrides to Vanuatu.* Suva: Institute of Pacific Studies. p. 32.

20   Ibid., p. 47.

21   For details of Mara's political ideology and vision, see Mara, Kamisese. 1997. *Pacific Way.* Honolulu: University of Hawai'i Press.

22   See Ratuva, 1999, op. cit.

23   Personal communication with Jeanette Bolenga (Walter Lini's sister), Electoral Fellow, University of the South Pacific (December 17, 2004).

24   Personal communication with Jeanette Bolenga (December 19, 2004).

25   See Lindstrom, Lamont and Geoffrey White (eds). 1994. *Culture, Kastom, Tradition: Developing Cultural Policy in Melanesia.* Suva: Institute of Pacific Studies, University of the South Pacific. pp. 67, 85.

26   See Roe, D., R. Regenvanu, F. Wadra and N. Araho. 1994. 'Working with Cultural Landscapes in Melanesia: Some Problems and Approaches in the Formulation of Cultural Policies.' In L. Lindstrom and G. M. White (eds), *Culture, Kastom, Tradition: Developing Cultural Policy in Melanesia,* Suva: Institute of Pacific Studies, University of the South Pacific. pp. 115–30.

27   Ratuva, Steven. 2004. *Storm in Paradise: The 1987 Military Coup* Uppsala: Life and Peace Institute.

POLITICAL CONSEQUENCES OF PACIFIC ISLAND ELECTORAL LAWS

3

Jon Fraenkel

AT FIRST SIGHT, the Pacific Islands seem like a graveyard for institutional determinist theories regarding the impact of electoral systems on party polarisation. Maurice Duverger's well-known 'sociological law' was that first-past-the-post electoral rules tend to deliver two-party systems. Proportional representation systems were more loosely associated by Duverger with multi-party settings.[1] Yet in the Pacific, countries using first-past-the-post systems, such as the Solomon Islands and PNG (1975–2002), have developed multiple-party systems. The proportional representation-using territories of New Caledonia, French Polynesia and Vanuatu have veered towards a two-camp polarisation around the issue of independence. Some first-past-the-post-using democracies, such as Palau and the FSM, have not witnessed the emergence of any party-based system at all. Neighbouring Kiribati, Nauru and Tuvalu have similar styles of loose and fluctuating parliamentary alliances but no election-oriented political parties, despite the first using a two-round electoral system, the second a unique simultaneously tallied preferential voting system, and the third a block-voting system in two-member constituencies. Electoral laws would appear to exert negligible sway over Pacific party systems.

On closer examination, Duverger's theory does shed some light on the direction of electoral incentives in some of the Pacific countries, once hedged with the necessary qualifications and confined to appropriate settings. Negative cases, where electoral laws do not bring about the anticipated party structures are not confined to Oceania. India and Canada, for example, have numerous political parties, but use first-past-the-post electoral systems. Guyana uses a list proportional representation system but has a two-party centred system, as did Austria from 1945–90. Much of the literature has consequently been aimed at revising Duverger's theories about the impact of electoral laws on party systems, either by emphasising that the critical association is in fact between district magnitude and the number of parties or by specifying the role of intervening variables, such as ethnic heterogeneity or the number of competing 'issue dimensions' to the political process.[2] It is in situations where a single salient political cleavage (such as labour/ conservative, or Catholic/Protestant) dominates the political order that distinct electoral laws might work in different directions, encouraging or limiting multi-partyism. In Fiji and New Caledonia, those varying electoral pressures on party systems exerted considerable control over the success or failure of compacts aimed at mitigating ethnic conflict.

In most South Pacific nations, the decolonisation issue did not prove an enduring ideological influence over post-independence politics (except in Vanuatu, and, if we include countries still under some kind of colonial rule, New Caledonia and French Polynesia). Class politics nowhere proved a central cleavage regulating post-colonial political organisation, except plausibly on one level within Fiji's Indian community during the 1990s. Nor — again except in ethnically bipolar Fiji — did other issues emerge that stimulated the formation of organisationally robust or durable alliances. In many cases, political parties remain either non-existent or they comprise only fleeting and regularly changing assembly groupings, commanding little loyalty or popular respect.[3] 'Party politics', to the extent that it exists, is frequently viewed with disdain, and charged with aggravating social tensions that run counter to Pacific traditions of consensus and compromise. Fluidity of parliamentary alignments, and the readiness of MPs to 'cross the floor', ensure a frequent turnover of governments, particularly in western Melanesia but also in Nauru and Kiribati. The Pacific Island states have consequently eminently passed Samuel Huntington's 'two turnover' test of democratic consolidation.[4] Indeed, they have done so to such a degree that the primary concern is endemic instability rather than the absence of regime change.

During the decolonisation era, colonial authorities frequently anticipated and encouraged the emergence of local political parties, identifying these as a necessary counterpart of the removal of official majorities and post-independence political stabilisation.[5] Drawing on experience in other parts of the world, analysts suggested that 'the appearance of political parties in a democratic political system tends to be associated with the expansion of the franchise and the introduction of a significant elective element in national decision-making councils'.[6] Party politics was often viewed as an evolutionary stage and any sign of the crystallisation of fleeting alliances or greater organisational rigour was seen as indicative of its imminent realisation.[7] The lessons from 20th century Western Europe or North America, after all, seemed to indicate the universality of party-centred political development, and elsewhere anti-colonial movements and/or labour movements often coalesced into political parties that served as governments-in-waiting and endured after the handover of power. Political parties are consequently frequently deemed indispensable for functioning democracies, to provide linkages between citizens and their representatives and to facilitate collective decision-making.[8]

Influenced by such ideas, contemporary Pacific governments have introduced a range of reforms designed to strengthen political parties. Fiji's 1995–96 Constitutional Review Commission, for example, gave a high priority to the 'recognition of the role of political parties' in its choice of institutions capable of achieving 'multi-ethnic government'.[9] Parties, it was hoped, would serve as agents of moderation and inter-ethnic conciliation, and, to accomplish this, they were provided with considerable control over the transfer of preference votes.[10] As part of the new electoral system adopted in 1997–98, a split-format ballot paper was introduced, with an 'above-the-line' section enabling voters to indicate their support for party-endorsed preference schedules. The hope was that this would enhance political parties' bargaining capacity and simultaneously encourage inter-ethnic deals on politically sensitive policy issues. Constitutional rules governing the post-election formation of cabinets in Fiji also potentially had repercussions for the party system. All parties with more than 10 per cent of seats were entitled to a proportional share of ministerial portfolios, implying a considerable disincentive for smaller parties and independent candidates.

PNG's *Organic Law on the Integrity of Political Parties and Candidates* (OLIPPC) is the most ambitious of the contemporary party engineering projects in the Pacific. MPs are given financial incentives to join political parties, and are required to toe the party line during critical votes in Parliament, including those on motions of no confidence, constitutional amendments and budgets. PNG's reforms, and the underlying concerns that inspire these, also influence the reform-oriented discourse elsewhere in the region. In Sämoa, the governing Human Rights Protection Party in 1995 facilitated the passage of legislation obliging candidates to specify their allegiance with the objective of enhancing the electoral significance of political parties. Sämoa, Fiji and New Zealand adopted laws against party-hopping, with a view to strengthening party parliamentary organisation and diminishing government instability.[11] The 'strengthening of parties' is frequently a smokescreen for reforms aimed at consolidating the grip of executives (or incumbent parties). Given the threat of instability associated with recurrent regime change and the often gridlocked nature of governments threatened by 'no confidence' challenges, such reforms (with or without the smokescreen) have often understandably found tacit support among donors and diplomats from neighbouring metropolitan powers.

This chapter surveys the range of electoral system types and party structures across the Pacific Islands and considers the viability of contemporary electoral reforms aimed at strengthening party systems. For each region, the chapter surveys in brief all countries, but focuses in detail on one or two countries in which particularly topical electoral issues arise. As an antidote to the approach of setting up the familiar party-based model, and then examining the extent to which Pacific politics achieves that style of organisation, we examine first the western and northern independent Pacific states where political parties are of least significance, then look at those Polynesian countries where political parties have assumed greater significance before focusing on the most strongly party-centred ethnically bipolar states of Fiji and New Caledonia.

Table 3.1 surveys the types of electoral system used in legislative elections across the region. First-past-the-post systems (used in single-member districts) are the most frequent arrangement, although often combined with a number of block-voting districts (with multiple members), where eligible citizens have as many votes as there are seats. Guam, where citizens have 15 votes to fill 15 places, has the most sizeable of such districts, but Majuro in the Marshall Islands elects five members and tiny Niue has a six-member island-wide constituency, as well as separate single-member village-based constituencies. Vanuatu and Pitcairn Island have multiple-member constituencies combined with only a single vote for each eligible citizen (i.e., single non-transferable vote systems). Kiribati has a multi-member block-vote district system, but uses a second round of voting where necessary. Fiji and PNG have adopted the alternative vote, which involves the redistribution of preference votes, either until majorities are secured (Fiji) or until ballots are exhausted (PNG).[12] Nauru's preferential system is distinctive, because it uses multi-member constituencies and because all preferences are simultaneously counted. New Caledonia, French Polynesia and Wallis and Futuna use list proportional representation systems for territorial elections. Voters back a single party, and the proportion of candidates elected from that party's list depends on its district percentage of the vote. These countries also have the largest constituencies in the Pacific: for example, 37 members are returned by French Polynesia's Windward Islands (Tahiti and Moorea), and 32 congress members are elected from New Caledonia's Southern Province. All three French territories also participate in metropolitan French elections, which entail a two-round system for legislative and presidential elections.

Table 3.1 also constructs an index for the 'effective' number of parties using an adjusted variant of the widely used Laakso/Taagepera Index combined with data covering distribution of seats by political party recorded in the 2005 *Political Parties of the World*. The Laakso/Taagepera Index aims at obtaining a meaningful composite number so as to establish whether each country has a two- or a multi-party system. For example, a country with three parties that secure 55 per cent, 45 per cent and 5 per cent of seats is shown as having a 2.2-party system, rather than a three-party system. The results are inevitably as good or as bad as the underlying data, in the sense that for some Pacific states the 'parties' recorded exist merely on paper.[13] Since party vote shares are impossible to establish meaningfully for the more fluid party systems, the index is calculated using party seat shares.[14] The standard Laakso/Taagepera Index is not well honed to deal with situations where a large number of independents enter parliament. To handle this, column three removes independents from the calculation while column four indicates the preponderance of the party system. Hence, for example, PNG's 22 parties that secured seats at the 2002 polls (including many single- or two-seat parties), once weighted to yield an adjusted Laakso/ Taagepera measure, suggest a 10-party system, whereas column four tells us that 79 per cent of PNG MPs were affiliated with political parties and that the residual, 21 per cent, were independents.

In terms of the robustness of party political organisation, the Pacific states straddle a range that extends from relatively strongly party-centred polities (such as Fiji and New Caledonia, where bipolar ethnic frictions have, historically, encouraged the emergence of relatively strong party organisations) to no-party or only nominally party-based systems (such as PNG, Solomon Islands, Palau, Nauru and the FSM). Political parties are regularly provided for in Pacific constitutions. Even where they are not envisaged, other legislative provisions might facilitate the emergence of assembly groupings. The cohesion of 'the opposition' is often encouraged, for example, by provisions regarding the establishment of an 'Office of the Leader of the Opposition', and laws regulating the competitive selection of the 'Leader of the Opposition'. In the Solomon Islands, provisions

Table 3.1: Electoral Systems, Effective Number of Political Parties and Extent of Party Preponderance in Pacific Island Legislative Assemblies.

Country/Territory	Electoral System (1)	Year (2)	'Effective' No. Parties (3)	Party Preponderance (4)
American Sämoa (US)	FPP	N/P	0.0	0.00
Cook Islands	FPP	1999	2.6	1.00
Fed. States of Micronesia	FPP	N/P	0.0	0.00
Fiji	AV	2001	2.7	0.96
French Polynesia (France)	LPR[1]	2001	2.3	1.00
Guam (US)	BV	2002	1.9	1.00
Kiribati	TRS[2]	1998	2.0	0.64
Marshall Islands	FPP/BV	1999	1.0	0.55
Nauru	STPV	N/P	0.0	0.00
New Caledonia (France)	LPR	1999	4.5	1.00
Niue	FPP/BV	N/P	0.0	0.00
Comm. Northern Marianas (US)	FPP	2003	2.5	1.00
Palau	FPP	N/P	0.0	0.00
Papua New Guinea	FPP	2002	10.0	0.79
Pitcairn Island (UK)	SNTV	N/P	0.0	0.00
Sämoa	FPP/BV	2002	1.9	0.73
Solomon Islands	FPP	2001	3.3	0.98
Tonga	FPP/BV	2002	1.0[3]	0.78
Tuvalu	FPP/BV	N/P	0.0	0.00
Vanuatu	SNTV	2004	6.9	0.85
Wallis and Futuna (France)	LPR	2002	1.8	1.00

Sources: Levine, S. and N. Roberts. 2005. 'The Constitutional Structures and Electoral Systems of the Pacific Islands.' *Journal of Commonwealth and Comparative Politics, Vol. 43, No. 3., pp. 276–95*; Szajkowski, B. (ed.) 2005. *Political Parties of the World*. 5th edition (1st edition, 1980).
Notes: FPP – first-past-the-post; AV – alternative vote; LPR – list proportional representation; BV – block vote; TRS – Two round system; STPV – simultaneously tallied preferential vote; SNTV – single non-transferable vote; N/P – no party system. The Laakso/Taagepera Index is one minus the sum of squared seat shares, with independents calculated as parties with single seats (Taagepera, R. 1989. *Seats and Votes: The Effects and Determinants of Electoral Systems*. New Haven: Yale University Press. pp. 78–9). The index shown here is adjusted by excluding independents, and by weighting parties by their share in the total seats secured by parties in assemblies. The party preponderance index (column four) shows party-affiliated MPs divided by total parliamentary membership (with 1.0 conveying an entirely party-centred system and 0.0 indicating an entirely non-party system). Election years are the latest recorded in the 2005 edition of *Political Parties of the World*.
1 With 30 per cent plurality Seat Bonus.
2 Block vote with second round in several multi-member constituencies.
3 Only the nine universal franchise seats are counted, and, in this context, the Human Rights and Democracy Movement is counted as a political party.

under the 1978 Constitution for the 'Leader of the Independents', oddly, encouraged the quasi-party-style functioning of reputedly non-aligned MPs. After general elections, independents operate virtually like the country's loosely knit political parties, and come together in the capital, Honiara, to select their own, or back another, candidate for the premiership. Similarly in Sāmoa, a Sāmoan United Independents Party emerged after the 2001 polls, although laws against post-electoral party formation were used by the Government to declare illegal its subsequent efforts to form a new party together with the major opposition party. As we have seen, legislation aimed at strengthening political parties has been adopted widely across the region, whether it be through direct financial incentives for party-aligned candidates or, indirectly, by 'grace periods', rules prohibiting 'party-hopping' and other restraints on 'no-confidence' votes.

Melanesia

PNG

PNG used an optional preferential voting system in elections held in 1964, 1968 and 1972, but then switched to a first-past-the-post system in 1975.[15] The number of candidates contesting elections subsequently increased at every election, reaching an average of 27 per constituency at the 2002 polls. Numbers of victors obtaining more than 50 per cent of the vote declined, with the majority of MPs being elected on the basis of less than 20 per cent of the vote in 1992, 1997 and 2002. National elections became vehicles for the articulation of clan rivalries, particularly in the Highlands. Parties proved, at most, loose associations, which politicians were readily willing to ditch in pursuit of ministerial portfolios. Customary 'big men' competed for wealth, influence and authority through electoral processes, driven by pecuniary rewards attached to state office-holding.[16] Whether or not they joined nominal political parties, victors' positions remained highly precarious. More than half of all MPs lost their seats at most elections after independence, with incumbent turnover reaching an all time high of 75 per cent at the 2002 polls.

Inside Parliament, politicians frequently steer clear of political parties, or form fleeting party attachments that play second fiddle to personal advancement. No single party has ever obtained an absolute majority in Parliament. PNG had 10 governments from 1975 to 2002, three of which were dislodged by votes of no confidence. Governments are frequently formed by backroom cabals ('lock-ups'), which proceed to divide among themselves the spoils of office. MPs on the Opposition benches thus have every incentive to, and little institutional inhibition against, plot the next no confidence bid. Many prefer to sit on the 'middle benches', in a twilight position between government and opposition, hoping to secure ministerial portfolios at the next reshuffle.[17] Instead of yielding the frequently anticipated advantage of strong and stable government (due to seat swings that enhance or magnify narrower vote swings), the first-past-the-post system provides the backdrop for a highly volatile parliamentary set-up, in which unscrupulous and opportunistic 'rubber band' or 'yoyo' politicians prove willing to repeatedly switch allegiances for personal or constituency gain.[18]

As a result, Papua New Guinean reformists have taken steps to strengthen the party system. The OLIPPC was enacted in 2002 and was aimed at strengthening political parties via controls over funding and restrictions on party-hopping. Those who contest elections as members of parties receive state financial support. Independents do not. Once a vote has been held for a prime minister, MPs are obliged to follow the party line on budgetary and constitutional votes, and in votes of no confidence. Cases involving MPs who cross the floor or fail to follow the party whip on these issues are heard by an Ombudsman Commission and, if necessary, are referred to a Leadership Tribunal, with the ultimate sanction being the forfeit of seats. New rules are aimed at restricting post-election horse-trading, by giving the party with the largest number of seats the first opportunity to form a government. One consequence, witnessed at the 2002 polls, was a sizeable increase in the official number of political parties, which rose from 12 in 1997 to 43 in 2002, although many of these existed only on paper and failed to obtain a single MP. The rules have proved difficult to implement, and, as in India after the introduction of similar legislation in 1985, much party side-switching continues, either illegally or (where this is sanctioned collectively by a party) legally.[19]

A limited preferential voting system (LPV) was also introduced in PNG, and came into effect in the wake of the 2002 general elections. It was aimed chiefly at avoiding the proliferation of MPs elected on the basis of less than 10 or 20 per cent of the vote. To cast a valid (or formal) ballot, citizens are required to list three candidates in order of prefer-ence (incomplete ballots with only one or two preferences marked are to be discarded as invalid or informal). If no candidate gets a majority of first-preference votes, the lowest-polling candidate is eliminated and his or her voters' second-preference votes are redistributed among the remaining candidates. This process of elimination of candidates and redistribution of votes continues until one candidate obtains 50 per cent plus one of valid votes or until ballots are exhausted. PNG's new electoral system is designed to encourage more moderate or conciliatory candidates, who reach out beyond their core bases of support in the hope of obtaining second- or third-preference votes from other communities. Both reforms, in different ways, anticipate and encourage a more issue-and/or party-based political culture. Just as the candidate with the broader appeal is anticipated, after the introduction of the LPV, to pick up preference votes outside his or her community, so too the more broadly aligned party MP is to receive financial encour-agement under the OLIPPC.

Implicit in the philosophy behind the introduction of the OLIPPC and the LPV was the view that Westminster-style political organisation and the first-past-the-post system were in fact responsible for vote-splintering among numerous candidates, high incumbent turnover and volatile allegiances inside Parliament.[20] If these are shown to owe their origin to inappropriate electoral laws or the constitutional set-up, then institutional change would appear to be a viable method of broadening the basis of parliamentary representa-tion and stabilising governments. If those features have other origins, the two reforms are likely to do more to change the form, rather than the substance, of PNG politics. Claims that electoral rules were responsible for PNG's hyper-fractionalised party space sit oddly next to the Duvergerian association between plurality rules and a two-party system, suggesting that the ultimate origin of vote-splintering lies elsewhere. Variations in the financial incentive structure made little difference in the past. As Ron May points out in

Chapter Five of this volume, even a tenfold rise in the PNG nomination fee in 1991 did little to arrest candidate proliferation.

Solomon Islands

In the Solomon Islands, as in PNG, the political spectrum at the national level lacks the enduring ideological cleavages necessary to facilitate the emergence of a stable party structure, partly because customary leadership systems are so individualised and partly because political allegiances are so localised. The political parties that emerged about the time of independence were loose associations clustered around political leaders such as Solomon Mamaloni and Bartholomew Ulufa'alu. Owing to the spread of parliamentary constituencies and the strength of regional loyalties, governments had to be formed that drew on alliances across the island group, in particular balancing the interests of populous Malaita against those of the Western Province and Guadalcanal. Those parties that did emerge usually lacked branch structures and did not have the kind of regional spread that would assist the formation of governments. Peter Kenilorea, a former civil servant from the Are'are District on Malaita who was initially an avowed opponent of 'party politics',[21] secured the premiership after elections in 1976 and 1980, although he lacked strong party backing. In 1981, ministerial defections brought down his government.[22] Archrival Solomon Mamaloni, from Makira, replaced Kenilorea as Prime Minister, and his three terms in office proved critical in shaping the post-independence style of Solomon Islands governance.

As Jeffrey Steeves has shown, the post-colonial Solomon Islands became an arena of so-called 'unbounded politics', based on the weaving together of fragile power bases that drew on personal allegiances.[23] As in PNG, party attachments proved of limited significance and loyalties changed regularly. MPs' positions were highly precarious, with about 50 per cent losing their seats at each election. Parliamentarians were much less likely to face defeat if they sat on the Government benches, and they were often prepared to abandon party allegiances to achieve that goal. Ministerial portfolios offered access to state funds or other government-controlled public service networks that permitted the forging of 'big man' networks of patronage. A Prime Minister's survival depended on judicious distribution of cabinet portfolios and other state appointments, as well as forging links with powerful local or foreign business interests.

Nevertheless, the Opposition was not entirely 'unbounded' by party or principle. In 1997, a reformist coalition came into office headed by Bartholomew Ulufa'alu. It sought to reduce the country's crippling debt, reduce the rate of log extraction and restructure government finances. From late 1998, however, the Solomon Islands became increasing engulfed in conflict, first on Guadalcanal and then also on Malaita and in the Western Province. On June 5, 2000, the Ulufa'alu Government was overthrown by a 'joint operation' involving the paramilitary wing of the police force and Malaitan militia groups, and replaced by a government under the control of the militia groups. After elections were held in December 2001, a new government, headed by former 'Mamaloni man' Allan Kemakeza, secured office, relying on support from the People's Alliance Party and independents. Both post-coup governments relied on personalised mechanisms for procuring political allegiance, although now with the added need to buy off increasingly intransigent militants roaming the streets of Honiara or hanging around with guns outside the Finance Ministry and the Prime Minister's office. Although the Australian-led Regional Assistance Mission to the Solomon Islands (RAMSI) arrived in mid-2003, disarmed and arrested most of the militants and took some steps to clean up government finances, Kemakeza served his full term as Prime Minister. Indeed, the stabilisation of the security situation initially strengthened his administration, with a number of former opposition leaders crossing the floor to join the Government.

Vanuatu

At independence, Vanuatu (formerly the New Hebrides) adopted an electoral system that is often believed to promote intra-party competition.[24] The single non-transferable vote system (SNTV) allows eligible citizens a single vote, but in multi-member constituencies.[25] The system has peculiar repercussions for party strategy. Parties must more or less accurately anticipate the extent of their electoral support in each constituency, and, where they are potentially able to secure more than one seat, they need to be capable of directing different groups of voters to support each strategically preferred candidate. If Party A potentially has 78 per cent support in a four-member constituency, it might obtain maximum advantage by fielding three candidates and directing precisely one-third of its potential voters to evenly back each favoured candidate (so that each gets 26 per cent). SNTV is crudely proportional, because Party B, if it has the residual 22 per cent support, is potentially capable of returning one of the four victorious candidates. The system was introduced at the time of Vanuatu's independence in 1980 in order to ensure some representation for the francophone minority, and to prevent a clean sweep in favour of the anglophone Vanua'aku Pati (as would have been likely under a first-past-the-post system). Although only crudely proportional, SNTV does have the advantage of simplicity, and removed the need to divide Vanuatu's ethnically mixed islands into separate constituencies.[26]

For the first 11 years after independence, Vanuatu's two major groupings were the predominantly English-speaking Vanua'aku Pati (VP) and an alliance of francophone-backed parties, the Union of Moderate Parties (UMP).[27] Despite exceptional ethno-linguistic heterogeneity and allegiances to varying Christian church denominations, the polarising issues of independence and land rights encouraged the temporary advent of a two-party system. Until the 1987 polls, the VP and UMP, taken together, accounted for an increasing share of the national vote, although with VP's share falling and the UMP's share steadily increasing. From then onwards, Vanuatu's two-party system splintered, with numerous rival party groupings emerging and a rising number of successful independent candidates. Owing to the emergence of an increasingly fractionalised party system, coalition governments became a permanent feature from 1991 and there were at least 18 wholesale changes of government between 1991 and 2004.[28]

Whether those splits and that instability are due to the usage of the SNTV system is debatable. SNTV rewards minor parties with concentrated regional bases of support and, potentially, promotes internal party rivalry and splintering.[29] But the late 1980s and early 1990s splits that arose in the VP in were the result of top level power struggles between Walter Lini, Barak Sope and the rest of the VP leadership, rather than grass-roots-driven splintering due to the incentives arising from the SNTV system.

Ni-Vanuatu politicians' frequent shifts of allegiance, the willingness of party-aligned MPs to cross the floor and continual real or threatened no-confidence challenges were, after all, characteristic also of neighbouring first-past-the-post-using Melanesian countries. SNTV provided a considerable degree of seats/votes proportionality at elections held in 1979, 1983 and 1987, and only in the subsequent years did it become less effective in this respect. As the number of candidates contesting elections rose, the former disciplined party adjustments to predicted voter base gave way to a free-for-all, with candidates potentially able to secure election on the basis of only a small share of the vote. Despite their distinct electoral systems, this cumulative and self-reinforcing candidate multiplication was common to Vanuatu, Solomon Islands and PNG.

Micronesia

In most of the North Pacific states that have 'Compacts of Free Association' with the US, plurality-based electoral systems have not triggered the emergence of political parties. The key bases for political organisation in the FSM are the separate states of Chuuk, Pohnpei, Kosrae and Yap, or further subgroupings, but the Federal Assembly is dominated by individual powerbrokers with fluctuating allegiances.[30] In Palau, the 'Compact of Free Association' with the US and the nuclear-free status question for a time proved strongly polarising issues. The compact was rejected at seven referenda, before being passed in 1993. During the 1980s and early 1990s, loose groupings did come together in support of, and in opposition to, the signing of the compact. Yet, as in the FSM, shifting loyalties were centred on 'family, clan and village ties more than party affiliation', and 'some elected leaders, who do not hold chiefly titles, win and hold office because they are supported by and represent the interests of traditional power structures'.[31] In the two northernmost territories, Guam and the Commonwealth of the Northern Marianas (CNMI), tighter integration with the US encouraged ascendancy of American-style parties.

Of the American-associated Micronesian countries, only the Republic of the Marshall Islands has developed a locally based two-party system. In the wake of the death of long-serving President Amata Kabua, local political struggles culminated in the formation of the reformist United Democratic Party (UDP), which won the 1999 election.[32] At fresh elections in 2003, the UDP was able to retain office, defeating the Kwajalein and other Ralik chain chiefs, who, for the first time, aligned themselves in a political party, the Ailin Kein Ad.[33] The renewal of the Marshall Islands' 'Compact of Free Association' with the US in mid-2003 and the issue of 'rental' payments for US usage of Kwajalein Atoll as a missile testing facility, alongside controversies about the decline of chiefly political authority, proved sufficiently polarising to, at least temporarily, bring about the development of a two-party system.[34]

Across the equator to the south, the Kiribati two-round electoral system coupled with a preferential ballot for the presidency was introduced to provide some choice despite the absence of organised party politics.[35] In the multi-member constituencies, candidates are elected if they obtain the required threshold of valid votes. If not, run-off elections are held for the top candidates.[36] Political parties initially proved occasional alliances of convenience between national politicians, lacking popular membership and regularly fading away.[37] Only after elections, when MPs gather together on the island of Tarawa did 'the factions behave most like political parties'.[38] Cleavages between Catholics from the northern islands and Protestants from the south underpinned early post-independence politics, but did not lead to the emergence of confessional parties.[39] Towards the turn of the century, parties assumed greater institutional coherence, adopting constitutions, establishing party offices, circulating newsletters and retaining a membership outside Parliament.[40]

Nauru's electoral system requires voters to rank all candidates in order of preference in seven two-member constituencies and one four-member constituency, a system that has been compared with that invented by 18th-century French mathematician Jean-Charles de Borda.[41] Voters' first preferences are counted as one, second preferences as a half-vote, third preferences as one-third of a vote, fourth preferences as one-quarter of a vote and so on, dependent on the number of candidates, and all votes are instantly summed with the victor being the candidate with the highest total. Unlike the Borda system, Nauru unusually allots fractional votes even to a candidate who comes last (e.g., the loser in a constituency with eight contestants gets one-eighth of the vote) and voters in multi-member constituencies only have a single vote.

Nauru is most frequently classified as a 'no-party' system.[42] After independence, traditional leaders, led by Hammer DeRoburt, most of whom were formerly councillors from the Nauru Local Government Council, were elected to the new Parliament, and dominated the country's politics for the next 20 years.[43] After DeRoburt's defeat in 1989, Bernard Dowiyogo served for six terms, with several breaks, until he was replaced by Rene Harris in March 2001. From then on, the once phosphate-rich territory experienced mounting financial crises and repeated regime change. In 2002 alone, for example, there were seven changes in the presidency.

Against this backdrop, a group calling itself the 'visionaries' eventually toppled the old guard politicians associated with Rene Harris in 2004, after a sequence of legal confrontations and controversies surrounding the role of the Speaker of Parliament. At the 2004 polls, there were few first-count leaders who were dislodged by the counting of lower-order preferences, suggesting that a first-past-the-post system would have yielded similar outcomes. Nauru's electoral system has been described as 'absurdly complex' for such a small country.[44] Yet much of the discussion about the merits of Jean-Charles de Borda's proposed voting system concerns its application to committee elections.[45] There is no particular reason why small size should be a deterrent to usage of complex systems. It is when they are applied to mass elections, or where the literacy is low, that elaborate voting rules potentially become troublesome.

Polynesia

Plurality-based electoral systems also prevail across Polynesia, with the exception of the French-controlled group towards the east. Largely block-vote-based systems exist in Tonga and Tuvalu, whereas Sämoa has a majority of single-member first-past-the-post-based districts with only a few multi-member constituencies.[46] Tonga's electoral system entitles 'commoners' to elect only nine representatives on a universal franchise. Another nine are returned by the holders of 33 noble titles,[47] and 12 are nominated by the King.

The King's nominees to Cabinet sit in the Legislative Assembly, but the Executive is not answerable to the Legislature. Contrary to popular belief, the prevailing seat distribution is not entrenched in the country's 1875 Constitution, and the balance between the different categories of members has witnessed major changes, most notably in 1915 when a revision of the composition of the assembly was aimed at enhancing the power of the monarch over that of the nobility.[48] Since the 1980s, a pro-democracy movement has emerged (lately calling itself the Human Rights and Democracy Movement). Pro-reform candidates took eight of the nine universal franchise seats in 2005, and, for the first time, two were allowed to join the Cabinet (and were required to forfeit their universal franchise seats to do so. They instead appeared among the King's nominees).

In Tonga, as in Sāmoa, the Cook Islands and Niue, overseas migration is a major influence on domestic politics. About 50 per cent of Tongans and Sāmoans reside outside their country, as do the overwhelming majority of Cook Islanders and Niueans. Tiny Niue has about 1,400 residents but about 18,477 migrants living in New Zealand who are not entitled to vote. It has a 20-member Parliament, with 14 members returned from single-member village constituencies and six 'common roll' MPs elected on an island-wide block vote. Party labels designate loose assembly groupings, although these are occasionally thought to be sufficiently robust for 'party politics' to be blamed for exacerbating social tensions.[49]

With a population of less than 10,000, Tuvalu has seven two-member constituencies and one single-member constituency, all of which return members by plurality voting (i.e., the block vote in the two-member districts).[50] There are no political parties, but both members from each of the seven dual-member constituencies tend to align themselves on the same side during prime ministerial elections. Although close to one-third of Tuvalu's population lives on Funafuti, where the capital is, citizens are obliged to vote on their home islands unless they own land or show evidence of five-years' residence elsewhere. Within Parliament, MPs frequently divide on north/south lines, with most prime ministers coming from the southern part of the group (and most governor-generals coming from the north).[51] Despite the absence of a party system, Tuvalu's Parliament has been finely balanced between pro- and anti-government MPs. Between 1999 and 2002, there were four different prime ministers, and parliamentary sessions were frequently cancelled or curtailed to avoid the threat of no-confidence challenges. That instability has generated local debate about introducing laws preventing MPs from switching sides, which, given the absence of parties, would presumably entail members sticking by whichever candidate they backed for the premiership after general elections.

The Cook Islands, with a plurality-based system, developed a two-party system shortly after self-government in 1965. Albert Henry's Cook Islands Party (CIP) controlled government but, during the 1970s, was opposed by the minority Democratic Party, which obtained office after a court ruling concerning electoral irregularities associated with using government funds to finance fly-in migrant voters from New Zealand at the 1978 polls. The CIP recaptured office in 1983, but defections and no-confidence challenges became an increasingly regular feature, encouraged by difficulties in securing parliamentary majorities after the emergence of a third party, the Alliance Party, in the 1990s.[52] The major electoral system changes during this period were (i) the abolition of block voting in multi-member districts in favour of single-member districts in 1981, a reform that has been claimed to have encouraged 'more parochial politicians',[53] and (ii) the introduction (in 1981) and subsequent abolition (in 2004) of a special seat for overseas voters. Despite having a party-based system, the Cook Islands suffers from the difficulties often attributed to the absence of party politics elsewhere: regular changes of government, fluid allegiances and parliamentary opposition groupings that are too preoccupied with overturning incumbent governments to play much role in scrutinising legislation.

Sāmoa

After independence, Sāmoa adopted a plurality-based system involving a mixture of single-member and block-voting two-member constituencies.[54] The country initially witnessed high levels of MP turnover and no-party-based contests as in many parts of Melanesia. The key difference was in the relationship between electoral processes and customary leadership. In 1961, a popular referendum backed usage of an electoral system in which only *matai* (chiefs) could vote and stand as candidates. In 1990, another popular referendum supported the introduction of a universal franchise, but retention of the *matai*-based qualification for candidates. Interestingly, the electoral system became much more competitive and party-based even before the 1990 extension of the franchise. Until the mid-1970s, large numbers of MPs were returned from non-contested constituencies, often based on a rotational principle of villages taking it in turns to fill seats. After the mid-1970s, the number of non-contested seats fell and the number of candidates contesting elections rose rapidly. Similarly, in the initial post-independence years, the premiership proved a unique preserve of *tama-a-'āiga* titleholders from Sāmoa's four leading dynasties, who were usually returned without contest in the 1960s. From 1976 onwards, prime ministers were all non-*tama-a-'āiga* titleholders, and the position tended to be filled by majority rule.[55]

After the 1979 polls, a party-based system emerged, first as a result of the rise to power of the Human Rights Protection Party (HRPP), and then because the Opposition also adopted party-style organisation. Despite the HRPP's continuing hold on power throughout the period from 1983 to the present (with a brief exception in 1986-87), party allegiances remained fluid. In 1988, only the last-minute defection of an opposition MP enabled the HRPP to retain its hold on office. In general, the number of successful candidates recorded as affiliated with the HRPP before prime ministerial elections tends to be far lower than that recorded once a new government has been formed. At that point, elected MPs gravitate towards the governing party in search of the rewards attached to office-holding. This process was actively encouraged by the HRPP, which increased the constitutionally allowed number of Cabinet portfolios from eight to 12 in 1991, introduced laws against party-hopping in 2005 and created new 'undersecretary' positions for government backbenchers.[56]

French Polynesia

French Polynesia, which has a majority Polynesian population and an 11 per cent white population, uses a list ticket system like that in New Caledonia, but in its present form it is deliberately not proportional. Gaston Flosse, an ally of French President Jacques Chirac, led the Government from 1991 and, owing to the difficulty in sustaining support for a French loyalist position in the predominantly Polynesian territory, favoured enhanced local autonomy. In the elections of May 7, 2001, his Tahoeraa Huiraatira won 29 seats, whereas the pro-independence Tavini Huiraatira (Union for Democracy) obtained 13 seats, resulting in Flosse serving his fifth term as President. In 2004, Flosse increased the number of seats from 49 to 57, introduced a 3 per cent threshold, and provided for a 30 per cent seat bonus for the party that received the most votes in each of the six multi-member constituencies, claiming that this would increase the stability of government.[57]

Believing that the new majoritarian electoral laws would enhance his majority, Flosse persuaded President Chirac to dissolve the French Polynesian Territorial Assembly. At the consequent elections, held in May 2004, Flosse again triumphed in the outer islands, particularly the Marquesas and Gambier Islands and the Tuamoto Archipelago — where Catholic allegiances and fears of Tahitian domination over an independent nation encouraged French loyalist affinities. But Tahoeraa Huiraatira was narrowly defeated in the large 37-member Windward Islands constituency by only 390 votes, thus missing out on the critical associated seat bonus.[58] Tahoeraa Huiraatira consequently failed to secure an absolute majority. Longstanding independence leader Oscar Temaru instead narrowly won the vote for the presidency. In the political battle that followed, Temaru was controversially ousted after a single defection from his Union for Democracy. Flosse regained the presidency, but tried to bolster his one-seat majority by calling fresh elections in the 37-member Windward Islands constituency (after Paris accepted his allegations of electoral irregularities in that constituency at the May 2004 polls). At a consequent by-election, held in February 2005, the Union for Democracy acquired an increased share of the vote, leading to the restoration of the Temaru Government.[59] Political controversy in French Polynesia came to centre less on the independence question (to be indefinitely postponed) and more on alleged corruption and nepotism under the Flosse Administration.

Ethnically bipolar configurations

Fiji

In Fiji, conflict between the 52 per cent indigenous Fijians and 44 per cent Indo-Fijians has centred on electoral outcomes, with constitutional crises (in 1977) and coups (in 1987 and 2000) following the election of governments backed largely by Indo-Fijian voters. Electoral reform has consequently been the most politically sensitive issue in the country since independence.

After colonisation in 1874, ethnic Fijians, who were suffering a catastrophic decline in population, were confined largely to their villages under a 'Fijian administration' governed by customary chiefs. From 1879, more than 60,000 labourers were brought from India as indentured labourers to cut sugar cane. Many stayed, and, after indenture ended in 1916, took up positions as tenant farmers supplying cane to the Colonial Sugar

Refining Company. As free labourers, living standards steadily improved and Indian population levels began to approach those of the Fijians. Demands for political rights led the colonial authorities to concede Indian elected membership in the Legislative Council in 1929, but from separate communal constituencies.[60] Subsequent agitation for a 'common roll', closely linked to demands from London- and Kenyan-based Indian organisations with regard to the East African situation, seemed in the Fiji context to entail a bid for political power. In response, local Europeans and colonial officials increasingly allied themselves with indigenous Fijians, an arrangement entrenched due to Fijian military participation during World War II. Fijian population levels had begun to recover from the early 1920s, and local Europeans and colonial officials in the postwar Legislative Council reinvented their role as one of protecting 'Fijian paramountcy' (a doctrine also inspired by the 1920s East African situation).

Only as the dismantling of the colonial order began were the issues of political institutions capable of enabling post-independence democracy addressed. In 1965, the official majority was removed and a 'cross-voting' system was introduced. Registered citizens had four votes each, one of which was in an ethnically reserved franchise constituency for their own 'Fijian', 'Indian' or 'general' candidate. The other three were for 'Indian', 'Fijian' or 'general' candidates, in common roll constituencies. The system was aimed at stimulating the emergence of a centrist Malaysian-style Alliance Party with strong roots in the different ethnic communities. It did not succeed in this objective. No centrist party emerged able to capture substantial support in both communities. Voting remained largely along ethnic lines. From 1970 to 1987, the consequence of having a first-past-the-post system with an ethnically bipolar structure was to encourage formation and retention of single homogenous ethnic parties. As one commentator put it, 'Political success in Fiji [became] … contingent upon maintaining solidarity in one's own ethnic community while actively promoting disunity among the opposition's.'[61]

The largely Fijian- and European-backed Alliance Party retained control of government throughout this period, with the exception of the two elections of April 1977 and 1987. The majoritarian electoral system ensured 'winner-takes-all' outcomes, which were not conducive to power-sharing arrangements. In 1977, the newly emergent Fijian Nationalist Party (FNP) acquired 25 per cent of the indigenous vote (in a manner that was notably disobedient to first-past-the-post's electoral incentives), and split the Alliance Vote. The National Federation Party (NFP) narrowly scraped to victory, with 26 of the 52 seats. Instead of enabling the NFP to form a government, Governor-General Ratu Sir Penaia Ganilau returned the defeated Prime Minister Ratu Mara to office at the head of a minority administration pending fresh elections held in September 1977, which the Alliance Party won. When, a decade later, a predominantly Indian-backed coalition between the Fiji Labour Party (FLP) and NFP won the general elections of 1987, the newly installed government was, within two weeks, dislodged by a military coup.

Backed by the country's Great Council of Chiefs, a new post-coup constitution was introduced in 1990, which reserved the position of Prime Minister and President for indigenous Fijians. The cross-voting (or national) seats were abolished in favour of a wholly communal-based district system. Fijians were granted 37 seats and Indo-Fijians

27 seats, provisions which, it was hoped, would guarantee Fijian 'paramountcy'. In fact, the electoral experience under the 1990 Constitution was a shift towards a multi-party setting. The coalition between the FLP and NFP broke down, with both parties vigorously competing for the Indian vote. Coup leader Sitiveni Rabuka's Soqosoqo ni Vakavulewa ni Taukei faced considerable internal party rivalry, and was challenged by several new Fijian parties, including the Fijian Association Party and the All National Congress as well as the earlier established FNP. Ironically, Rabuka found himself dependent on FLP support to secure his majority after the 1992 polls.[62] Domestic political difficulties, as well as international pressures, encouraged the Rabuka Government to embark on a mid-decade review of the 1990 Constitution.

As part of the new 1997 Constitution, Fiji introduced the alternative-vote system (AV), along with provisions for mandatory power-sharing. As with PNG's LPV system (outlined above), voters rank candidates in order of preference and, during the count, lowest-polling candidates are progressively eliminated until a victor is established. The main differences are that (1) Fiji's system requires voters who mark preferences to rank 75 per cent of candidates numerically to cast a valid ballot (whereas PNG's system requires only three candidates to be ranked)[63] and (2) Fiji's ballot papers have an 'above-the-line' section enabling voters to place a simple tick endorsing a political party, thereby delegating decisions about subsequent preferences to that political party. More than 90 per cent of Fiji's voters took the latter option in 1999 and 2001, giving party officials extraordinary control over the reallocation of preference votes. The system was designed, under the influence of questionable theories about the benefits of the AV system in mitigating ethnic conflict, to encourage pre-election deals between political parties representing the ethnic Fijians and Indo-Fijians. Local parliamentarians, however, were not convinced that the AV system alone would ensure multi-ethnic government. As a result, provisions were added for mandatory power-sharing. All parties with more than 10 per cent of seats in the House were entitled to Cabinet portfolios. The widely expected result was the re-election of Rabuka's Government, but with Indo-Fijian Opposition Leader Jai Ram Reddy's NFP henceforth playing a junior role in Cabinet.

Instead, the centrist Rabuka-Reddy coalition was defeated heavily at the May 1999 polls. The FLP, relying mainly on first-preference support from the 44 per cent Indo-Fijian community combined with transfers of lower order ethnic Fijian preference votes under the control of party officials, found itself with an absolute majority (despite obtaining only 32.3 per cent of the nationwide first-preference vote). The country's first ever Indo-Fijian Prime Minister, Mahendra Chaudhry, took office, at the head of a reformist coalition including several small Fijian-backed parties. Precisely one year later, that government was overthrown in a coup perpetrated by indigenous Fijian extremists, backed notably by many rank-and-file members and backbench MPs from parties whose leaders had joined the Coalition Government.[64]

After the May 2000 coup, the Constitution was restored by Fiji's Court of Appeal, paving the way for fresh elections, again held under the alternative-vote system. At the 2001 polls, two exclusively ethnic Fijian-backed political parties, the Soqosoqo ni Duavata ni Lewenivanua (SDL) and the Conservative Alliance- Matanitu Vanua

(CAMV), secured the largest number of seats, and formed a coalition government (despite obtaining together only 35.7 per cent of the first-preference vote). A centrist alliance that called itself the 'Moderates Forum' fared poorly. Moderate parties' preferences served instead to elect the extremist Fijian parties in key marginal constituencies.[65] The FLP, reliant almost exclusively on the Indo-Fijian vote (i.e., without the preference transfers from its now largely defunct allied Fijian parties) was left with 27 seats. Unable to form a government, it nevertheless insisted on its right to inclusion in Cabinet, based on the constitutional provision entitling all parties with 10 per cent or more of parliamentary seats to participate in Cabinet. The result was a succession of legal challenges to the SDL-CAMV Government, with the courts in each case upholding the FLP's right to ministerial portfolios. The SDL responded by offering to incorporate the FLP by increasing the size of Cabinet to 36 members, so as to avoid sacking CAMV ministers and thus preserve intact its governing coalition. The FLP was to be awarded a host of minor portfolios, with controversial figures such as party leader Mahendra Chaudhry excluded from participation. Further court battles followed, culminating in the FLP finally opting for a position on the Opposition benches as scheduled elections in 2006 loomed closer.

New Caledonia

Like Fiji, New Caledonia is an ethnically bipolar society, but with a 34.1 per cent white population and 44.1 per cent Melanesian population and a more substantial 'other' grouping comprising Wallisian (9 per cent), Indonesian (2.5 per cent) and French Polynesian (2.6 per cent). Since the abolition of the *Code de l'Indigénat* in 1946, New Caledonia has not had the rigid compartmentalisation by ethnic group characteristic of Fiji. In 1951, the French National Assembly passed legislation resulting in the enfranchisement of close to 9,000 Melanesians. In response, conservatives briefly secured a 'double electoral college' system in 1952, with ethnically separate constituencies for the 80 per cent majority Kanak east coast, but this was soon abandoned. Also in 1952, the two-round (or double-ballot) system was replaced with a list proportional representation system with five electoral zones returning 25 members.[66]

For most of the postwar years, the New Caledonian Territorial Assembly was dominated by the multi-ethnic and pro-autonomy Union Calédonien (UC), which was able to secure Melanesian and liberal European support. Kanak calls for independence in the late 1970s, influenced by the inability of the UC to achieve much in the way of self-government, led to the formation of a variety of breakaway socialist and pro-independence parties. In 1977, the UC itself adopted a pro-independence position. Most European UC members left the party during the 1970s, many joining the conservative and anti-independence settler party, the Rassemblement pour la Calédonie dans la Republique (RPCR).[67] Electoral laws promulgated by conservatives in the late 1970s raised the threshold required to secure seats in the Territorial Assembly to 7.5 per cent and abolished proportional representation in the Governing Council. The objective was to exclude smaller Melanesian parties such as Parti de Libération Kanak (Palika — with 6.5 per cent of the vote in 1977).[68] Instead, it precipitated their unification: pro-independence groups aligned themselves behind a newly formed Front Indépendantiste

(FI), which obtained 14 seats compared with the RPCR's 15 seats in the 1979 Regional Aassembly (the FI was renamed Front de Libération Nationale Kanak et Socialiste [FLNKS] in 1984). During the 1980s, growing social conflict including land occupations, roadblocks, assassinations, industrial sabotage and electoral boycotts culminated in the 1988 Ouvéa crisis, which resulted in the death of 19 pro-independence demonstrators and four members of the government security forces and precipitated greater efforts by political leaders on both sides to secure a negotiated settlement.

The 1988 Matignon Accord, agreed between RPCR and FLNKS leaders, included a 10-year 'rebalancing' program, entailing development projects for the majority Kanak north and the Loyalty Islands, and promised a referendum on independence a decade later. For electoral purposes, the territory was divided into three provinces, one each covering the south and north of the Grand Terre (main island) and another covering the Loyalty Islands. These returned, respectively, 32, 15 and seven members to the 54-member New Caledonian Congress as well as electing members to separate provincial assemblies. Indigenous Kanaks predominate both in the Northern Province and in the Loyalty Islands, whereas all other ethnic groups reside largely in the more populous Southern Province, which is also the most prosperous region and location of the capital, Noumea.[69] With substantial support from minority groups as well as European settlers and some Melanesians, the RPCR was able to obtain the largest share of the vote in the Southern Province (52.5 per cent in 1989, 46.4 per cent in 1995, 49.6 per cent in 1999), and secured significant minority support in the Northern Province and even in the overwhelmingly indigenous Loyalty Islands.[70] It was able to retain control over Congress, either alone or in coalition, through the 1990s.

The FLNKS, by contrast, saw its support decline in the Northern Province (62.7 per cent in 1989, 34.3 per cent in 1995 and 22.2 per cent in 1999), owing to internal fissions centring on the coalition's longstanding leftist orientation and collaboration of senior leaders with the RPCR. The signing of the Noumea Accord in 1998 further accentuated those divisions, with the breakaway Fédération des Comités de Co-ordination des Indépendantistes (FCCI) coalescing with the RPCR to control the Congress. The Noumea Accord put back the scheduled vote on independence for a further 15-20 years, established a Senate for Kanak chiefs and provided for mandatory power-sharing, with all parties receiving in excess of six seats in the 54-member Congress securing representation in government.[71] At the 2004 polls, 31 distinct lists were fielded in the three provinces, with divisions becoming particularly acute among the Melanesian-backed parties. Inability to agree on a unified list ensured that no Kanak party crossed the 5 per cent electoral threshold in the Southern Province, and all six FLNKS senators in the south lost their seats.[72] Fragmentation was not confined to the Kanak parties. Jacques Lafleur's Rassemblement UMP (the renamed RPCR) saw its overall vote share fall from 38.8 per cent to 24.4 per cent, and it lost eight of its 24 seats at the 2004 polls. The newly formed centrist Avenir Ensemble secured 23.8 per cent of the overall vote (and 16 seats), and led the post-election Government. Avenir, argues Nic Maclellan, is shifting the political agenda away from divisive ethnic issues towards a greater concern with 'issues of corruption, cronyism and gender politics'.[73]

Repercussions of electoral laws

The contemporary political history of the Pacific is, as we have seen, littered with misconceived electoral reform initiatives and institutional changes that had outcomes that varied markedly from what was anticipated by their architects. In New Caledonia, raising the threshold required for parties to secure representation in 1979 was intended to disadvantage radical Kanak parties. Instead, it brought them together and enabled them temporarily to enter the local government in the early 1980s. Gaston Flosse's introduction of a 30 per cent seat bonus for the winning party in French Polynesia was devised to bolster the fortunes of his Tahoerra Huiraatira. Instead, it enabled his archrival, Oscar Temaru, to take office in May 2004. Fiji's 1965–87 cross-voting system was intended to facilitate the emergence of a Malaysian-style Alliance Party. Instead, it strengthened communal party machines, which became adept at finding puppet candidates from the other ethnic group to field in the appropriate constituencies.[74] The post-coup 1990 constitution was intended to entrench indigenous Fijian 'paramountcy'. Instead, coup leader Rabuka soon found himself reliant on support from the largely Indian-backed FLP to retain office. The alternative-vote system was intended to encourage moderate candidates and coalitions based on policy agreements on ethnically sensitive issues. Instead, it sent its centrist architects to a crashing defeat in May 1999, and, in 2001, facilitated victory for an ethno-nationalist coalition that included supporters of the failed coup of May 2000.

The anticipated Duvergerian interrelation between the electoral system and party polarisation did play some role in the political history of the bipolar countries, but, everywhere, other factors were of primary significance. Vanuatu's francophone/anglophone divisions, and the indigenous/settler-descended cleavages in Fiji and New Caledonia in the 1980s provided the critical impetus towards the formation of two-party systems, not the logic of electoral laws. Even the no-party systems, whether or not they used single-member districts, often witnessed loosely bipolar-style cleavages centred on distinctions between those on the Government side or on the opposition benches (for example, Tuvalu, Kiribati and Sämoa). Executive instability in such states was indicative of a tendency for government to *only just* secure its majority in Parliament, providing other members with the incentive to group together to plot the next no-confidence challenge (a trend that can occur in *any* parliamentary system, whatever the electoral system). In the bipolar and party-based territories, electoral systems worked their influence at the margin, facilitating multi-partyism in situations already prone to greater political fragmentation or entrenching bipolarity in circumstances where political allegiances were already such as to pit two sides against each other.

Nevertheless, the marginal influence was important. Electoral arrangements that served to break down polarised alignments in the political sphere eased the way to ethnic accommodation. In Fiji, inter-ethnic electoral alliances, which had become possible due to the introduction of the 25 new open or common roll constituencies in 1997, broke down after the first election under the AV system, and were in ruins after the May 2000 coup. The more centrist of the two largely Indian-backed parties, the NFP, did form a coalition with other 'Moderates Forum' parties in the run up to the 2001 polls, but it was emphatically defeated, and left for a second time with no seats in Parliament.[75] New Caledonia's political parties, including both conservatives (for most of the postwar years) and Melanesian-backed pro-independence parties (from the 1970s) had a long history of infighting and splintering. The impact of electoral incentives in promoting greater unity among Melanesian parties was evident in 1979 when the threshold was raised to 7.5 per cent. As polarisation increased in the 1980s, elections served as referenda on the independence issue, and the bipolar division became more entrenched. In the wake of the Matignon and Noumea Accords, an increasing number of parties again emerged and, as they did so, coalitions became increasingly unavoidable. Whereas Fiji, under AV, saw increasing numbers of voters line up behind ethnic political parties, one representing Indo-Fijians[76] and the others representing ethnic Fijians,[77] New Caledonia's ethnic fissures have become less marked in the wake of the electoral boycotts and violence of the mid-1980s, with centrists securing control over Congress in a multi-party coalition in 2004.[78]

Other technical aspects of the electoral system also influenced Pacific party constellations. Laws on party finances, crossing the floor and official designations on ballot papers served to alter parliamentary balances between independents and party-aligned MPs. Constitutional provisions for parliamentary offices for opposition or independent leaders encouraged greater coherence among MPs not in government. French Polynesia's list proportional representation system, with its 37-member Windward Islands constituency, did not encourage multi-partyism after the introduction of a 30 per cent majority seat bonus (which turned the classic proportional representation system into its opposite). Electoral thresholds in the French territories discouraged tiny parties. Split-format ballots in Fiji gave party officials an extraordinary influence over the distribution of preference votes. Mandatory power-sharing provisions regarding cabinet composition, if anticipated in pre-election party alignments, discouraged smaller parties that might diminish broader ethnic representation in cabinet. Only once all these influences are weighed up, together with the extent of heterogeneity and the electoral laws, can one establish the likely repercussions for party polarisation.

A key issue in many of the Pacific countries is not whether the electoral system encourages a two-party system or a multi-party constellation, but whether it encourages any party system at all. Single-member districts might have eased the path to the retention of no-party systems, with MPs often selected, at least in rural areas, on the basis of their position within local hierarchies or community standing.[79] Yet such responses were also evident in countries with multi-member districts, such as Nauru, Tuvalu or Kiribati. The multi-member single non-transferable vote (SNTV) in Vanuatu initially coexisted with what was probably the strongest party-based system in the post-colonial Pacific, but as the independence issue faded parties splintered and independents proliferated. The rise and fall of Vanuatu's two-party-based system had little to do with the logic of electoral laws, although SNTV might have encouraged feuding politicians to fall back on regional fiefdoms. Where electoral laws had most impact in encouraging the formation of political parties was in New Caledonia and French Polynesia, but here too other complementary influences were the inheritance of strong traditions of party politics from mainland France and polarisation around the independence issue.

Leaving aside the ethnically bipolar states (which face distinctive problems), contemporary reform objectives in most Pacific Island countries might focus on encouraging the emergence of party systems, but the primary objective is usually strengthening executive authority. In this, Sāmoa's HRPP has proved most successful, having survived in office, with only one brief exception, for more than one-quarter of a century. Sāmoa initially witnessed a high degree of incumbent turnover and, until 1979, had an Assembly dominated by independents. The HRPP proved able to diminish scope for parliamentary and extra-parliamentary challenges to its rule, by extending parliamentary terms from three to five years, by expanding Cabinet size and, most controversially, by use of the fruits and achievements of office to procure political support. Although the Opposition also improved political party organisation from 1982 onwards, the *itu Malo* (the Government or 'victorious side') triumphed over the *itu Vaivai* ('losing side'). Sāmoa increasingly has a single executive party dominating a loosely party-aligned assembly with many 'independents'. After elections, the Government consolidates control over the assembly, by drawing hitherto non-aligned or opposition MPs across the floor. The system strengthens executive authority, but not to such a degree as to empower an authoritarian regime (although some political controversy centres on this possibility). Most importantly, the Sāmoan party system was not a top-down creation of institutional engineers, but a home-grown product of shifting political forces and the decline of *tama-a-'āiga* (ruling chiefly families) parliamentary authority during the 1970s.

Party-centred political development is not an inevitable accompaniment of human history. Pacific nations are sometimes compared with Greek city-states,[80] but ancient Athens, that 'cradle of democracy', did not have a party-based system. Many Pacific states are similar in size to shire counties or town councils in metropolitan countries, which often have more fluid and personalised alignments than national parliaments or lack political parties altogether. Where domestic issues have emerged around which party systems crystallise, as in the Marshall Islands or Sāmoa, these on balance probably assist effective government. But there seems to be little logic in forcing party organisation on countries such as the FSM, Palau or Tuvalu on the dubious grounds that political parties are indispensable for democracy or stability. Government instability in the Cook Islands, despite the party-centred system, indicates that legislation aimed at obliging MPs to join political parties is unlikely to be greatly effective. Where political parties are nothing more than vehicles for ambitious leaders to capture power, they inevitably remain weak and lack broad legitimacy. Elaborate institutional engineering projects are much more likely to create these types of parties than genuine watchdog parties or truly hegemonic governing parties. The notion that *collective* action and *ideological* affinity can be forced top-downwards by statute is indicative of a topsy-turvy style of thinking.

More effective reform proposals would aim instead at harnessing existing local pressures for greater choice, enhancing direct popular controls over representatives and governments, and experimenting with new checks and balances over executive authority. A greater separation of executive and legislative powers, coupled with effective popular recall systems and a strong judiciary, offers a better way of avoiding the problem of hamstrung assemblies that serve only as arenas for the pursuit of personal ambition rather than institutional experiments designed to conjure into being party-based systems.

Footnotes

1 Duverger, M. 1954. *Political Parties: Their Organisation and Activity in the Modern State.* London: Methuen. pp. 217, 239; see also the discussions in Grofman, Bernard and Arend Lijphart (eds). 1986. *Electoral Laws and Their Political Consequences.* New York: Agathon Press; Neto, Amorim O. and G. W. Cox. 1997. 'Electoral institutions, cleavage structures and the number of parties.' *American Journal of Political Science,* Vol. 41, No. 1. pp. 149–74.

2 Taagepera, R. and M. S. Shugart. 1973. *Seats and Votes: The Effects and Determinants of Electoral Systems.* New Haven, Conn: Yale University Press; Lijphart, A. 1994. *Electoral Systems and Party Systems; A Study of Twenty-Seven Democracies, 1945–1990.* Oxford, UK: Oxford University Press; Taagepera, R. 1999. 'The Number of Parties as a Function of Heterogeneity and Electoral System.' *Comparative Political Studies,* Vol. 32, No. 5. pp. 531–48; Neto and Cox, op. cit.; Ordeshook, P. C. and Olga V. Shvetsova. 1994. 'Ethnic Heterogeneity, District Magnitude, and the Number of Parties.' *American Journal of Political Science,* Vol. 38, No. 1. pp.100–23.

3 Ghai Y. 1988. 'Systems of Government — 1.' In Y. Ghai (ed.), *Law, Government and Politics in the Pacific Island States.* Suva, Fiji: Institute of Pacific Studies, University of the South Pacific. p. 69.

4 Huntington, S. 1991. *The Third Wave; Democratization in the Late Twentieth Century.* Norman, OK, and London: University of Oklahoma Press. pp. 266–7. The much-debated two-turnover test finds 'democratic consolidation' in situations where the governing party is ousted by another party and that second party is subsequently defeated at the polls and gives way to the victor.

5 This was, however, often not the case *during* the colonial era, as Ron May points out in Chapter Five of this volume, when political parties were sometimes seen as a potential threat to foreign rule.

6 Premdas, R. and J. Steeves. 1981. 'The Solomon Islands: First Elections after Independence.' *Journal of Pacific History,* Vol. 16, No. 4. p. 193.

7 Ibid., pp. 194, 202; Macdonald, B. 1996. 'Governance and Political Processes in Kiribati.' *Economics Division Working Paper,* No. 96/2. Canberra: RSPAS-ANU. p. 6; Lawson, S. 1996. *Tradition Versus Democracy in the South Pacific; Fiji, Tonga and Western Sämoa.* New York: Cambridge University Press. p. 148.

8 Lipset, Seymour Martin. 2000. 'The Indispensability of Political Parties.' *Journal of Democracy,* Vol. 11, No. 1. pp. 48–55; Schattschneider, E. 1942. *Party Government.* New York: Farrar & Reinhart. p. 1; Lijphart, A. 2004. 'Constitutional Design for Divided Societies.' *Journal of Democracy,* Vol. 15, No. 2. pp. 96–109, at p. 102.

9 Reeves, Paul Vakatora, R. Tomasi and Brij V. Lal. 1996. 'The Fiji Islands: Towards a United Future.' *Report of the Fiji Constitutional Review Commission, Parliament of Fiji, Parliamentary Paper,* No. 34 of 1996. p. 310.

10 Ibid., p. 320. The way this system worked is outlined in the Fiji section below.

11 For New Zealand, see Geddis, A., 'Gang Aft A-Gley: New Zealand's Attempt to Combat "Party Hopping" by Elected Representatives', *Election Law Journal,* 1 (4), 2002, pp. 557–71.

12 Table 3.1, however, shows PNG as having a first-past-the-post system, since this was still in use at the 2002 polls, with AV adopted only for the following general election and intervening by-elections.

13 Solomon Islands Prime Minister Kemakeza's PAP is shown, in the *Parties of the World* data set used here, as having 20 MPs after the 2001 Solomon Islands elections, whereas this in fact included at least seven so-called 'shadow' members, whose allegiance was far from certain (see Fraenkel, J. 2004. *The Manipulation of Custom.* Melbourne: Victoria University Press. p. 137).

14 Even here, however, timing is often critical to measurement; in the Solomon Islands or Sämoa, for example, the number of seats secured by each party differs markedly depending on whether one estimates this straight after a general election or closer to the time when Parliament gathers to select a prime minister or during the subsequent process of government formation (when previously unaligned MPs tend to cluster towards the victor).

15 This section draws on Fraenkel, J. 2004. 'Electoral Engineering in Papua New Guinea; Lessons from Fiji and Elsewhere.' *Pacific Economic Bulletin,* Vol. 19, No. 1. pp. 122–33.

16 Standish, B. 2002. 'Papua New Guinea Politics: Attempting to Engineer the Future.' *Development Bulletin,* 60. pp. 28–32.

17   Okole, H. 2002. 'Institutional Decay in a Melanesian Parliamentary Democracy: Papua New Guinea.' *Development Bulletin*, 60. pp. 37–40, at p. 39.

18   May, R. J., chapter in this volume.

19   In India, more defections occurred *after* the introduction of anti-defection legislation than before-hand. While individual defections diminished from 1985, collective defections increased in number ('Advisory Panel on Electoral Reforms; Standards in Political Life, Review of the Electoral Law, Processes and Reform options, consultation paper prepared for the National Commission to Review the Working of the Constitution, New Delhi, 8 January 2001, Section 19.1, http://lawmin.nic.in/ncrwc/finalreport/ v2b1-9.htm).'

20   Reilly, B. 1996. 'The Effects of the Electoral System in Papua New Guinea.' In Y. Saffu (ed.), *The 1992 Papua New Guinea Election: Change and Continuity in Electoral Politics*, Canberra: ANU, pp. 43–76; Reilly, B. 1997. 'The Alternative Vote and Ethnic Accommodation: New Evidence from Papua New Guinea.' *Electoral Studies*, Vol. 16, No. 1. pp. 1–11; Reilly, B. 2001. *Democracy in Divided Societies; Electoral Engineering for Conflict Management.* Cambridge: Cambridge University Press. pp. 58-94. For an alternative perspective, see Standish, B., op. cit.

21   Kenilorea, P. 1972. 'Political Development.' In R. J. May (ed.), *Priorities in Melanesian Development*, papers delivered at the sixth Waigani Seminar, Port Moresby: UPNG and ANU. pp. 24–5; Herlihy, J. M. 1980. 'Decolonization Politics in the Solomon Islands: The Model that Never Was.' In R. J. May and H. Nelson (eds) *Melanesia; Beyond Diversity*, Vol. 2, Canberra: ANU. p. 6.

22   Premdas, R.R. and G. Steeves, op. cit., pp. 190–202; Chick, J. D. 1980. 'Electoral Politics in the Solomons.' *Pacific Perspectives*, Vol. 8, No. 2. pp. 21–30.

23   Steeves, J. 1996. 'Unbounded Politics in the Solomon Islands.' *Pacific Studies*, Vol. 19, No. 1. pp. 133–8.

24   Reynolds, A., B. Reilly and A. Ellis. 2005. *Electoral System Design; The New International IDEA Handbook.* Stockholm: IDEA. Annex A. pp. 113–7, 166–73.

25   In Vanuatu, there are in fact six single-member and 11 multi-member districts, so that the former function, in effect, as first-past-the-post districts, while only the latter employ the single non-transfer-able vote system.

26   See Van Trease, H. 2005. 'The Operation of the Single Non-Transferable Vote System in Vanuatu.' *Commonwealth and Comparative Politics*, Vol. 43, No. 3. pp 296–332.

27   Morgan, Michael G. 2004. 'Political Fragmentation and the Policy Environment in Vanuatu, 1980–2004.' *Pacific Economic Bulletin*, Vol. 19, No. 3. pp. 40–8; Morgan, this volume.

28   See Van Trease, H., op. cit., figure 2, p. 316.

29   See Grofman, B., S-C. Lee, E. A. Winckler and B. Woodall. 1999. *Elections in Japan, Korea and Taiwan Under the Single Non-Transferable Vote; The Comparative Study of an Embedded Institution.* Ann Arbor: University of Michigan Press.

30   Hanlon, D. and W. Eperiam. 1988. 'Federated States of Micronesia: Unifying the Remnants.' In R. Crocombe and A. Ali (eds), *Politics in Micronesia*, Suva: IPS-USP. pp. 85–106.

31   Quimby, F. 1988. 'The Yin and Yang of Belau: A Nuclear Free Movement Struggles with the Quest for Economic Development.' In R. Crocombe and A. Ali (eds), ibid. pp. 113, 114; Anckar, D. and C. Anckar. 2000. 'Democracies Without Parties.' *Comparative Political Studies*, Vol. 33, No. 2. p. 229; Shuster, D. R. 2001. 'Palau.' In D. Nohlen, F. Grotz and C. Hartmann (eds), *Elections in Asia and the Pacific; A Data Handbook*, Oxford: Oxford University Press. p. 742.

32   For further detail, see Fraenkel, J. 2002. 'Strategic Registration from Metropolis to Periphery in the Republic of the Marshall Islands.' *Journal of Pacific History*, Vol. 37, No. 3. pp. 299–312.

33   Johnson, G. 2004. 'Marshall Islands National Election 2003 — Trends and Implications.' Paper presented at *Political Culture, Representation and Electoral Systems in the Pacific Islands*, PIAS-DG Conference, Port Vila, Vanuatu, July 2004.

34   Beyond the 2003 polls, rallies and public demonstrations have continued to figure as a regular feature of Marshallese political life, focused on Kwajalein rents, the compact and nuclear compensation (see 'Protestors Buck Tradition in the Marshalls', *Yoke Online*, February 7, 2005).

35   Macdonald, B. 1996. 'Governance and Political Processes in Kiribati.' *Economics Division Working Papers*, No. 96/2. Canberra: RSPAS-ANU. p. 12.

36   In a three-member constituency with no first-round victors, the top five contest a second round. In two-member constituencies, the top four candidates contest in round two (Brechtenfeld, N. 1993. 'The Electoral System.' In H. Van Trease (ed.), *Atoll Politics; The Republic of Kiribati*, Canterbury and Suva: Macmillan Brown Centre and IPS-USP, p. 44.

37   Macdonald, B., op. cit. pp. 6, 19, 24; Somoza, A. 2001. 'Kiribati.' In D. Nohlen, F. Grotz and C. Hartmann (eds), op. cit. pp. 674–5.

38   Van Trease, H. 1993. 'The General Election.' In H. Van Trease (ed.), op. cit. p. 80.

39   Somoza, A., op. cit.

40   Mackenzie, U. N. 2004. 'Kiribati 2004.' *National Integrity Systems, Transparency International Country Study Report.* Transparency International 2004. pp. 13-4.

41   Reilly, B. 2002. 'Social Choice in the South Seas: Electoral Innovation and the Borda Count in the Pacific Island Countries.' *International Political Science Review*, Vol. 23, No. 4. p. 357.

42   Anckar, D. and C. Anckar, op. cit.

43   Kun, R., W. Togomae and R. Kun. 2004. 'Nauru 2004.' *National Integrity Systems, Transparency International Country Study Report.* Transparency International. 2004. p. 15.

44   Hughes, Helen. 2005. 'Nauru's Future, Submission to the Constitutional Review Committee, Republic of Nauru.' The Centre for Independent Studies, www.cis.org.au, accessed May 7, 2005. Nauru's counting system was computerised, and eight members of staff were employed in the Computer Bureau (*Naoero Bulletin*, 03/04 Special Issue, October 22, 2004).

45   Black, D. 1958. *The Theory of Committees and Elections.* Cambridge: Cambridge University Press.

46   In Tuvalu and Sämoa, resort to block-voting constituencies have been methods of accommodating population increase by adding extra members rather than subdividing constituencies.

47   Some nobles hold multiple titles and are therefore entitled to multiple votes.

48   Campbell, I. 2001. 'Tonga.' In D. Nohlen, F. Grotz and C. Hartmann (eds), op. cit. pp. 810–11.

49   'Niueans Vote Against Party Politics.' *Fiji Times*, April 2, 2002.

50   Constituencies with more than 500 voters are entitled to two members, a threshold all except one have reached.

51   Taomia, Fakavae. 2005. 'Tuvalu.' Speech given to the Asian Development Bank, Suva, May 6. 2005.

52   Hassall, G. 2001. 'Cook Islands.' In D. Nohlen, F. Grotz and C. Hartmann (eds), op. cit.

53   Crocombe, R. and J. T. Jonassen. 2004. *Political Culture, Representation and the Electoral System in the Cook Islands.* Paper delivered at the conference 'Political Culture, Representation and the Electoral System in the Pacific Islands', Port Vila, Vanuatu, July 2004.

54   Initially, an 'individual voters' constituency had five members, but this was reduced as numbers of voters falling into this category declined, due partly to those of foreign descent opting to join the 'territorial' (i.e., Sämoan) rolls.

55   For further details, see So'o, A. and J. Fraenkel. 2005. 'The Role of Ballot Chiefs (Matai Palota) and Political Parties in Sämoa's Shift to Universal Suffrage.' *Commonwealth and Comparative Politics*, Vol. 43, No. 3. pp. 333–61.

56   'Dump Under-secretaries: Le Mamea.' *Samoa Observer*, February 7, 2005.

57   Chappell, D. 2005. 'French Polynesia; Polynesia in Review.' *The Contemporary Pacific*, Vol. 17, No. 1. p. 198.

58   As Sémir Al Wardi and Jean-Marc Regnault point out ('La Crise Politique en Polynésie Française (2004–2005)', forthcoming paper, p. 2), Flosse would have won the election under the former electoral arrangements.

59   Radio New Zealand. 2005. 'French Polynesia elects Oscar Temaru President.' March 3, 2005.

60   Fijians had, since 1903, been represented only by non-elected members nominated by the Council of Chiefs, and did not secure elected representation until 1963.

61   Lal, B. V. 1988. 'Before the Storm: An Analysis of the Fiji General Election of 1987.' *Pacific Studies*, Vol. 12, No. 1. p. 90.

62   Lal, B. V. 1995. 'Rabuka's Republic: The Fiji Snap Elections of 1994.' *Pacific Studies*, Vol. 18, No. 1. p. 49; Lal, B. V. 1993. 'Chiefs and Indians: Elections and Politics in Contemporary Fiji.' *The Contemporary Pacific*, Vol. 5, No. 2. pp. 294–7.

63 Hence, Fiji's system makes it much more likely than PNG's system that absolute majorities will be secured in constituencies. In PNG, ballots can be exhausted before majorities are secured. Even Fiji's system, however, does not ensure that the party that wins the election obtains a majority of national votes cast.

64 For further details, see Fraenkel, J. 2001. 'The Alternative Vote System in Fiji: Electoral Engineering or Ballot-Rigging?' *Journal of Commonwealth and Comparative Politics*, Vol. 39, No. 2. pp. 1–31.

65 This was often because Labour was ranked last and the SDL or CAMV were in penultimate position. As in 1999, negative ranking proved a critical determinant of electoral success in the most marginal seats.

66 Dornoy, M. 1984. *Politics in New Caledonia*. Sydney: Sydney University Press. p. 163; but see the slightly different account in Thomson, V. and R. Aldoff. 1971. *The French Pacific Islands; French Polynesia and New Caledonia*. Berkeley, Los Angeles, and London: University of California Press. p. 298. In 1957, an open list proportional representation system was adopted 'in which electors could mark their whole ballot in the order of their preference' (Thomson and Aldoff, *The French Pacific*, p. 305).

67 Dornory, M., op. cit., pp. 170–1.

68 Connell, J. 1987. 'New Caledonia or Kanaky? The Political History of a French Colony'. *Pacific Research Monograph*, No. 16. Canberra: NCDS, ANU. p. 278.

69 In 1996, Melanesians formed 96.2 per cent of the voting-age population in the Loyalty Islands, 76 per cent in the north, but only 23.4 per cent in the south.

70 McCallum, W. 1992. 'European Loyalist and Polynesian Political Dissent in New Caledonia: The Other Challenge to the RPCR Orthodoxy.' *Pacific Studies*, Vol. 15, No. 3. pp. 55–6n.

71 For further details, see Maclellan, N. 1999. 'The Noumea Accord and Decolonisation in New Caledonia.' *Journal of Pacific History*, Vol. 34, No. 3. pp. 245–52.

72 Maclellan, N. 2005. 'From Eloi to Europe: Interactions with the ballot box in New Caledonia'. *Commonwealth and Comparative Politics*, Vol. 34, No. 3. pp. 394–417.

73 Ibid., p. 412.

74 For a more detailed analysis, see Fraenkel, J. 2003. 'Electoral Engineering and the Politicisation of Ethnic Frictions in Fiji.' In Bastian, S and R. Luckham (eds), *Can Democracy Be Designed? The Politics of Institutional Choice in Conflict-Torn Societies*, Sussex: IDS, Zed Books Ltd. pp. 220–52.

75 The NFP did gain Nadi Open, but lost this after a court-ordered recount of invalid ballots.

76 The FLP secured 66 per cent of the Indo-Fijian vote in 1999, 75 per cent in 2001.

77 The SDL secured 50 per cent of the Fijian vote in 2001, with the CAMV taking another 20 per cent.

78 This section summarises the arguments in Fraenkel, J. Forthcoming. 'Fiji and New Caledonia; A Microcosm of the Global Electoral Engineering Debate.'

79 Ghai, Y., op. cit. pp. 60, 69. It might be noted, however, that there was not much sign of a decline in the party-based system in the Cook Islands when the country switched to a single-member-based system in 1981.

80 Larmour, P. 1994. '"A Foreign Flower?" Democracy in the South Pacific.' *Pacific Studies*, Vol. 17, No. 1. p. 49.

ANATOMY OF POLITICAL PARTIES IN TIMOR-LESTE[1]

Joao M. Saldanha

Introduction

While Fretilin, the main group to resist Indonesian dominance between 1975 and 1999, still dominates Timor-Leste (earlier, East Timor) politics overwhelmingly, the transition to democratic elections in 2001 under the authority of the United Nations Transitional Authority in East Timor (UNTAET) has witnessed the re-emergence of multi-party politics. While Fretilin maintains hold of more than 60 per cent of the seats in the fledgling legislature, representatives of the several minority parties also won seats. Of these, most have their origins in the initial emergence of Timor-Leste from Portuguese control in the 1970s, while others represent former factions of Fretilin. While Timor-Leste has faced many hurdles in its attempts to install multi-partyism and functioning democracy, not least from the spectre of a one-party state, the present composition of the National Parliament reflects these various interests vying for national influence.

Timor-Leste gained full independence only in May 2002, nearly three years after the overwhelming majority of Timor-Leste voted for independence in a UN referendum held on August 30, 1999. The referendum was followed by the tragic destruction of the country, inflicted by the Indonesian military and its supporters. In October 1999, UN Security Council Resolution No. 1272/1999 established UNTAET to prepare Timor-Leste for independence as well as to oversee reconstruction efforts. One of UNTAET's major tasks was to create the foundations for a democratic Timor-Leste.[2] To assist in achieving this goal, it organised elections for a Constituent Assembly, whose mandate was to write the Constitution of Timor-Leste.

Sixteen political parties registered to participate in the elections for the Constituent Assembly on August 30, 2001. Twelve gained enough votes to be represented in the Assembly. The clear winner was the Frente Revolucionaria Timor Leste Independente (Fretilin), which won 55 of the 88 seats. With this majority, Fretilin formed the Second

Transitional Administration and dominated the process of drafting a constitution for the Democratic Republic of Timor-Leste.

This chapter examines the role political parties have played in promoting democracy in Timor-Leste. First, it documents the emergence of political parties in Timor-Leste since 1975. It then discusses the ideological spectrum and programs of the parties. This section also analyses party representation and the question of what is an effective number of parties in the new democracy. Next, the future of political parties in Timor-Leste is considered by evaluating their current positions and the potential for opposition parties to build coalitions. A conclusion is offered in the last section of the chapter.

The emergence of political parties in Timor-Leste

The emergence of political parties in Timor-Leste dates back to April 1974, when a military coup took place in Portugal. The coup leaders granted freedom to all Portuguese colonies, including Timor-Leste. Now able to decide their own future, five political parties emerged in Timor-Leste, namely Uniao Democratica de Timor (UDT); Associacao Social Democratica de Timor (ASDT), which later transformed into Fretilin; Associacao Popular Democratica de Timor (APODETI); Klibur Oan Timor Asuain (KOTA); and Trabalhista (Labour).

UDT's objective was to turn Timor-Leste into a federated state of Portugal with independence to come later. Fretilin wanted immediate independence, while APODETI aimed at integrating Timor-Leste into Indonesia as an autonomous state. KOTA and Labour wanted to maintain strong ties with Portugal.

The Portuguese Government planned to complete the decolonisation process in 1976, but UDT interrupted that timetable by staging a coup in August 1975. This was followed by a counter coup. On November 28, 1975, Fretilin unilaterally proclaimed the independence of Timor-Leste, precipitating the Indonesian invasion and occupation on December 5, 1975.

Under the dictatorship of Suharto, Indonesia ceased the activities of all Timor-Leste-based political parties. The three Indonesian parties — Golkar, Indonesian Democratic Party (PDI) and United Development Party (PPP) — operated in the province without a strong following, although the people of Timor-Leste were forced to participate in the five-yearly election process, known in Indonesia as the 'festival of democracy'.

Even during the occupation, new parties — Partido Nacionalista Timorense (PNT) and Uniao Democratica Cristao (UDC) — did emerge in Timor-Leste and in exile, especially in Portugal. Further, in the 1980s, Xanana Gusmao, the leader of the resistance within Timor-Leste, established with another exiled resistance fighter, Jose Ramos-Horta, the Concelho Nacional da Resistencia Nacional (CNRM) to accommodate groups other than Fretilin who were resisting Indonesian rule. In 1998, CNRM was replaced by Concelho Nacional da Resistencia de Timor (CNRT)[3] as the umbrella organisation of the resistance movement. CNRT gained large support internationally and domestically and, in elections on August 30, 1999, it was the CNRT flag, not Fretilin's, which was used at the ballot box.

The Indonesian authorities, while not officially allowing the operation of parties other than the three registered blocs, did allow PNT to be established in 1999. A coalition of the UDC and Partido Democratico Crista (PDC) was established in Portugal in 1998 as a splinter of UDT. Subsequently, that coalition divided into two parties — UDC representing the Catholic wing and PDC the Protestant one — in order to be able to register separately to participate in the 2001 elections. Another party to emerge in the 1990s, during the Indonesian occupation, was Partido Socialista de Timor (PST). It conducted its activities underground.

It was when UNTAET began to organise the Constituent Assembly elections that political parties in Timor-Leste were revived. Sixteen parties registered to participate in that election (see Table 4.1). These included parties established during the Portuguese period, namely Fretilin, KOTA, Trabalhista and UDT. APODETI did not register but a breakaway faction, APODETI Pro-Referendum — founded in the 1990s to fight the Indonesian occupation — did. In addition, Associacao Social Democratica de Timor (ASDT) revived itself in 2001 and registered as a separate party from Fretilin with Francisco Xavier do Amaral, the founding president of both parties leaving Fretilin to resume his position as ASDT president.

Eight new parties emerged to participate in the 2001 elections. These were: the Liberal Party, Partido Democratico (Democratic Party or PD), Partido Democratico Cristao (PDC), Partido Povo Timor (PPT), Partido Social Democratica (PSD), Partido Democratico Maubere (PDM), Parentil and Uniao Democratica Crista/Partido Democratico Cristao (UDC/PDC).

Of the 16 registered political parties that stood for election in 2001, only 12 won enough votes to be represented in the Constituent Assembly (see Table 4.2).

The ideology of political parties

The history of Timor-Leste has been shaped by colonialism and occupation. When the elections were held, pro-independence parties attracted the support of the people, but ideology per se was of less influence. This is reflected by the dominance of Fretilin in the elections of 2001. With the independence issue resolved, however, a degree of ideological difference is emerging, even if all parties still have similar platforms.

The narrow ideological divide among the parties might be attributed to the fact that, with the exception of Fretilin, UDT and APODETI Pro-Referendum, all are newcomers to politics, and might represent regional elites rather than contending ideologies.[5] Given that the elections of September 2001 were based more on emotional issues connected to the long Indonesian occupation and the suffering it caused and less on ideology and programs or the ability to govern, the new parties are still in the process of articulating their ideological positions.

The established party, Fretilin, has changed from a radical, revolutionary and left-wing party to a moderate one, with a less dogmatic ideology. Indeed, Fretilin might be facing something of a crisis in ideology now that it has to cope with new domestic and international circumstances. Its latest *Political Manual*[6] strongly emphasises mainstream economics and liberal democracy, including multi-partyism. On the other hand, conser-

Table 4.1: Political Parties in Timor-Leste, June 2004.

Party	General Characteristics		Year
	Vision/Objectives	Origins	established
ASDT	Defence of independence, democracy and pluralism.	From ASDT to Fretilin then ASDT	1974/2001
Fretilin	Independence and democracy based on social justice.	From ASDT	1974/2001
KOTA	Defence of an independent, sovereign and stable state with balance of power.	Strong ties with UDT	1974/2000
Liberal	Liberal and individual rights at centre.	Youth movement	2001
PD	Nation-building based on freedom, democracy and a just society.	Fretilin, Student and youth movements	2001
PDC	Build a society within peace, democracy and justice.	Splinter of UDC/PDC	2000
PNT	Democracy.	Splinter of Fretilin	1999/2001
PPT	n.a.	Several parties	2001
PSD	Creating a state based on national unity and consensus.	Splinter of Fretilin and UDT	2000
PST	A socialist & classless state free from colonialism, imperialism and exploitation.	Splinter of Fretilin	2000
UDC	Establishment of democratic system.	Splinter of UDT	1998/2001
UDT	Democracy and justice.	First party in East Timor	1974/2001
Trabalhista	Democracy to eliminate exploitation.		1974/2001
Povu Maubere	n.a.	APODETI Pro-Referendum	2001
Parentil	n.a.	Splinter of Fretilin	2001
APODETI-Pro-Referendum	Defence of democracy, tolerance and non-violence.	Splinter of APODETI	2001

vative parties such as UDT have maintained their ideology largely consistently since the 1970s, paying more attention to the role of traditional authorities.

If we place political parties in Timor-Leste along a left-right axis, we can identify three groupings at the left, centre and right; and then three further parties (PDC, PNT and PPT) without clear ideologies or stated platforms. The most left-wing party is the Socialist Party of Timor (PST), which aims for a socialist and classless state. Other parties ideologically close to PST are Fretilin and ASDT.

Fretilin started out as a revolutionary movement that later became a political party calling for radical changes in Timor-Leste society, although, as mentioned above, its stance has been tempered by the realities of independence. Fretilin wants a free and mandatory school system and, in regard to health policy, advocates the use of 'green' (traditional) medicine. It argues that Timor-Leste should become a member of the International Socialist Organisation of centre-left parties around the world.

Table 4.2: Political Parties in Timor-Leste, May 2001.

Party	Selected principles and policies	Tendency	President
ASDT	Liberal politics and open market economics, attention to veterans of independence.	Centre-left	Francisco Xavier do Amaral
Fretilin	Revolutionary. Mandatory and free primary education, agriculture, cooperatives, literacy, natural resources and foreign investment. Membership in ASEAN and South Pacific Forum.	Left	Francisco 'Lu-Olo' Guterres
KOTA	Promote culture and tradition, agriculture, tourism and good relations with neighbouring countries.	Right	Leao dos reis Amaral
Liberal	Individual freedom, government should not intervene in economy, business and trade.	Extreme right	Armando da Silva
PD	Democracy, pluralism and individual rights. Market economy with selective intervention of the Government. Transparent and responsible government. Membership in ASEAN and South Pacific Forum. Mandatory primary schooling, recognition of veterans, primary health care and standardisation of Tetum. Investment policy with attention to small and medium enterprises. Priority on agriculture, poverty reduction and elimination of famine.	Centre	Fernando 'Lasama' de Araujo
PDC	Christian values. People-oriented economy and universal health policy.	Unclear. Seems to be centre-left	Olinda Guterres
PNT	Investment and Bahasa Indonesia as official language.	Unclear. Seems to be centre-left	Abilio de Araujo
PPT	Not available.	Not available	Jacob Xavier
PSD	Minimum wage and state role in economic development. Prioritise education, health, housing and good governance. Membership in ASEAN and South Pacific Forum. Oppose death penalty and abortion.	Centre-right	Mario Viegas Carrascalao
PST	Socialist and classless state. Compulsory education, development of Tetum, divorce legalised and equality between men and women, equal distribution of land, free and universal health system, against death penalty.	Extreme-left	Pedro Soares
UDC	Establishment of democratic system and Christian humanism, market economy, basic education and free health care, and promotion of local culture. Membership of ASEAN, CPLP, and other democratic regimes.	Right	Vicente Guterres
UDT	Just distribution of income, centralised system of government, pensions for retired FALINTIL widows and orphans, also for ex-Portuguese and Indonesian civil servants. Application of customary law and role of elders in solving problems.	Right	Joao Viegas Carrascalao

Source: Political parties' manuals, speeches of party leaders, and Walsh.[4]

ASDT has made a dramatic shift to the right. Its party manual states that, while still a vanguard party, it values liberal politics and an open market economy. This is very different from ASDT's initial position in 1974 when it was established as a leftist party (becoming further radicalised when it was absorbed into Fretilin). Now, ASDT is seeking to establish itself as a centre-left party, which embraces mainstream political and economic ideas. ADST's leader is Francisco Xavier do Amaral, the man who founded the party and then became President of Fretilin, until he was captured and imprisoned first by antagonistic Fretilin cadres and then by the Indonesians. Unable to return to this position after independence, he decided to revive ASDT as his personal political vehicle.

The party most clearly on the right is the Liberal Party, which values individual freedom and argues against any state intervention in the economy. Other parties apparently tilting to the right — despite not yet fully defining their positions — are UDT, UDC and KOTA.

UDT was a large party in 1974, but, in 2001, was among the smaller ones, with its leadership — made up of former bureaucrats who had worked for the Portuguese Colonial Government and traditional village heads — having partly contributed to its decline in support. Apart from having shifted from its original position that Timor-Leste should be a federated state of Portugal to joining the CNRT in the 1990s, its ideological stance is little changed. It is a strong proponent for the application of customary law and of a significant role for elders in the nation's governance.

UDC and KOTA are both splinters from UDT. UDC talks about Christian humanism, with an emphasis on democracy and justice. It is market oriented but, like UDT and KOTA, defends local culture and tradition. KOTA is a strong proponent of Timor-Leste as a federation of kingdoms.

Two new parties — the Democratic Party (PD) and Social Democratic Party (PSD) — seem to be placing themselves at the centre. PD was founded just two months before the elections of September 2001. It was formed by former students, intellectuals and clandestine activists who were disenchanted with Fretilin tactics and ideology:

> There was resentment against the returned Fretilin exiles, such as the party's secretary-general, Mari Alkatiri, because they were perceived as arrogant, privileged, and authoritarian … They were seen as marginalizing the younger generation who were educated in Indonesian. They were also discounting the contribution of the student movement and of urban East Timorese against Indonesian rule, e.g., the demonstrations in 1991 that drew worldwide attention to human rights violations perpetrated by the Indonesian army.[7]

The Democratic Party (PD) is also strengthened by intellectuals educated in the West, especially in Australia, the US, UK, Portugal and Indonesia. Another major component of PD are middle-level resistance figures, many of whom came from the clandestine Internal Political Front (FPI) of the CNRT and had therefore held leadership positions at district, subdistrict and village level. Many among this group were members of Fretilin but opted for PD because of its spirit of national unity and inclusiveness.

PD managed to attract the second-largest number of votes after Fretilin and is currently the main opposition party in the Parliament, with seven seats. Although PD's ideas are still in the formative stages, its position tends towards left of centre. It supports mandatory primary schooling and calls for assistance to veterans of war and war victims. It is in favour of a market economy with selective intervention from government. In his latest policy speech, the President of PD, Fernando 'Lasamo' de Araujo, stressed the development of an investment climate that favoured small and medium enterprises through tax incentives and less regulation.[8] The PD, however, suffers from leadership problems and lacks a systematic policy approach to managing the country. This might be explained partly by the lack of experience of its leaders in governance matters, drawn as they are from the ranks of political activists.

The Social Democratic Party (PSD) is also in the central grouping, although it is still grappling with its precise orientation. It defends minimum-wage policy and state intervention in economic development, and is against the death penalty and abortion. Younger leaders have also been arguing that the PSD should approach the International Socialist Organisation. It is interesting to note that the PSD has attracted supporters from UDT, which might have reduced the latter's votes in the 2001 elections.

The remaining three parties in the National Parliament do not have clear positions on socioeconomic matters. The Partido Povu Timor (PPT), whose supporters come mainly from Hatudu, a subdistrict in Ainaro District, is sympathetic to a kingship model of governance.

Religious orientation has not been a particularly influential factor in contemporary Timor-Leste politics. Most parties, including the major ones such as Fretilin, PD, PSD and ASDT, defend the idea of a secular state and the separation of church and state. Even the parties that have adopted Christian references in their names — Uniao Democratica Crista (UDC) and Partido Democratico Crista (PDC) — do not articulate their religious beliefs strongly and have only three seats in the Parliament.

Similarly, attachment to customary law and traditional kingdoms have so far been peripheral election issues, though it remains to be seen if these will emerge as more significant matters in the future. At the moment, however, KOTA, with its platform based on kingship, and UDT, which wants to see elders play a role in national affairs, have only two seats each in the Parliament.

With regards to foreign policy, most parties view ASEAN favourably for security and trade reasons. This represents a shift from the view in 1999, when Timor-Leste leaders, especially Jose Ramos-Horta (at the time, the CNRT's foreign spokesman), stated that an independent Timor-Leste would become part of the South Pacific Forum. Now, the PD has a firm position on joining ASEAN, and PSD has also indicated that membership would be desirable. Fretilin still has reservations, given Indonesia's prominence in ASEAN. Nevertheless, the current Fretilin Government has developed a strong relationship with Malaysia, which might facilitate entry into the grouping.

Fretilin dominance and the opposition of PD and PSD

Timor-Leste has a multi-party system with 12 parties represented in the National Parliament. UNTAET Regulation 2001/01 determined a unicameral Constituent Assembly (later called the National Parliament), with 88 seats, of which 75 were contested through party lists, and the remaining 13 seats were allocated to the districts and elected on the basis of proportional representation.

The results of August 30, 2001, elections saw Fretilin emerge as the majority party with 55 seats, while the rest of the seats were divided among 11 other parties (see Table 4.3), with the next largest party, the Democratic Party (PD), gaining seven seats, followed by ASDT and PSD securing six seats each.

Table 4.3: Timor-Leste: Parties in the National Parliament.

This figure shows the number of seats held by each party and their political orientation, from left to right.

PST	Fretilin	PNT	ASDT	PD	PSD	UDT	KOTA	PPT	PDC	UDC	Liberal
1	55	2	6	7	6	2	2	2	2	1	1

Why did Fretilin gain such a majority? Several factors can explain the outcome. First, it is the party that has consistently defended independence since 1974. Anecdotal evidence suggests that people thought Fretilin should be rewarded for this position, although people also encouraged their children to vote for other parties. This does not completely explain Fretilin's victory given that the party had experienced leadership problems and a weakened organisational structure, especially in the late 1970s and early 1980s, when it suffered crushing military defeats against Indonesia. There were also atrocities associated with Fretilin leaders during the same period, which reduced its influence. And then Xanana Gusmao and Jose Ramos-Horta decided to form the CNRM to unify all resistance forces fighting against Indonesia. In 1987, Xanana Gusmao went further by declaring FALINTIL no longer a military wing of Fretilin but instead a nationalist force fighting against Indonesia. The change in FALINTIL's position was also a way to accommodate several guerrilla leaders who were not members of Fretilin. From the late 1980s, the resistance movement was revitalised and attracted more popular and international support compared with the exclusivity of Fretilin in the late 1970s and early 1980s. From there, the face of resistance changed forever and Xanana Gusmao became a national not just a party leader.

And so, secondly, there was the Xanana factor. Many voters, especially in rural areas, thought that Xanana was still the leader of Fretilin and that the elections were about choosing Xanana to be president. In fact, leading up to the elections, Xanana had stated that a big majority by Fretilin would not be healthy for democracy in Timor-Leste.[ix] This stance might well have prevented Fretilin winning the 88 per cent of votes predicted by the party's leaders, Francisco Lu-Olo Guterres and Mari Alkatiri.

Thirdly, there was, again particularly in rural areas, a fear of revenge if people did not choose Fretilin. In late 2000 and early 2001, Fretilin activated its dormant membership and completed a national registry of all militants and sympathisers. Some citizens felt there was high degree of intimidation in this process.[10]

At any rate, the results of the elections turned Fretilin into the dominant party in the Constituent Assembly and later the National Parliament, with major influence over the drafting of laws, including the Constitution. Fretilin's strength in the Legislature was further increased through its alliance with ASDT, PNT and PDC.

As mentioned above, it is the Democratic Party (PD) that represents the major opposition party in the Parliament. PD draws its support from the grassroots and the middle class. Recently, a number of intellectuals and former guerrilla leaders also joined the party. It is an open party that can accommodate people with different backgrounds and, as such, has the potential to become a serious alternative to Fretilin in the next election. A poll by the American-based International Republican Institute (IRI) in 2003[11] showed that PD has gained 4 per cent support since 2001, especially among the youth and in the urban areas, despite not having staged any major activities since September 2001. The same poll shows that Fretilin has lost almost 5 per cent of voters and PSD has gained 2 per cent additional support.

The Social Democrat Party (PSD) is the second opposition party with six seats in the Parliament. Its leader, Mario V. Carrascalao, a former Portuguese official, Timor-Leste Governor and ambassador under the Indonesian occupation, and Vice-President of CNRT, is a competent technocrat who could easily lead Timor-Leste. In addition, Carrascalao has a charismatic personality, which has been a major factor in attracting followers. PSD draws support from former UDT members, Fretilin, some clandestine and FALINTIL members and independents. The party could also emerge as a strong alternative party if it can overcome its internal divisions.

It is conceivable that PD and PSD could form a centre-right coalition in order to form a strong front against Fretilin and its allies. It was this idea that led both parties to spearhead the National Unity Platform in 2003 comprising five parties, including ASDT, a key Fretilin ally. Weighed down by conflicting agendas and personality politics, their platform never became a serious threat to Fretilin's dominance.

Fretilin and ASDT represent a centre-left coalition, although for the time being, as the dominant party, Fretilin does not need to rely on coalitions to secure the passage of any laws that require a simple majority. When it needs to get an absolute majority in the National Parliament, it can look to ASDT, PNT and PDC for support.

At present the alliances of political parties in the National Parliament are fluid. While it might be expected that parties such as PST at the extreme left would vote with parties of similar ideological persuasion — such as Fretilin and ASDT — in fact, PST often votes with centre-right parties such as PD and PSD. Similarly, the Christian parties do not always ally themselves with the centre-right parties. For example, PDC regularly votes with Fretilin. The conclusion we can draw from this is that the party system in Timor-Leste has not yet solidified along a left-right political spectrum.

How many parties?

What is an ideal number of parties in Timor-Leste? While the presence of 12 parties in the Parliament might appear excessive, four parties (Fretilin, PD, PSD, ASDT) control 84 per cent of the seats, with the remainder divided between eight minor parties.

Interestingly, the Laakso/Taagepera Index, which measures the average number of parties for comparative purposes, notes that Timor-Leste has 2.44 effective parties.[12]

The small number of effective political parties reinforces the notion that the party system in Timor-Leste is not so fragmented as to cause serious problems of coordination. As Haggard notes, policy coordination requires time and incentives and can be undermined if there are too many coalitions that need to be juggled.[13] In the case of Timor-Leste, a coalition system could be successful because there are only four effective parties. But for the time being, the strength of the governing coalition is unmatched because of Fretilin's sizeable parliamentary majority (65 per cent).

The future of political parties

What is the future of political parties in Timor-Leste? Fretilin's current supremacy leads some to argue that Timor-Leste could become a one-party state, similar to the situations in Malaysia and Singapore, where the United Malays National Organisation (UMNO) and the People's Action Party (PAP), respectively, are dominant. This is a distinct possibility for the following reasons.

First, the Opposition is being weakened through direct and indirect intimidation. For example, civil servants who attended opposition party activities, especially those of the Democratic Party, during holidays in Suai in March 2004, have been suspended. In the same month, PSD activity in Uatu-Lari, Viqueque, was disbanded by local authorities and police. In addition, when accusations of bribery were made about Prime Minister Mari Alkatiri, the Government suggested the Opposition was behind the claims. Similarly, when former Commander L-7, the alias of Cornelio Gama, a former FALINTIL commander who fought against Indonesia for 24 years, staged a demonstration in July 2004, demanding wide-ranging reforms in the police and in the Government, the Government's response was to use force to disband the demonstration and to claim that L-7 had been used by the Opposition — in particular, Mario Carrascalao, head of the PSD and a Fretilin rival since the 1970s. In the words of Prime Minister Alkatiri, 'L-7 is not the culprit in this regard. It is the opposition who have used him for political purposes. So we will take care of them.'[14]

Secondly, there has been persecution of the media: for example, when the Government attempted to relocate the *Suara Timor Lorosae* newspaper from its current premises because it was running stories critical of the Government. Individual journalists have also been threatened.

Thirdly, the current leadership of Fretilin is controlled by the Mozambican clique led by Alkatiri. With few exceptions, this group has been exposed to the dictatorial practices of the African continent of failed states and vast poverty. One of the frequent explanations for sustained poverty in Africa is that despotic regimes run their countries by stealing public wealth. The tendency towards working without consultation is demonstrated by Fretilin's refusal to take any constructive part in the CNRT after 2000. Fretilin had always seen the CNRT as a threat to its power. The disbandment of the CNRT therefore offers Fretilin further opportunity to forge itself into a dominant party.

There are, however, also reasons why Fretilin might not remain as powerful as it is today. The electorate is already growing disenchanted. While the Fretilin Government benefited from the unqualified support of the international community during the reconstruction period, more recently there has been a decline in international aid and economic growth, as well as increased unemployment. These trends are being reflected in reduced support for the party, which, according to IRI polling in 2003, is about 50 per cent, down 7 per cent from the results of the 2001 elections. As noted above, that support is being transferred to the Democratic and Social Democratic parties. Early indications of the village head (*chefi suco*) elections in Maliana and Oe-Cusse districts in December 2004 were that very few Fretilin candidates were elected as heads of villages — this despite Fretilin often being the only party to put up candidates, because other parties encountered bureaucratic obstacles to even registering to participate in the poll. Thus, most of the other candidates were independents, possibly associated with opposition parties.

Fretilin's national leaders, especially Francisco Lu-Olo Guterres (the party's president as well as President of the National Parliament) and Mari Alkatiri (its secretary-general and Prime Minister) are not popular. The IRI polling shows Lu-Olo's popularity rating at 64 percent, well below the 68 per cent for Mario Carrascalao (PSD President) and also below other prominent political leaders such as Jose Ramos-Horta (Minister of Foreign Affairs and Cooperation), Taur Matan Ruak (Commander of Armed Forces) and Xanana Gusmao (Timor-Leste's President). Mari Alkatiri's rating is even worse, at less than 50 per cent. Incumbency, lack of personal appeal and incompetence might have contributed to the decline in popularity of these two leaders. After all, the dominance of Fretilin in the last legislative elections is arguably less about the quality of its leaders and more about the party's long standing in the struggle for independence.

Looking to the next parliamentary elections in 2006, it must be noted that the Xanana factor, as at least an indirect vote-getter for Fretilin in 2001, will not exist. Even in the presidential elections in April 2002, the differences between Fretilin and Xanana Gusmao were obvious and became amplified when Fretilin leaders urged voters to vote for both presidential candidates, namely Xanana Gusmao and Francisco Xavier do Amaral. Mari Alkatiri went further, urging voters to destroy the ballot — a call that drew criticism from observers.[15] It is also to be hoped that the fear of not voting for Fretilin will have dissipated.

Finally, the 2001 elections were characterised by emotion. Campaigns were not based on the quality of programs and candidates. People chose Fretilin reward it regardless of its leadership quality and is platform. In the next elections, the opposition, especially PD and PSD, will be better organised. Both parties have been active in districts across Timor-Leste. Recently, PD commemorated its third anniversary in Samaletek (Ermera), a former Fretilin stronghold. Such activities will intensify as the election year approaches. In addition, a new party, comprised of resistance veterans and intellectuals educated in the West, might also emerge and appeal to voters, including those who voted for Fretilin in the past.

Fretilin leaders are not popular, strong or capable enough to forge a single dominant-party state as Lee Kuan Yew did in Singapore and Mahathir Mohamad and his predecessors did in Malaysia. Indeed, without the UN presence in Timor-Leste during the past three years, the Government of Fretilin might well have not survived, especially after the riots of December 2002.

Fretilin might still win in 2006, albeit with the likelihood that its majority will be reduced, however, should the party engage in tactics of intimidation, vote-rigging and money politics in future campaigns, it might maintain its current levels of control, although these strategies will necessarily challenge its legitimacy. Unfortunately, there is already evidence of government intimidation as noted above. And Fretilin is building up a war chest unmatched by opposition parties. Money alone, however, cannot buy votes. This was demonstrated in the 1999 referendum, when Indonesia tried to buy voters but failed. The people of Timor-Leste took the money but walked away by voting for independence.

Conclusion

Political parties in Timor-Leste emerged in response to the 1975 military coup in Portugal, with domestic hopes for a democratically governed state for Timor-Leste. But they had little opportunity to become established in the country, given that during the Indonesian occupation, all the Timor-Leste-based political parties were disallowed. They began to flourish only after UNTAET initiated the 2001 Constituent Assembly elections. Those elections resulted in Fretilin becoming the government party, with 11 other parties represented in the Constituent Assembly. Later, the Constituent Assembly transformed itself into the National Parliament. Thus, Timor-Leste now operates on a multi-party system, albeit with only a small number of effective players. The ideology of the political parties is informed primarily by socioeconomic issues, with positions held across the left-right spectrum but with a convergence towards the centre.

As far as the future of political parties in Timor-Leste is concerned, it is likely that Timor-Leste will not be a single-party state unless intimidation, vote-rigging and money politics are used in the 2006 elections. Instead, it is to be hoped that the main opposition parties can develop coherent party platforms that will be able to compete with those of the Fretilin Government, especially now that the high emotions of newly and bloodily acquired independence are replaced by a more sober mood in the electorate.

Footnotes

1   I thank Paulino F. Guterres for research assistance and Roland Rich, CDI, ANU, Australia, for supporting this research. All errors are mine.

2   See Gorjao, Paulo. 2002. 'The Legacy and Lessons of the United Nations Transitional Administration in East Timor.' *Contemporary Southeast Asia*, Vol. 24, No. 2. pp. 313–36.

3   The CNRT comprised three fronts, namely the armed wing, Forcas Armadas para Libertacao Nacional (FALINTIL), the clandestine wing named Internal Political Front (FPI, a Portuguese abbreviation), and the diplomatic front.

4   'KOTA: Manifesto aos Membros do Partido e aos seus simpatisantes (Novembro 2000).' Dili; 'Manifesto Politik PST.' 1999, Unpublished (political pamphlet); 'Manual Politik Partido Democrata Cristao.' Juli-2003; *Partido Associacao Social Democrata Timorense (ASDT). 2003.* Eastatuto: Republica Democratica de Timor-Leste; 'Resultado do I Congresso Nacional do Partido Social Democrata de Timor Leste (6–8 de Novembro de 2003).' Dili; 'Komemorasaun Tinan Partido Socialista de Timor (1999–2000).' Aileu–Atsabe; *Manual Politico da Fretilin e Estatuto.* Aprovado No. 1 Congresso Nacional Extraordinario da Fretilin. Dili, 10–15 de Julho de 2001; Lasama de Araujo, Fernando. 2004. 'Forsa PD: Hamutuk ho Povu Hari Nasaun (Go PD: Together with People Build the Nation).' Political Speech. Samaletek, Ermera, Timor-Leste, June 12; Walsh, Pat. 2001. 'East Timor's Political Parties and Groupings.' Briefing Notes. April. Unpublished.

5   Walsh, Ibid.

6   *Manual Politico da Fretilin e Estatuto,* op. cit.

7   King, Dwight. 2003. 'East Timor's Founding Elections and Emerging Party System.' *Asian Survey,* Vol. 43, No. 5. California: University of California Press. p. 755.

8   Lasama de Araujo, op. cit.

9   For more discussion of the contention between Xanana and Fretilin leaders, see Smith, Anthony L. 2004. 'East Timor: Elections in the World's Newest Nation.' *Journal of Democracy,* Vol. 15, No. 2. pp. 145–59.

10 Walsh, op. cit.

11 International Republican Institute. 2003. *Public Opinion Poll.* Dili, Timor-Leste.

12 Laakso, M. and Rein Taagepera. 1979. 'Effective number of parties: a measure with application to Western Europe.' *Comparative Political Studies,* Vol. 12. pp. 3–27; Saldanha, Joao M. 2003. 'Political Party and Electoral System.' *Module 5 Basic Leadership Training.* Dili: Timor Institute of Development Studies.

13 Haggard, Stephan. 2000. 'Interests, Institutions, and Policy Reform.' In Anne Krueger (ed.), *Economic Policy Reform: The Second Stage,* Chicago: University of Chicago Press. pp. 1–60.

14 *Suara Timor Lorosae,* July 21, 2004.

15 Smith, op. cit.

POLITICAL PARTIES IN PAPUA NEW GUINEA

R. J. May

AT THE TIME of PNG's independence in 1975, there was a small number of recently established political parties. The Australian Colonial Administration had had some doubts about encouraging the growth of parties in the emerging state, but, in the late 1960s, as parties spontaneously emerged, it extended its political education program to cover them. There was a widespread expectation, at independence, that a two- or three-dominant-party system would develop, in the context of a first-past-the-post electoral system, though there were some who feared that PNG, like much of post-colonial Africa, would succumb to military rule or a dominant one-party regime. In fact, as in a number of post-colonial states, a coherent political party system has not taken root in PNG. This is so despite the fact that elections have been held regularly and have produced orderly changes of government, and that, despite some pre-independence predictions, the country has maintained a democratic parliamentary system.

In a paper written in 1984, I questioned the apparently widespread assumption that the 'party system' in PNG was in a state of transition from an 'undeveloped' to a 'developed' system (that is, essentially one like Australia, the UK, the US and some European countries), and specifically challenged the view that the party system would solidify along emergent social class lines.[1] Some 20 years later, political party development in PNG — or the lack of it — has tended to strengthen those convictions. This chapter, therefore, attempts, after presenting a brief history of political parties, to examine the main features of political parties in PNG, to look at attempts to strengthen the political party system through legislation, to explain why parties have not developed as many predicted in the 1970s and 1980s, and, finally, to speculate on the future for political parties in the country.

A brief history of political parties[2]

In the lead-up to PNG's independence, the Australian Administration progressively, if perhaps somewhat belatedly, established the institutions of an essentially Westminster parliamentary democracy. A part-elected, part-appointed House of Assembly was created in 1964, replacing an appointed Legislative Council, and further elections were held in 1968 and 1972, the latter producing the country's first wholly elected Parliament.

Initially, there was little enthusiasm for political parties. As late as 1967, Australia's External Affairs Minister, Charles Barnes, suggested that 'the Territory would be better off without [political] parties',[3] and this view was shared by many field officers of the Australian Administration, who tended to be wary of any indigenous political organisation and disparaging of attempts to establish political parties.[4] Recalling his unsuccessful electoral campaign in 1967, Albert Maori Kiki said:

> Many people had told me that it was unwise to campaign on the Pangu platform, that the administration had tried to discredit us and that it could be used against me. In fact most of the Pangu candidates, even the ones from the inner circle, campaigned as individuals in order not to expose themselves to this kind of attack.[5]

Even as the 1972 elections approached, some officials of the Australian Administration 'foster[ed] the attitude that parties were detrimental to the country'.[6]

Despite this, political education material prepared by the Administration before the elections of 1968 and 1972 commended political parties, specifically supporting the idea of two or three parties over one or many,[7] and, after a visiting UN mission in 1971 had recommended that parties be promoted on a nationwide basis,[8] the Administration distributed a booklet on parties that contained the platforms of the three major parties at that time. Indeed, by the early 1970s, it might be said that the Administration was propagandising for the institution of political parties as some well-informed Papua New Guineans were arguing against parties as being potentially disruptive.

Inhibiting factors aside, mass-based political movements did emerge in the pre-independence period. Among the various political organisations to appear on the scene vefore the elections for the second House of Assembly in 1968, two — the United Christian Democratic Party (later United Democratic Party — UDP) and the Papua New Guinea National Union (Pangu Pati) — might be described as the first indigenous, mass-based parties. The UDP, an ideologically conservative party identified with the Catholic mission, was established in the East Sepik Province in 1966, but proved to be short-lived, fading away after a disappointing showing in the 1968 election. Pangu was more successful: when the second House of Assembly sat in 1968, 10 of the 84 members were Pangu members, and the party declared itself to be the 'loyal opposition' to the Administration-dominated 'government'. Nevertheless, a study of the 1968 election, echoing Kiki's comments, minimised the influence of parties in the election:

> Outside a handful of towns, there was little sign of the 'political parties' so hastily inaugurated during 1967 ... At worst ... it was an electoral liability for a candidate to be publicly associated with them, and candidates ... avoided or even denied such association.[9]

And Ted Wolfers observed:

Parties probably had a real impact at the popular level only in the East Sepik, Bougainville and Morobe districts.[10]

Between 1968 and 1972, two other mass-based movements emerged, which were described at the time as political parties.[11] These were the Mataungan Association of East New Britain and Napidakoe Navitu of the North Solomons. But though both movements fielded candidates in the election of 1972 (and the Mataungans again in 1977), they were not formed as political parties to contest elections.[12] Before the end of the 1968–72 House of Assembly, three more political parties had emerged. The first of these, the United Party, had its origins in an Independent Members' Group (IMG) established in the House in 1968 among a group of members brought together essentially by their opposition to Pangu's demand for early independence. The group consisted largely of Highlands members together with some of the more conservative expatriate members. In 1968–69, attempts were made by members of the IMG to create local groups to support a political party centred on the IMG and, in early 1970, the formation of a coordinating body, Combined Political Associations (Compass), was announced. Its chairman and secretary were both Highlanders. The next year, Compass changed its name to United Party (UP). By mid 1971, UP claimed the backing of 45 parliamentary members. A second party also emerged from within the IMG in 1970: the Business Services Group, under the leadership of Julius Chan, comprised 10 members, mostly from the New Guinea Islands, who, it was suggested 'seemed to represent a regional distrust of the highlands leadership implicit in Compass'.[13] The Business Services Group subsequently founded the People's Progress Party (PPP). The association of Highlanders with a 'go-slow' attitude to independence, which Compass represented, also prompted the formation among a group of generally younger and more progressive Highlanders of the New Guinea National Party (NP), which was generally regarded as 'the highlands equivalent of Pangu.'[14]

The 1972 election was thus, for the first time, contested by parties. About 150 of the 611 candidates who nominated were endorsed or selected and helped by parties,[15] and in his overview of the election David Stone concluded that 'Undoubtedly … what marked the 1972 general election from its predecessors was the prominent and active participation by political parties and associations'.[16] Nevertheless, some candidates were still hesitant about publicly admitting party membership, and party organisation was still weak: as in 1968, a number of electorates fielded more than one candidate from the same party, and no party had a nationwide organisation. In the event, no party emerged from the 1972 elections with a clear majority and, notwithstanding the expectations of the UP (which had anticipated up to 60 seats and in fact won about 37), after some intense lobbying of members elected without formal party commitment, Pangu leader Michael Somare was able to cobble together a National Coalition Government, which embraced Pangu (with 18 endorsed candidates winning, and additional pro-Pangu members bringing its numbers to 26), PPP (11), NP (eight), the Mataungan Association (three) and eight independents. This post-election lobbying of apparently unattached members set a precedent for all subsequent elections. The UP accepted the role of Opposition, and this party alignment was broadly maintained during the life of the 1972–77 Parliament (though in 1975 some UP members supported the Government on critical divisions).

In 1972, a Constitutional Planning Committee was appointed to begin the process of preparing a constitution for the independent state. Its *Final Report* (1974) contained only a brief comment on political parties, proposing that parties be registered and supporting the idea of public funding for parties. The Constitution subsequently provided that organic laws would make provision to ensure the integrity of political parties and candidates,[17] but 25 years later this had not been done.

Between 1972 and the first post-independence election in 1977, there were several significant developments in the incipient party system. One was the emergence of the Nationalist Pressure Group (NPG) in 1974. The NPG represented a coalescence of members who supported the proposals of the Constitutional Planning Committee against modifications put forward by the Government.[18] Although it voted as a cohesive group on 'national' issues in 1974–75, the NPG specifically avoided the label 'party' and its 18 core members — drawn from the four major parties plus the Mataungan Association and a newly formed Country Party (whose members were recruited mostly from the UP) — retained their party affiliations. Another development was the election, in a by-election in 1976, of a second member representing the separatist Papua Besena movement, whose leader, Josephine Abaijah, had been elected in 1972, and the subsequent announcement of a Papua Party.[19] A third was the split and virtual collapse of the NP in 1976, after Somare had dismissed from Cabinet its leader and deputy leader, and a move by them to withdraw all NP members from the coalition failed. The NP split provides an early example of the way in which parties have fractured when some party members have jockeyed for a place in a new coalition while others have wanted to hold on to ministerial portfolios. By the end of the 1972–77 Parliament, party allegiances, as well as coalition ties, were looking fragile and there were calls for variously an all-party system and a no-party system.

In 1977, the party mass organisations, which had generally atrophied since 1972, were revived for the country's fourth and inaugural post-independence election. This time, of the 879 candidates who contested the 109 seats, 295 (30 per cent) were endorsed by one, or more, of the three major parties.[20] In addition, a number of Papuan candidates stood for Papua Besena, which in 1977 appeared to have evolved from an ill-defined separatist movement to a fully fledged political party. Observers of the 1977 poll seem to have been generally agreed that political parties had a substantial impact on the election,[21] though in an interim report on the election Bill Standish concluded that while in the towns, competition 'was more in terms of modern associations', in rural areas 'clan voting prevailed'.[22] In 1977, as in 1972, uncertainties about the political allegiances of some candidates resulted in intense post-election lobbying among those who hoped to be able to put together a government. One proposal was for a 'National Alliance' including UP, Papua Besena, the Country Party and NP. Another was for an Islands-based Alliance for Progress and Regional Development, led by the two former NPG spokesmen, John Momis and John Kaputin. In the event, the successful combination was a coalition of the enlarged Pangu and PPP membership (38 and 20 respectively) with most of the Mataungan and North Solomons members and two UP defectors, led by Somare. After several months of infighting within the Opposition, former NP

minister Iambakey Okuk emerged as Opposition Leader. Having attempted unsuccess-
fully to bring together his Highlands supporters, Papua Besena members and some
others in a People's United Front, Okuk revived the NP and, as its leader, waged an
aggressive campaign against the Coalition.

In November 1978, after a growing unease in the relationship between PPP and
Pangu (which had probably more to do with personalities and leadership styles than with
policies), PPP withdrew from the Coalition. Pangu was maintained in office by a split
within the UP, which brought about half of that party's members across the floor to the
Government. In 1978–79, the Somare Government survived three no-confidence
motions initiated by Okuk, but in January 1980, after a Cabinet reshuffle, Momis and
Kaputin withdrew from the Coalition, forming a new party, the Melanesian Alliance
(MA), and, two months later, with their support, a no-confidence vote against the
Somare Government succeeded. Chan became Prime Minister as the head of a National
Alliance Government comprising PPP, NP, MA, Papua Besena and part of UP.

The Alliance was able to hold on to office until the scheduled elections of 1982, but
it was, to say the least, an improbable coalition. PPP and NP, broadly aligned in support
of capitalist development and foreign investment (though with little personal empathy
between Chan and Okuk[23]), were at one end of a political spectrum from the MA,
which regarded itself as being to the left of Pangu and whose leaders were strongly identified with economic nationalism and the aim of self-sufficiency; and Papua Besena, which
owed its origins in large part to fear and distrust of Highlanders,[24] was a strange
bedfellow for a coalition in which Highlands members were a large component and
whose deputy leader (Okuk) was a staunch Highlands nationalist.

Between 1977 and 1981, extra-parliamentary party organisation, such as it was,
had again atrophied, but party organisations were resuscitated in the lead-up to the 1982
elections and several new groupings appeared. Indeed, in the 1982 elections, parties
seemed to be more salient than ever. Pangu, PPP, UP, NP, MA and Papua Besena/Papua
Party all fielded candidates, while two new groups — a Papua Action Party (which had
links with the NP) and a predominantly Papuan 'Independent Group' headed by former
Defence Force Commander Ted Diro — emerged as significant contenders. Some 59 per
cent of the 1,125 candidates who stood in 1982 were endorsed by one or more of these
eight parties.[25] My own observation of the 1982 campaign in the East Sepik suggested
not only that nearly all candidates sought a party label (some, indeed, more than one)
but that a high proportion of voters could accurately attach party labels to most candidates; nevertheless, 'party organization was still fairly rudimentary and … local and kin
ties and exposure to the electorate were still critically important'.[26]

Notwithstanding this, party attachment for most candidates seemed still to be loose
and it was not rare for a candidate who failed to get endorsement or assistance from one
party to turn to another; for some parties and in some electorates, party attachment
meant little more than the use of a label. Further, in a number of instances, party
members stood against endorsed candidates of their own party against their party's interests (though in some cases, parties — especially Pangu — supported more than one
candidate in order to split the local vote of opponents of their endorsed candidate).

Overall, it seemed that although there was in 1982 some increase in party voting, personal and local loyalties were still considerably more important for the majority of voters.[27]

The outcome of the 1982 election was a victory for Pangu, which — apart from the recently established MA — was the only party to increase its representation in the Parliament. Somare was duly re-elected to the Prime Ministership, heading a government comprising Pangu (with 50 members), UP (six) and a number of members who were either elected as independents or switched from other parties after the election. Diro emerged as Opposition Leader, and, surprisingly, Parliamentary Leader of the NP, after Okuk had lost his seat in Simbu; but when, in 1983, Okuk was returned in a by-election, Diro stepped down from both posts in Okuk's favour. The MA aligned itself with the NP/Independent Group and Papua Party in opposition, but the PPP for a while occupied the middle benches.

In 1985–86, Pangu Pati suffered two splits. The first occurred when a group of 15 members led by Deputy Prime Minister Paias Wingti (a Highlander, who had been elected as a UP candidate but switched to Pangu in 1977) left to form a new party, the People's Democratic Movement (PDM). The second came in early 1986 when a small group of senior Pangu members, led by Somare's Sepik colleague Anthony Siaguru, formed a Pangu Independent Group (PIG). The PIG sought acceptance as an 'affiliate' of Pangu, but when this was refused they broke away to form the League for National Advancement. The Somare Government survived a vote of no confidence early in 1985 with support from the NP and MA, but in November a vote of no confidence went against Somare, and Wingti became Prime Minister, leading a coalition consisting of PDM, PPP, NP and some Pangu, UP and MA defectors. During 1986, there was tension within the Coalition, particularly between Wingti, Okuk (until his death in late 1986) and Chan, but the Coalition was still intact when Parliament rose for the 1987 election.

As the 1987 election approached, five new parties emerged, including the People's Action Party (PAP), a Papuan-based party led by Diro, which drew on the support for the earlier Papuan Action Party and Diro's Independent Group, and the Morobe Independent Group (MIG) headed by former student leader and Morobe Premier, Utula Samana. This gave a total of 15 parties. Despite the increased number of parties, the percentage of party-endorsed candidates among the 1,513 candidates nominating dropped to 37, and independents won 22 of the 109 seats. In a pre-election survey of voters conducted by Yaw Saffu, to the question 'What is it that you would look for in the candidate you will be voting for?', only 3.4 per cent of respondents answered 'Party'.[28] When votes were counted, Pangu had 26 seats, PDM 17, NP 12, MA seven, PAP six, PPP five, MIG four, LNA three, Papua Party three and UP one. Elections for the three remaining seats were postponed. It was widely expected that Somare would be able to put together a winning coalition, but in the event it was Wingti who was successful, emerging as the leader of what Somare described as 'a ramshackle gaggle of unruly independents',[29] which included the PPP and a newly formed Papuan Bloc led by Diro, which included PP, PAP and some independents.

In the next months, the governing coalition came under severe strain. Diro, who had served as Minister for Forests in the previous Wingti Government, had been named in an investigation into the forestry industry and faced a leadership tribunal as well as perjury charges; it was also disclosed that he had received 'campaign contributions' of almost $A180,000 from Indonesian Armed Forces Commander, Benny Murdani, contrary to the provisions of PNG's Constitution. Notwithstanding this, Diro continued to press for appointment as Deputy Prime Minister and for more Cabinet posts for the Papuan-dominated PAP, and failed to dissociate himself from rumours of an impending coup, after Wingti had removed the commander of the PNG Defence Force (PNGDF) and three colonels, all of whom were Papuans. Kaputin, who had been expelled from the MA for joining the Wingti Coalition in 1985, initiated a meeting of New Guinea Islands' members (attended by 10 of the 17 Islands members), which called for 'political stability, social justice and a return to the principles of democracy'. And there were defections from the governing coalition, one member referring to the Government as 'morally corrupt'. Facing a vote of no confidence, the Government adjourned Parliament. During the adjournment there were, first, moves for a 'grand coalition' including PDM, PPP and Pangu, over which talks collapsed, and then the signing of an 'irrevocable memorandum of understanding' for the formation of a Government of National Reconciliation, embracing PDM, PPP, Pangu, PAP and Samana's renamed Melanesian United Front (MUF). But while Wingti was signing an agreement with Pangu, he was secretly negotiating with the NP (then led by Wingti's fellow Highlander Michael Mel), and, in a Cabinet reshuffle in June 1988, NP was dealt in and Pangu excluded.

A motion of no confidence was foreshadowed as soon as Parliament met later that month, and there was a spate of defections from PDM. The NP also split, again. In the subsequent vote, a combination of Pangu (including a few members who defected *back* to Pangu), most of the Papuan Bloc, the MA, LNA, a faction of NP and a few others prevailed over Wingti's leadership, and Rabbie Namaliu, who had replaced Somare as Parliamentary Leader of Pangu in July 1988, became PNG's fourth Prime Minister.

Despite the enlightened leadership of Namaliu, and the passage of a budget of 'unity, reconciliation and reconstruction', the period from mid-1988 to 1992, when the next election took place, was turbulent. It saw the start of the Bougainville rebellion, unrest within the PNGDF, economic downturn and escalating problems of law and order. Several votes of no confidence were initiated, and Parliament was adjourned for further long periods in 1989 and 1990. In 1991, the Constitution was amended to extend the initial grace period for votes of no confidence from six months to 18. There were several Cabinet reshuffles, which, among others, saw Diro eventually achieve the position of Deputy Prime Minister, a position he held until April 1991, when he was found guilty of 81 counts of misconduct under the Leadership Code. The decision of the Leadership Tribunal in the Diro case precipitated a brief constitutional crisis when the Governor-General, a Papuan and former president of the PAP, refused to sack Diro. The tensions brought about by all this political activity saw a split in the PAP, defections from PDM and PPP, and from Pangu, and several parties expelled rebellious MPs.

Commenting on Wingti's political machinations in mid-1988, Saffu suggested that 'Wingti's *modus operandi* had helped to raise the levels of cynicism and deception in PNG politics'.[30] Indeed, the well-publicised comings and goings in the Parliament of

1987–92 left many people cynical about political parties, and, although there was, once more, something of a revival of extra-parliamentary party activity in the lead-up to the 1992 election, parties seem to have been less salient in 1992 than in the previous two or three elections.[31] Six of the parties that had contested in 1987 had disappeared (including Samana's MIG/MUF, Papua Besena and the Papua Party), and several new parties emerged, including the People's Solidarity Party (PSP), a breakaway from the PAP. The PSP polled well (probably in part at the expense of the PAP), but failed to win a seat and subsequently faded away.

In 1992, the fee for candidature was raised from K100 to K1,000 in an attempt to counteract the growth in the number of candidates standing, but the number continued to rise, to 1,655. Of these, 75 per cent chose to stand as independents. In 1987, the seven major parties (Pangu, PPP, PDM, MA, PAP, LNA and NP) won 51 per cent of votes and 76 seats; in 1992, their share of the vote fell to 32 per cent and they won 68 seats.[32] Pangu was the most successful party, but its percentage of the total vote fell from 34 to 9 per cent and seats won from 50 to 20. In the vote for Prime Minister, Wingti, in coalition with the PPP, LNA and a group of independents, defeated Namaliu by a single vote. As in every Parliament to date, there was a mid-term change of government in 1994 when, having resigned and been re-elected as Prime Minister in a move to avoid a vote of no confidence, Wingti was removed after a Supreme Court ruling against his action. In the reshuffling that followed, PPP leader Chan became Prime Minister, outvoting prominent Port Moresby politician Bill Skate of the Papua New Guinea First Party (PNGFP); Chan headed yet another coalition government, in partnership with Pangu. Chris Haiveta, who had succeeded Namaliu as Pangu leader, became Deputy Prime Minister.

In 1997, there was a major political upheaval when the Chan Government, having secretly negotiated a contract with 'military consultants' Sandline International to bring an end to the Bougainville rebellion, was challenged by the Commander of the PNGDF, Brigadier General Singirok. Singirok denounced the contract, detained the Sandline mercenaries and called on Chan, Haiveta and the Defence Minister to stand down. An inquiry was set up and a major crisis averted, but in the ensuing election Chan lost his seat.

Once again, there was a proliferation of parties on the eve of the 1997 election. New parties included the People's National Congress (PNC), which replaced the PNGFP as Skate's Papuan-based party; the Movement for Greater Autonomy (MGA), a New Guinea Islands-based party headed by former Manus Premier, Stephen Pokawin; and the National Alliance (NAL). In 1995, Somare, then a member of the Chan Government, had opposed legislation that fundamentally changed the country's provincial government system. As a result, he was dropped from Cabinet and became alienated from some of his Pangu colleagues. He subsequently founded the NA as a new political grouping, comprising the MA, the MGA (which also had its origins in the provincial government debate), some Pangu supporters and progressive independents. Somare used the NA as his electoral vehicle in 1997. Of the 2,372 candidates contesting, 712 were listed as having party attachment, though parties in 1997 seemed to have fewer resources to offer and party leaders seemed to be less active outside their own electorates. On these figures, the proportion of independents fell slightly, to 70 per cent, though the actual number rose. PAP fielded the largest number of candidates; surprisingly, given its Papuan origins, more than half of these were in Highlands electorates, where there were multiple PAP candidates in a number of electorates.

When votes were counted, PPP (which had won eight seats in 1992 but had seen its support grow to 32 before the parliamentary recession of 1997) had 16 seats; Pangu had also lost ground, gaining 13 seats; the NA had 11 (including four MA seats); PDM nine; NP seven; PNC six (all in Papuan electorates); PAP six, and there were 38 independents. In the scramble for numbers prior to Parliament sitting, it looked as though Somare would emerge on top. The NA-led coalition failed to get the numbers in Parliament when Skate, who had promised support for Somare, took his PNC into a rival grouping and was rewarded with the Prime Ministership.

The Skate Government faced several minor crises between 1997 and 1999 — mostly self-made. In December 1998, there was another long adjournment of Parliament designed to avoid a vote of no confidence (between July 1998 and June 1999, Parliament met for only 17 days). Tensions had emerged between Skate and Haiveta, and when, in 1999, Skate dropped Haiveta from Cabinet, Pangu withdrew from the Coalition and backed the PDM in a successful move to oust Skate. Wingti having lost his seat in 1997, the leadership of PDM was assumed in 1998 by former Treasury Secretary and Central Bank Governor, Sir Mekere Morauta, who had stood as an independent in 1997 and had been a minister in the Skate Government before becoming one of 12 ministers sacked by Skate. In the vote for Prime Minister, Morauta won by 99 votes to five — with Skate voting for him! Morauta thus became PNG's sixth Prime Minister. In 2001, a number of members switched allegiance to the PDM, giving it for a while an absolute majority in Parliament, but the 2002 elections saw a shift away from the party (see below).

Characteristics of political parties in PNG

It is impossible, within a short space, to detail the constant comings and goings of members, defecting from one party and joining another, sometimes only temporarily, and the constant wheeling and dealing among party leaders seeking to advance their party's interests or their own ministerial aspirations through the formation of new coalitions or the preservation of existing ones. The brief history above conveys something of the flavour of party politics in PNG and provides a broad context within which some of the particular characteristics of political parties and the 'party system' in PNG can be highlighted.

Party organisation
Typically, political party organisation in PNG has been weak. Although, on paper, some of the larger parties have had organisational structures based on party branches, most parties have been essentially parliamentary alliances and have been dominated by prominent parliamentary members (or, in a few cases — the PPP with Julius Chan and the PDM with Paias Wingti — by former MPs who hoped to be re-elected). In between elections, party organisations in the electorate, such as they exist, have tended to lie dormant. Even

Pangu, which in the 1970s and 1980s probably came closest to maintaining an effective organisation — at least in its strongholds of East Sepik and Morobe Provinces — found it difficult to sustain popular support.

As a result, the textbook functions of a political party in formulating policy options, recruiting supporters and selecting candidates have seldom been fulfilled in PNG. Indeed, rather than having party branches that select candidates from among their numbers for the open and provincial electorates, in most parties it is the party leader who seeks out and recruits likely candidates for party endorsement, frequently from outside the party.

Lack of mass membership has also affected party finances. In the elections of 1968 to 1987, the larger parties were generally able to offer financial and logistical support during election campaigns — financing candidate deposits and the printing of posters, providing vehicles, boats or outboard motors for campaigning and sometimes providing T-shirts or cash. Indeed, in the 1970s, several major parties had established 'business arms' to generate campaign funds. In the 1990s, most business arms seem to have been depleted and party funding for endorsed candidates seems to have substantially dried up. When funds *were* forthcoming to support party candidates, party leaders seem to have been the predominant source, strengthening the personalistic tendency in party identity.

In Parliament, party discipline has generally been weak, the institution of party whips not having become well entrenched, and, from an early stage, 'party-hopping' or 'yoyo politics' has been fairly commonplace.

Associated with the fluidity of party attachment has been a rise in the number of candidates standing as independents. Often such 'independents' have known party leanings and might have accepted campaign support from parties that might have endorsed another candidate, but have left themselves relatively free so that, if elected, they can 'sell' their parliamentary support to the party that makes the best offer. This has given rise to a particularly Papua New Guinean practice: after the declaration of candidates after elections, two or three camps are set up, generally well away from Port Moresby (even as far as Australia), by powerbrokers for the major parties, and attempts are made to physically assemble winning coalitions of elected members. Substantial inducements might be offered to attract members to a coalition, and, on occasion, there have been complaints that members have been held at such camps against their will (hence the term sometimes used for such occasions — 'lock-ups').

Bases of party differentiation

The ease with which some MPs have changed party allegiance reflects partly a lack of clear ideological (or other) differences between parties. In the period before independence, Pangu, together perhaps with the NP, was differentiated from the other parties primarily by its critical attitude towards the Australian Administration and its demand for early independence. The UP preferred a longer transition to independence, reflecting the view of its predominantly Highlander membership that they needed more time to 'catch up' with the coastal people, who had had a longer period of contact with the Colonial Administration and enjoyed higher levels of education and public sector employment. With the achievement of independence in 1975, this ceased to be a point of differentiation. Otherwise, the UP and PPP were generally regarded as more 'business' oriented and more favourably disposed towards foreign participation in the economy than Pangu, whose associations included trade unionists. But in practice the differences were not substantial, as the record of the first coalition government (1972-77) demonstrated. Indeed, on the one occasion that substantial differences on important policy issues did arise — namely, during the constitutional debates of 1974–75, which gave rise to the NPG — alignments cut across party lines. The nature of the coalition that replaced Somare in 1980 (see above) suggested further that issues were secondary to strategies for achieving parliamentary office, a view reinforced by the 1978 split in the UP and demonstrated in political behaviour ever since.

Among later-established parties, the MA, under the leadership of former Catholic priest John Momis and Bernard Narokobi, has been seen as a relatively socially progressive party; there have been several 'labour' parties, the most recent, the Papua New Guinea Labour Party, linked to the Papua New Guinea Trade Union Congress; there was a short-lived Socialist Democrat Party, 'The True People's Party', established by former student leader Gabriel Ramoi; a Christian Democratic Party was launched in 1995, 'with the vision to provide Christian Leadership in all levels of government'; and a United Resources Party emerged during the 1997-2002 Parliament with a platform that emphasised equitable returns from resource development. But none of these has done much to further the cause of issue-based politics. In the 1980s, there were suggestions that emerging social class divisions might provide a basis for political party development, but subsequent developments have not provided the evidence for such a view.

In the absence of class or ideological cleavages, ethnic or regional divisions seemed to be a likely base for political aggregation. The visiting UN mission in 1971 expressed concern at the regionalist tendencies in political party development,[33] and the next year a local scholar forecast that 'it will not be ideology or class interests which separate the parties — if there are more than one … regional interests are the most likely source from which political parties will derive their mass base'.[34] Commentaries on the 1977 election tended to support this judgment: Hegarty observed that in the pre-election period 'considerable social differentiation had become apparent', but went on to conclude, 'The basic cleavages in PNG politics are not ideological or class based but regional',[35] and Premdas and Steeves ventured the opinion, 'It would be difficult for anything but an ethnically-based party system to emerge.'[36] By the 1980s, the regional concentration of party support appeared to have been diluted somewhat,[37] nevertheless, there was still evidence of a regional element in party support: Pangu had its strongest support from the East Sepik and Morobe Provinces (in the case of East Sepik, Pangu support merged with loyalty to the provincial member, Pangu leader and 'father of the nation', Michael Somare), though from 1982 it began gaining support in parts of the Highlands; PPP and MA were strongest in the New Guinea Islands region; and UP, NP, Country Party, and subsequently PDM were associated primarily with Highlands politicians. More specifically, a Morobe District People's Association (MODIPE) had been established in 1973 with the objective of preventing people from outside Morobe Province becoming parliamentary members for Morobe electorates (at this time, the Pangu member for Lae was a

Papuan), and, in 1987, this sentiment was revived by former Morobe Premier, Utula Samana, who launched a Morobe Independent Group (MIG) and led it successfully into the election that year. A more substantial regional influence has been that exercised by Papuans. This began with the election of Papua Besena leader, Josephine Abaijah, and the formation of the Papua Party; it continued with the formation of the NP-associated Papua Action Party and Diro's Independent Group, and the subsequent emergence of a Papuan Bloc in Parliament; these in turn provided the base of the PAP (initially a Papuan-dominated party, though in recent years it has received substantial support from the Highlands); after being elected in 1992 as an NP candidate, Skate formed the PNGFP, a Papuan-based party, and, in 1997, as leader of the PNC — a party with six Papuan MPs — he became the country's first Papuan Prime Minister.

Longevity of parties

Not surprisingly, in this context, the majority of parties that have emerged over the years has been short-lived. There has been a proliferation of parties at each election, but those that do not achieve electoral success mostly disappear soon after the election. Many of these are essentially one-person parties.

Of the parties currently represented in the National Parliament, Pangu has enjoyed a continuous history as a major player since 1967, though it has suffered two major break-aways and is currently (early 2005) split into two factions; PPP also has a continuous record as a major party, though it too, is currently divided between two factions: UP and NP have survived, but with periods of low activity and records of factionalism; the MA has been a small but significant actor since its formation in 1980; and the PDM, PAP and NA have now been around, if sometimes fractious, for several years. Beyond that, parties have tended to come and go quite rapidly, mostly just before and just after elections.

The OLIPPC, LPV and parties since 2002

In the latter half of the 1990s, there was considerable dissatisfaction within PNG about the country's lack of social and economic progress and growing problems of lawlessness and corruption, and growing criticism from outside. On becoming Prime Minister, Morauta vowed to address these issues and 'to restore integrity to our great institutions of state'. A major plank in his government's reform platform was an *Organic Law on the Integrity of Political Parties and Candidates* (OLIPPC). A secondary measure was an amendment to the *Organic Law on National and Local-level Government Elections* to change the electoral system from one of first-past-the-post voting to one of limited preferential voting.[38]

In each national election in PNG since 1972, there has been a steady increase in the number of candidates contesting, notwithstanding an increase in the required fee for candidature in 1992, from K100 to K1,000 (then roughly equal to per capita GDP). While some of these candidates might have been put up to split the local vote of a rival candidate in another clan or another part of the electorate, with voter support being localised there are often several candidates with a good chance of winning if they can hold their support base together. There has also been a fairly steady increase in the proportion of candidates who have stood — at least overtly — as independents. These developments have had at least two adverse effects on elections: first, with the number required for victory sometimes relatively small in open electorates with many candidates, holding one's bloc together is critical, and this has encouraged voting irregularities and violence in parts of the country, especially in the Highlands. In 2002, this caused the declaration of failed elections in six of the nine electorates in the Southern Highlands. Secondly, with many candidates competing, the percentage of the total vote that winning candidates have obtained has been, on average, steadily falling. Concerns about these issues lay behind the OLIPPC.

After widespread public consultation, organised through a Constitutional Development Commission, and parliamentary debate, the OLIPPC and associated constitutional amendments were passed in December 2000 and came into force in 2001, in time for the country's sixth post-independence elections. In a foreword to an explanation of the proposed legislation by the CDC, Prime Minister Morauta described the initiative as 'the most important Constitutional change this country has made since independence'.[39] Its broad objectives were to strengthen the party system and help return stability and integrity to politics.

The OLIPPC contains four main provisions.

Party registration

Political parties must be registered with the Registrar of Political Parties, an office created under the OLIPPC and independent of the Electoral Commission. An unregistered party cannot nominate candidates for election. Parties must submit details of membership and a constitution, and provide financial returns on an annual basis. Membership is not to be confined to people from a particular province, region or group and the party must not encourage regionalism or secession.[40] Party offices are to be 'elected in a democratic manner' (spelled out in the legislation). Party members must be paid-up, and a person cannot be a member of more than one party. Provision is made for cancellation of registration (inter alia, if a party fails to file financial returns for two consecutive years), for dissolution of a registered party (where a majority of party members or 75 per cent of party MPs agree), and for amalgamation of registered parties. In addition to the Registrar, the OLIPPC set up a Central Fund Board of Management (renamed Commission on the Integrity of Political Parties and Candidates), whose membership comprises the Registrar, the Electoral Commissioner, the Clerk of the National Parliament, the chair of the National Economic and Fiscal Commission, and church and women's representatives. The board appoints the Registrar and is responsible for dealing with registration applications and management of the Central Fund. By August 2001, 43 parties had registered (though not all had supplied the necessary documentation).

Funding of parties and candidates

The OLIPPC established a Central Fund, from which parties receive public funding. The sources of income available to the Central Fund comprise an annual appropriation from the national budget and (unlimited) contributions from citizens, international organizations and non-citizens. The allocation to parties is on the basis of K10,000 for each elected MP. In 2003, the Central Fund Board of Management approved the distribution of K990,000 to 20 parties, at the same time complaining that 'The government has miserably failed to adequately fund the Board and its Secretariate [sic]'.[41]

In addition, registered parties and candidates can receive contributions from citizens and non-citizens of up to K500,000 in any financial year, in each case — a somewhat generous provision, especially considering that the Constitution in 1975 precluded non-citizen contributions, and the CDC initially recommended a limit of K100,000. The donor and the recipient are required to provide details of such contributions to the Registrar, though there have been complaints that the Registrar has not been fully informed. Successful candidates are also required to submit a detailed financial statement within three months of election.

Strengthening political parties in Parliament

Probably the most important provisions of the OLIPPC were those intended to prevent 'party-hopping'. Under the organic law, a Member of Parliament who was elected as a party-endorsed candidate cannot withdraw or resign from that party during the life of the Parliament (unless he/she can establish that the party or an executive of the party has committed a serious breach of the party's constitution or that the party has been adjudged insolvent) and cannot vote against a resolution of the party concerning a vote of no confidence, the election of a Prime Minister, approval of the national budget or a constitutional amendment (a member can, however, abstain from voting). Contravention of this provision is regarded as resignation from the party and sets in motion a series of procedures that can culminate in the member having to reimburse the party for all campaign and other expenses received from the party, exclusion from appointment as a minister or committee chair, or dismissal from Parliament. A member elected as an independent can join a party after the initial vote for prime minister, and then incurs the same obligations to the party as a party-endorsed candidate. A member elected as an independent who remains independent, but who supported a particular candidate in the vote for prime minister, must not vote against that candidate or his/her government in a subsequent vote of no confidence, nor against a budget brought down by that government, nor against a constitutional amendment proposed by that government.

These provisions were tested in December 2003, when the Somare Government, already facing threats of a vote of no confidence, sought to extend, from 18 months to 36, the grace period within which an incoming government was free from a vote of no confidence. The proposed constitutional amendment was defeated, but several parties split over the issue. Some members who voted against their party leader defended themselves by arguing that there had not been a formal party resolution on the issue. The issue has not to date been resolved.

The OLIPPC also provides that, after an election, the Head of State shall invite the party with the greatest number of endorsed candidates elected to form a government and to nominate a candidate for election by the Parliament as Prime Minister. This was intended to minimise the post-election lobbying that had produced the 'lock-ups' after earlier elections.[42] In 2002, this probably gave an advantage to Somare, as leader of the NA, and Somare was duly elected Prime Minister, but it did not eliminate the post-election machinations and it did not necessarily ensure a victory for Somare.

Incentives for female candidates

In an effort to address the massive under-representation of women as electoral candidates and in the National Parliament, the OLIPPC provided that where a party-endorsed female candidate received at least 10 per cent of the votes cast in her electorate, the Central Fund would reimburse up to 75 per cent of the campaign expenses outlaid on her by the party. In 2002, the number of female candidates (mostly independents) rose from 45 to 74, but the number elected fell from two to one, and only received 10 per cent of the vote.

Before the 2002 national elections, 43 parties had registered with the Registrar for political parties, though many of these had very small membership and, on the eve of polling, a number had not provided the Registrar with the required list of candidates. In the event, with 'failed elections' declared in six seats in 2002, 24 parties were represented in the new Parliament: the NA with 19 members, PDM 13, PPP eight, Pangu six, PAP five, People's Labour Party four, nine parties with two or three members and another nine with one member each. Seventeen candidates were elected as independents. By December 2003, the number of parties had been reduced, through amalgamations, to 18.[43] As the leader of the party with the most winning candidates in 2002, Somare was invited to form a government, and he was subsequently elected Prime Minister by a vote of 89 to nil, with 14 members abstaining. The PDM, under Morauta, joined the small Opposition group, subsequently changing its name to the Papua New Guinea Party (PNGP). Wingti was re-elected in 2002, but he stood as an independent and did not seek to regain leadership of the party he had established.

The shift from first-past-the-post voting to limited preferential voting (LPV) was affected in the general belief that such a change would bring about greater cooperation between candidates, reducing the number of candidates and lessening the violence associated with recent elections — though the rationalization of this belief has never been made very clear.[44] LPV came into effect after the supplementary elections in the Southern Highlands in 2003. By December 2004, there had been six by-elections held under LPV. All were fairly peaceful affairs, with fewer candidates than in the 2002 national elections, but since that is usual in by-elections it would be premature to take these outcomes as a validation of this particular piece of social engineering.

Why has a coherent party system failed to develop in PNG?

The question, why have parties not developed, implicitly assumes that political parties are an inherent part of a parliamentary system. Certainly, the process of majority decision-making encourages groups of like-minded members to come together to ensure the numbers necessary to push legislative agendas, and when there are significant lines of social cleavage — class, ideology, ethnicity, religion, region — and corresponding clearly differentiated collective group interests, these might form a natural basis for party organisation. This has been the history of political party development in most developed nations. But it does not describe politics in PNG.

First, as Hegarty has argued, PNG lacked the galvanising influence on politics of an independence struggle, through which parties have often been defined elsewhere,[45] and, after the early differences between Pangu-NP and UP over the speed of transition to independence became irrelevant in 1975, party platforms, as we have seen, tended to converge. Class has not emerged as a major social cleavage in a country where about 85 per cent of the population is at least partly involved in subsistence agriculture and even the urban elite tend to retain their links with the village. Undoubtedly, there is a growing gap between rich and poor, but Western class models are largely irrelevant in explaining the dynamics of economic inequalities in PNG. Regionalism has had more impact on PNG politics, especially in relation to a continuing Papuan identity, but it has not provided a systematic basis for party organization. Indeed, to achieve office, all coalitions need to put together a group representative of all four regions, and this to some extent cuts across regionalism as a base for party organisation. In the absence of such social or geographic cleavages, collectivities have developed primarily from personal networks. Since politicians also compete for office, these personal networks are typically fragile, especially among aspiring leaders.

Secondly, and not unrelated, politics in PNG remain essentially parochial. While I have argued elsewhere that the view of electoral outcomes in PNG being determined by clan or 'tribal' loyalties is an oversimplification, electoral success nevertheless seems to be determined primarily by local factors: local reputation, local perceptions of a candidate's ability to deliver goods and services to his or her electorate and the effectiveness of electoral campaigning. Successive studies of PNG national elections have provided little evidence of a party vote – even of a strong Pangu vote in Pangu's stronghold of East Sepik — and only occasionally (as perhaps in the case of Sir Michael Somare, the country's first Prime Minister) has a national reputation translated into local votes. Added to this, a high turnover of parliamentary members means that most MPs seek a quick return from their period in office, and this places a premium on being in government, preferably with a Cabinet portfolio. Indeed, MPs' constituents generally *expect* their member to be in government, regardless of party attachment. After several Opposition MPs defected to governing coalition parties in 1990, they explained: 'We are elected to Parliament to be in government.'[46]

As a result, MPs are driven less by the desire to implement a particular policy agenda than by the desire to maximise the returns, for themselves and their constituents, from being in office. And as every government since 1972 has been a coalition and, until 2002, no government has survived a full parliamentary term, with MPs hopping from one party to another and parties shifting allegiance from one coalition to another, the potential for individual interest outweighing party loyalty is substantial. This has been reflected in the frequency of votes of no confidence. In such a volatile atmosphere, party loyalties are difficult to sustain. OLIPPC sought to address this problem by strengthening parties, but developments since December 2003 have so far suggested that MPs are not willing to accept the constraints of the OLIPPC and that the State is either incapable of enforcing the provisions of the organic law or unwilling to pursue them.

Prospects for future party development

If political parties in PNG could play a role in mobilising electors and defining issues that cut across narrow clan or local identity interests, if they could play a role in selecting capable and effective candidates to become MPs, if they could provide an organisation and discipline to control the parliamentary behaviour of MPs — the functions traditionally associated with parties in liberal democracies — they could make a substantial contribution to the achievement of a less fractious political system, in which the Legislature legislates and the Executive takes the lead in governing. There is no real evidence that this happening, or, in the light of experience to date with OLIPPC, that it will happen. As has been argued above, since the 1980s, political parties seem to have become more, rather than less, fluid, weaker in terms of organisation and finance, and have a shorter life expectancy. Those inside and outside PNG who argue, largely on the basis of developed Western country experience, that parties *will* develop but that, as in developed Western countries, the process 'will take time', have not produced a convincing argument to support this social Darwinist assumption. Almost 30 years after independence, political allegiances are still heavily personalised and significantly localised, with a poorly developed sense of national identity. State institutions are mostly weak, and, in the absence of the sort of major social cleavages that characterised political party development in the West, there is no obvious reason why this should change. Moreover, PNG is not unique: in many countries, mass-based political parties are weak and play a secondary role to personalised parliamentary factions.

In 1970, a frustrated young political organiser, Michael Somare, observed: 'The administration is the giver of all things and people do not care so long as they are at the receiving end. Our people are so accustomed to getting things for nothing that … they do not see why they should organise as political groups.'[47] Thirty years later, people were not 'so accustomed to getting things for nothing', but they still tended to see the State as the source of things, and getting access to the State meant getting *their* candidate elected. Once in Parliament, MPs hope to improve their access to things by becoming part of government, and, with weak party allegiance and discipline, parliamentary alliances are constantly shifting. Institutional change, through the OLIPPC, has so far done little to change this pattern. What is needed to bring about change is a fundamental shift in behaviour, and, in the foreseeable future, it is not clear what could bring about such a change.

Footnotes

1   May, R. J. 1984. 'Class, ethnicity, regionalism and political parties.' In R. J. May (ed.), *Social Stratification in Papua New Guinea*, Working Paper No. 5, Canberra: Department of Political and Social Change, Research School of Pacific Studies, The Australian National University. pp. 174–90 (reprinted in May, R. J. 2001. *State and Society in Papua New Guinea: The First Twenty-Five Years*. Adelaide: Crawford House Publishing. pp. 127–146).

2   For a more detailed history of political parties in Papua New Guinea, see Wolfers, E. P. 1970. 'A short history of political party activity in Papua New Guinea.' In M. W. Ward (ed.), *The Politics of Melanesia*, Fourth Waigani Seminar. Canberra: The University of Papua New Guinea and ANU. pp. 439–88; Stephen, D. 1972. *A History of Political Parties in Papua New Guinea*. Melbourne: Lansdowne Press; Loveday, P. and E. P. Wolfers, 1976. 'Parties and Parliament in Papua New Guinea 1964–1975.' *IASER Monograph*, No. 4. Port Moresby: Institute of Applied Social and Economic Research; May, 1984, ibid.; Okole, Henry T. 2004. 'The Fluid Party System of Papua New Guinea: Continuity and Change in a Third Wave Democracy.' Unpublished PhD thesis, Northern Illinois University; and May, R. J. 2004. 'Papua New Guinea.' In Alan J. Day and Henry W. Degenhardt (eds), *Political Parties of the World*, London: John Harper Publications. Also see Faircloth, Susan, Hartmut Holzknecht and R. J. May. 1978. 'Politics and Government in Papua New Guinea.' *IASER Bibliography*, No. 4. Port Moresby: Institute of Applied Social and Economic Research. pp. 141–6. The role of political parties is also discussed in a series of studies of PNG's national elections: Epstein, A. L., R. S. Parker and M. Reay (eds). 1971. *The Politics of Dependence: Papua New Guinea 1968*. Canberra: ANU Press; Stone, David (ed.) 1976. *Prelude to Self-Government. Electoral Politics in Papua New Guinea 1972*. Canberra: RSPAS-ANU, and UPNG; Hegarty, David (ed.) 1983. *Electoral Politics in Papua New Guinea. Studies on the 1977 National Elections*. Port Moresby: UPNG Press; King, Peter (ed.) 1989. 'Pangu Returns to Power: The 1982 Elections in Papua New Guinea.' *Political and Social Change Monograph*, No. 9. Canberra: DPSC, RSPAS-ANU; Oliver, Michael (ed.) 1989. *Eleksin. The 1987 National Election in Papua New Guinea*. Port Moresby: UPNG; Saffu, Yaw (ed.) 1996. 'The 1992 PNG Election: Change and Continuity in Electoral Politics.' *Political and Social Change Monograph*, No. 23. Canberra: DPSC, RSPAS-ANU; May, R. J. and Ray Anere (eds). 2002. *Maintaining Democracy: The 1997 Elections in Papua New Guinea*. Port Moresby: Department of Political Science, School of Humanities and Social Sciences, UPNG and State, Society and Governance in Melanesia Project (SSGM), ANU. From 1967 to 1991, the *Australian Journal of Politics and History* contained a regular chronicle of developments in PNG written by various Port Moresby-based authors, which provides valuable source material; these chronicles have been brought together in Clive Moore with Mary Kooyman (eds). 1998. *A Papua New Guinea Political Chronicle 1967–1991*. Bathurst: Crawford House Publishing [references to these chronicles in this paper will be to the Moore with Kooyman volume].

3   *Canberra Times*, June 23, 1967.

4   Wolfers recalls that during the 1960s, police Special Branch personnel 'were regularly to be observed taking notes' at meetings of political parties (see Epstein, Parker and Reay, op. cit., p. 30).

5   Kiki, Albert Maori. 1968. *Ten Thousand Years in a Lifetime*. Melbourne: F. W. Cheshire. p. 175. Also see Somare, Michael. 1970. 'Problems of political organization in diversified tribes in Papua-New Guinea.' In M. W. Ward (ed.), op. cit.; and Somare, Michael. 1982. 'The role of political parties in Papua New Guinea.' *Administration for Development*, Vol. 9. pp. 3–8.

6   Stone (ed.), op. cit. p. 51.

7   See R. J. May. 'The political education programme.' In Stone (ed.), ibid., pp. 107–26.

8   United Nations. 1968. *Report of the United Nations Visiting Mission to the Trust Territory of New Guinea*. Document T/1717. p. 66.

9   Epstein, Parker and Reay (eds), op. cit., p. 326.

10   Wolfers, E. P. 1998. 'Political Chronicle January–April 1968.' In Moore with Kooyman (eds), op. cit. p. 36.

11   See Wolfers, E. P. 1970, op. cit.; and Stephen, D., op. cit.

12   The leaders of several other 'micronationalist' movements that emerged about this time also contested elections, some successfully, but did not see themselves as political parties (see R. J. May [ed.] 1982. 'Micronationalist Movements in Papua New Guinea'. *Political and Social Change Monograph*, No. 1. Canberra: DPSC, RSPAS-ANU. Chapter 1).

13   Loveday and Wolfers, op. cit. p. 21.

14   Ibid.

15   Ibid. p. 74.

16   Stone, op. cit. p. 535.

17   Sections 129–130 of the Constitution of the Independent State of Papua New Guinea stipulated that parties were to be registered and political contributions limited; contributions to parties and candidates by non-citizens were specifically precluded.

18   See Hegarty, D. 'Political Chronicle January–June 1975.' In Moore with Kooyman (eds), op. cit. pp. 236–40.

19   See McKillop, R. F. 1982. 'Papua Besena and Papuan separatism.' In May (ed.), 1982, op. cit. pp. 329–58.

20   Hegarty, D. 'Political Chronicle January–June 1977.' In Moore with Kooyman (eds), op. cit. p. 300.

21   See Hegarty, ibid. and Hegarty (ed.), 1983, op. cit. Chapter 1.

22   Standish, W. 1977. 'Independent Papua New Guinea's first national elections: an interim report.' *Dyason House Papers*, Vol. 4, No. 1. p. 4.

23   See, for example, *Post-Courier*, June 21, 1983.

24   See Daro, B. B. 1976. 'The Papua Besena movement; *Papua dainai, tano dainai, mauri dainai.*' *IASER Discussion Paper*, No. 7, Port Moresby: Institute of Applied Social and Economic Research; McKillop, op. cit.

25   Hegarty, David and Peter King. 1998. 'Political Chronicle January–June 1982.' In Moore with Kooyman (eds), op. cit. p. 357.

26   See May, R. J. 1989. 'The East Sepik electorates.' In Peter King (ed.), *Pangu returns to power: the 1982 elections in Papua New Guinea*, Canberra: DPSC, RSPAS-ANU, pp. 221–7.

27   Hegarty and King, 1998, op. cit. p. 361.

28   See Saffu, Yaw. 1989. 'Survey evidence on electoral behaviour in Papua New Guinea.' In M. Oliver, op. cit. pp. 15–36.

29   *Post-Courier*, August 6, 1987.

30   Saffu, Yaw. 1998. 'Political Chronicle January–June 1988.' In Moore with Kooyman (eds), op. cit. p. 455.

31   See May, R. J. 1996. 'Election in the East Sepik: Mit na Bun.' In Yaw Saffu (ed.), 1996, op. cit. pp. 219–39.

32   Saffu, Yaw. 1989. 'Survey evidence on electoral behaviour in Papua New Guinea'. In Michael Oliver (ed.), *Eleksin: The 1987 National Election in Papua New Guinea*. Port Moresby: UPNG. p. 30–31.

33   United Nations, op. cit. p. 176.

34   Waddell, J. R. E. 1973. 'Constitutions and the political culture.' In A. Clunies Ross and J. Langmore (eds), *Alternative Strategies for Papua New Guinea*. Melbourne: Oxford University Press. p. 96.

35   Hegarty (ed.), 1983, op. cit. pp. 454, 461.

36   Premdas, R. R. and J. S. Steeves. No date. *Political parties and electoral politics in Papua New Guinea. The case of the Moresby North-East electorate*. Port Moresby: UPNG. p. 35.

37   Cf. Jackson, Richard and David Hegarty. 1983. 'From geography to ideology?' *Australian Geographer*, Vol. 15, No. 5. pp. 334–6.

38   In an unpublished paper ('Political change in Papua New Guinea: Is it needed? Will it work?') presented to a conference at the Divine Word University, Madang, 2003, I questioned some of the assumptions underlying the 2001 reforms. Some of those questions remain valid. For more recent analyses of the operation of the OLIPPC, see Baker, Louise. 2003. *Political Integrity in Papua New Guinea and the Search for Stability*. Canberra: AusAID; and Gelu, Alphonse. 2005. 'The failures of the Organic Law on the Integrity of Political Parties and Candidates.' Unpublished paper presented to the Pacific Islands Workshop, Asia Pacific Week, RSPAS/International Centre of Excellence-Asia Pacific, ANU, January–February 2005.

39   *Explaining the Proposed Political Integrity Laws Prepared by the Constitutional Development Commission*, Waigani, July 2000. p. 1.

40   The term 'regionalism and secession' is taken from Bengo, Paul. 2002. *Brief on Provisions of the Organic Law on the Integrity of Political Parties and Candidates for Members of the Seventh Papua New Guinea National Parliament* by the Registrar, July 2. p. 4. The Organic Law itself (S.7 [a]) does not specifically mention 'regionalism'.

41   Central Fund Board of Management. 2003. 'Press Release on Financial Returns of and Funding to Registered Political Parties for 2002.' March 11.

42   Another provision of the OLIPPC made it an offence to force, threaten, intimidate, detain or otherwise interfere with the free movement of an MP in the performance of his parliamentary duties.

43   A list of parties and some detail on the larger parties can be found in R. J. May, 2004, op. cit.

44   Cf. Rumsey, Alan. 1999. 'Social Segmentation, Voting, and Violence in Papua New Guinea.' *The Contemporary Pacific,* Vol. 11, No. 2. p. 327; Reilly, Benjamin. 2001. *Democracy in Divided Societies: Electoral Engineering for Conflict Management.* Cambridge and New York: Cambridge University Press. pp. 88–9.

45   See Hegarty, David. 1979. 'The political parties.' In A. Amarshi, K. Good and R. Mortimer (eds), *Development and Dependency. The Political Economy of Papua New Guinea,* Melbourne: Oxford University Press. p. 187.

46   *Post-Courier,* April 17, 1990, quoted in Saffu, Yaw. 1998. 'Political Chronicle January–December 1990.' In Moore with Kooyman (eds), op. cit. p. 488.

47   Somare, 1970, op. cit. p. 490.

PARTIES, CONSTITUTIONAL ENGINEERING AND GOVERNANCE IN THE SOLOMON ISLANDS

Tarcisius Tara Kabutaulaka

IN LATE JUNE 2004, the then Opposition Leader in the Solomon Islands National Parliament, John Martin Garo, announced that he was 'crossing the floor' to join the Government.[1] About a week later, on July 8, Garo was sworn in as Minister of State assisting the Prime Minister and took his oath of allegiance to a government he had spent the past year opposing.[2]

In many other parliamentary democracies, the defection of the Leader of the Opposition to the Government side, and his immediate appointment as Cabinet Minister, would have attracted widespread political debate. This was not the case in the Solomon Islands, where the incident passed with just murmurings from a few disgruntled politicians and citizens. Ironically, the most profound expressions of concern — most of them not publicly expressed — came from government backbenchers who were not keen on having a former Opposition Leader taking up a Cabinet position that they would have wanted for themselves.[3] For the rest of Parliament and the country, however, the Opposition Leader's defection was '*politiks nomoa ia*' (just politics). Not long afterwards, a new Leader of the Opposition, former Prime Minister Francis Billy Hilly, was elected and parliamentary business continued largely as usual.

The Opposition Leader's defection did not raise many eyebrows in the Solomon Islands because most Solomon Islanders are familiar with tactics like this. The previous Leader of the Opposition, Patteson Oti, also resigned as Opposition Leader and leader of the Solomon Islands Alliance for Change (SIAC) Party in May 2003 and later joined the People's Alliance Party (PAP) — the leading party in the ruling coalition. He was appointed

Minister for Communication, Aviation and Meteorology.[4] Garo was, therefore, simply following his predecessor's footprints across the floor of Parliament. This raises a number of points. First, these events illustrate the porous nature of the boundary between the Opposition and Government, and the fact that Solomon Islands politicians, generally, have weak loyalty to parties. Second, it demonstrates the weakness of the country's party system. This is what Jeffrey Steeves referred to as an 'unbounded' political process in which parties 'are not sufficiently strong in binding the loyalty of elected members to ensure that the party controls their legislative behaviour'.[5] Consequently, political allegiances change regularly and political instability is endemic, making it difficult to make and implement medium- and long-term policy and program plans. Because coalition governments are usually fragile, time and effort are spent building and sustaining clientelistic relationships to ensure the maintenance of power. This affects democratic efficiency and the effectiveness of governments.

To avert political instability and enhance democratic efficiency, it is often suggested that countries such as the Solomon Islands need to politically engineer the development of parties by instituting statutory mechanisms that would regulate their formation and operation. Such political engineering, it is envisaged, could also transform the behaviour of politicians and voters and create organised and broad-based parties that are effective in structuring issues and aggregating and representing diverse interests. Further, it is argued that political engineering could also make citizens more aware of the role of parties in the political process.

This chapter discusses how political engineering could strengthen parties and their participation in the promotion of representative democracy in the Solomon Islands. It examines, in particular, how the introduction of statutory mechanisms might affect not only party developments but also governance processes and outcomes overall. First, the chapter provides a brief history of the development of parties in the Solomon Islands and how they have influenced the country's political landscape and its governance processes and outcomes. Second, it provides an overview of the experiences of some countries in the Asia-Pacific. Third, it discusses some of the lessons that Solomon Islands could learn from countries that have attempted to politically engineer the development of parties, and some of the issues that need to be considered when introducing statutory mechanisms to regulate political parties in the Solomon Islands.

I agree that there is a need to politically engineer the development of parties in the Solomon Islands. But, in establishing institutional means to strengthen parties and enhance their participation in the political process, it is also important to note that institutional changes from above will not, by themselves, lead to political stability and effective and efficient governance. Rather, there is also a need to link institutional changes at the top to changes in political culture on the ground, and an enhancement of the masses' understanding of the democratic process and the role that parties play in it. This is important because Solomon Island politicians are influenced not only by the statutes that regulate parties, but by the local political cultures and the demands that constituents place on them. Such societal changes will require mass education that depends on the improvement of the standard and accessibility of education and the development of mass-media communications.

Parties and governance in the Solomon Islands

Like other new democracies, Solomon Islands political parties are relatively new, and tend to be small, organisationally thin, elite-based, highly personalised, and have few (if any) institutional or ideological links to the electorate. Many parties are formed, or become active, only before elections. After elections, most parties become quiescent or disappear completely from the public arena. They function largely as institutions for recruiting candidates for elections and for lobbying support for the formation of coalition governments and maintaining power, and only second as vehicles for the electoral mobilisation of the masses, or for structuring issues, aggregating, representing and articulating diverse interests, and translating diverse public views into coherent public policies, for waging election campaigns, forming and maintaining stable governments, and implementing policies. Many politicians, in fact, declare their membership to a party after rather than before elections.

There are a number of factors that influence the nature and development of parties in the Solomon Islands and their participation in the political process. First, (as stated above) parties are relatively new in the Solomon Islands and are still in their early evolutionary stage. The first 'political party' — or, what closely resembled one — was formed as recently as 1965. This development was associated with the Solomon Islands' political transformations to self-government, the introduction of elections and the inclusion of indigenous Solomon Islanders in the political process. Sam Alasia provides an elaborate account of the historical development of parties and how the introduction of elections and the involvement of Solomon Islanders led to the emergence of parties.[6] In 1960, the Legislative Council was established to replace the former Advisory Council that had been set up to advise the High Commissioner, who was the British colonial representative in the country. The Legislative Council consisted of 21 members, six of whom were indigenous Solomon Islanders. Two of the Solomon Islanders were included in the eight-member Executive Council. This was the first time that Solomon Islanders participated in the Colonial Government as policy-makers. In 1964, the first direct election was introduced in Honiara to select a representative for the Legislative Council. Eric Lawson, an expatriate, emerged as winner, and, in early 1965, in an attempt to lobby support to form a government (the Executive), Lawson and the member for North Malaita, Mariano Kelesi, formed the Democratic Party (DP). The party revolved around Lawson and Kelesi, did not have a formal institutional set up and relevance beyond the Legislative Council and was used primarily as an attempt to lobby for support in forming a government. After the election of the Executive, the party ceased to exist because the purpose for which it was set up had been achieved.

After the 1967 election, however, Bill Ramsay, the man who replaced Lawson as Member for Honiara, teamed up with David Kausimae, the Member for South Malaita, and formed the Solomon Islands United National Party (SIUNP). Again, the function of the party was primarily to lobby support for the formation of government. It was not formally registered — because there were no statutory requirements for it to do so — and, like the previous Democratic Party, it had no organisational structure beyond the Legislative Council.

In 1973, the structure of government was further transformed when the High Commissioner became Governor with only nominal power. The Executive power was given to the newly established position of Chief Minister. In preparation for the 1973 general elections, two parties were formed: the People's Progressive Party (PPP), led by Solomon Mamaloni, and the United Solomon Islands Party (USIPA), led by Benedict Kinika. After that election, no party had a clear majority and the two new parties had to lobby for support from the independent members, led by Willie Betu, to form a coalition government. Mamaloni was subsequently elected the country's first Chief Minister, leading a coalition government that consisted of the PPP and some independent members.

In January 1976, the Solomon Islands achieved self-government and in July that year the last election of the colonial era was held. The two parties — PP and USIPA — had disintegrated before the election and their members stood as independents. A new party emerged when a recent graduate from the University of PNG (UPNG), and Union leader, Bartholomew Ulufa'alu, formed the National Democratic Party (NADEPA). The new party won eight of the 38 seats in the House and was able to act as the parliamentary powerbroker. On July 14, 1976, Peter Kenilorea, then a relative newcomer to politics, was elected as Chief Minister and led the country to independence. Ulufa'alu became the Leader of Opposition, with his NADEPA members and some independents.[7]

Independent Members of Parliament have played crucial roles in Solomon Islands politics. In most instances, they have held the balance of power in coalition governments, and have, in some cases, caused the collapse of governments by withdrawing their support. Independent members provide an interesting insight into the nature of Solomon Islands (and Melanesian) politics where allegiance is given to individuals rather than to parties. These independent members are attracted to and support individuals (big men) whom they see as having the potential to assert their interests and those of their constituents. They could withdraw their support when they see that another big man could promote their interests much better. In preparation for the 1980 general elections, for example, the Kausimae-led USIPA merged with the Mamaloni-led PPP and formed the new PAP. Kenilorea formed the Solomon Islands United Party (SIUP). The SIUP won 16 seats, the PAP 10, NADEPA two, and the independents 10. The independents and NADEPA held the balance of power and a coalition was inevitable. The SIUP attracted some independent members and formed the Government, and Kenilorea was subsequently elected as Prime Minister. To strengthen the Coalition, the leader of the independents, Francis Billy Hilly, was selected as Deputy Prime Minister. Mamaloni became Leader of the Opposition.[8]

In these situations, the ability to form coalitions depends on the individual big man, rather than on party policies or ideologies.[9] In this case, Kenilorea was perceived as a much better choice, however, Kenilorea's Government did not stay in power for long. In August 1981, after only 14 months, the Coalition collapsed. Differences between leaders saw the withdrawal of the independents' support. They realigned themselves with the Opposition and Mamaloni took over as Prime Minister, forming a government that consisted of the PAP, NADEPA and the independents. They stayed in power from 1981 to 1984.

Second, Solomon Islands political parties are largely elite-based. Bartholomew Ulufa'alu, a former Prime Minister and veteran Solomon Islands politician, says that, '[t]he parties were divorced from the masses. The Solomon Islands elites were then [in the early days of party development] paying more attention to trying to unseat their colleagues, and looked for support upwards towards the colonial administration, rather than outwards to the people.'[10] Parties have not found a way to connect with the people. This is partly because the parties are Honiara-based and oriented to middle-class Solomon Islanders who live and work in Honiara. They do not have organisational links or branches outside of the capital.

Third, the absence of mass media communications makes it difficult to mobilise rural constituents. The print media consists of only one daily newspaper (*Solomon Star*) and one weekly newspaper (*Solomons Express*), which are circulated primarily in Honiara and provincial towns such as Auki, Gizo, Lata and Buala. There is only one radio station — the Solomon Islands Broadcasting Corporation (SIBC) — that broadcasts nation-wide. Apart from this there are three FM radio stations that broadcast only in Honiara. There is no local TV, although the Telekom relays the British Broadcasting Corporation (BBC) and the Australian Broadcasting Corporation (ABC) TV programs to Honiara residences. Communications and transportation are also made difficult by the dispersed nature of the country's geography.

Parties' abilities to reach the population are also limited by the fact that most do not have the financial (and other) resources to undertake public relations campaigns. After the 1980 general elections, NADEPA attempted to expand its power base beyond the union movement to the rural areas by campaigning nationwide. Its popularity, however, was affected by widespread misconceptions that it was a 'communist' party,[11] and its ability to reach out was limited by the lack of resources and the absence of a decentralised organisational structure.

From the mid-1980s onwards, many small, thinly organized and highly person-alised parties emerged. These affected the ability of parties to establish support among the masses. Just before the 1984 election, for example, a new party, the Solomone Ago Sagefenua (SAS), was formed, increasing the number of parties competing in the election to four: United Party (UP), PAP, NADEPA, SAS and the independents.

In the 1989 general elections, the number of parties participating in the elections further increased to six: PAP, UP, SAS, NADEPA (which had changed its name to the Liberal Party), plus two new parties — the Nationalist Front for Progress (NFP), led by Andrew Nori, and the Labor Party, led by Joses Tuhanuku.

Most of these parties revolve around particular individuals, rather than certain political ideologies. The UP, for example, was organised around Kenilorea, while PAP was organised around Mamaloni, NADEPA around Ulufa'alu, NFP around Nori, and the Labor Party around Joses Tuhanuku. There was no attempt to establish organisational structures that would detach the parties from these individuals.

The 1989 election saw for the first time the emergence of one party, PAP, as the winner of the majority of seats in Parliament. The party's parliamentary leader, Mamaloni, was subsequently elected as Prime Minister. Steeves attributes this to voters' choice: 'Solomon Islands voters opted for dramatic change, selecting the PAP partly on the basis of its emphasis of its established leadership, including former PM Solomon Mamaloni.'[12] I think, however, that PAP's emergence as the majority party had little to do with voters' choice. Rather, it was more to do with the ability of the PAP leadership to persuade elected Members of Parliament to join the party. Many of those who joined did not have party affiliations during the election and only declared their membership to PAP after. It was, therefore, a result of the political ingenuity of PAP leaders more than the ability of the party to persuade voters. Yet, PAP's parliamentary dominance was only short-lived: in October 1990, barely a year into its term in office, the party's hold on government disintegrated during a no-confidence motion before the party's national executive, seeking Mamaloni's removal as PAP's parliamentary leader. For the first time, a party showed enough internal organisation to challenge its own parliamentary leader. Mamaloni was being challenged from within his own party rather than on the floor of Parliament. Steeves describes what happened:

> The bonds of party unity, loyalty, and discipline were fractured for all to see. In a dramatic and bold stroke, Mamaloni headed off the challenge by resigning from the party and, using his power as prime minister, forming a 'Government of National Unity and Reconciliation' (GNUR). Mamaloni displaced five members from his cabinet including Deputy Prime Minister, Danny Philip, to make room in the ministerial ranks to build a new governing coalition.[13]

In the 1993 election, the number of parties that competed increased to eight: the PAP, GNUR, UP, NFP, National Action Party of Solomon Islands (NAPSI), the Liberal Party (formerly NADEPA), the Christian Leadership and Fellowship Group, and the Solomon Islands Labor Party. The number of independent members was still significant and, after the election, an independent, Francis Billy Hilly, was elected as Prime Minister, leading a fragile collection of parties that formed the Coalition Government, referred to as the National Coalition Partnership (NCP) Government. By the beginning of October 1994, however, six Members of Parliament, including five ministers, had left the NCP Government. In an attempt to stay in power while lobbying for support, and because of fears that he might be voted out in a motion of no confidence, Hilly did not convene Parliament. In October 1994, however, the then Governor-General, Moses Pitakaka, convinced that Hilly no longer had the majority to rule, sacked him. In November 1994, Parliament convened and elected Mamaloni as Prime Minister.[14]

The 1997 elections saw Ulufa'alu elected Prime Minister on August 27, leading a coalition that called itself the Solomon Islands Alliance for Change (SIAC) Government. Ulufa'alu's Government was shaken in mid-1998 with the defection of six MPs to the Opposition after the dismissal of the Minister of Finance, Manasseh Sogavare, in July. For the next two months, the Opposition, which now claimed to have a majority, pushed for the convening of a special parliamentary session in order to introduce a vote of no confidence in Ulufa'alu's Government. The vote on September 18, 1998, resulted in a tie, which, under parliamentary standing orders, meant that the motion was defeated and Ulufa'alu narrowly survived. His SIAC Government's term in office was, however, short-lived, and he was ousted in a coup in 2000 after civil unrest on Guadalcanal.

Party fluidity

Parties in the Solomon Islands are very fluid and lack the organisational structures needed to establish mass support and maintain stable governments. Steeves provides an elaborate discussion of how the fluidity of parties has affected the nature of governance in the Solomon Islands. Since independence, the country has predominantly had (except for a brief period after the 1989 election) coalition governments that are generally unstable. Politicians, because of their general lack of allegiance to political parties, tend to move from one party to another causing an unstable political situation. Nearly every government since independence has not served its full term in office, having been voted out in motions of no confidence, or realignments causing a Prime Minister to alter his political affiliations in order to continue in office. As discussed above, a case in point is when, in 1990, after the resignation of his ministers, Mamaloni resigned from his PAP, pulled in members from other political parties and continued as Prime Minister leading the GNUR.[15]

This is what Steeves referred to as 'unbounded politics'. As a result, there is no cohesion of the Cabinet or government regarding consensus, and little interest in policy-making. This is because, in most cases, coalition governments are formed, posing problems in agreeing on policy within the Cabinet and insecure parliamentary majorities have made it difficult to steer legislation through the Legislature.

But, politicians' political behaviour and the nature of their alliance to parties are also influenced by the national and local political culture. Politicians are motivated predominantly by local issues and the enhancement of cliental relationships that might have little to do with parties and party policies. Much of what influences national politics — including party politics — in the Solomon Islands are often local and parochial issues. As Steeves notes, 'elected members have to cultivate their community bases of support very carefully',[16] because they depend on that to get into and stay in Parliament. To gain community support, a Member of Parliament does not necessarily have to join a party. Rather, he simply needs to build cliental relationships with big men in his constituency and be perceived to be serving the community's interests.

The country's ethnic and cultural diversity and lack of developed mass media compound the problem further, making it difficult to develop common ideologies that would sustain parties with a large popular base. This could, however, change as citizens identify more with a common nationality and parties become more organised and are able to use the mass media to construct and disseminate common ideologies, or at least, inform electorates about how they would address issues of common concern.

Because parties are organisationally thin, and because candidates are influenced largely by local (rather than national) issues, governments will continue to be built on coalitions rather than single parties. While this might be perceived as a drawback for the political stability necessary to implement development programs,[17] it has also ensured that no party or individual has become hegemonic or has monopolised power enough to use the State to enhance particular interests and suppress others. This, however, also means that effective and efficient governance is compromised because politicians are often preoccupied with trying to stay in power, rather than with governing.

Engineering party developments in the Solomon Islands

To alleviate the problems of political instability (as discussed above) and improve the effectiveness and efficiency of governments, the Solomon Islands could follow the examples of other countries and politically engineer the development of parties. This could be done by providing statutory mechanisms that would ensure that parties take root, are mass based, have loyal membership and play a better role in structuring issues, aggregating and representing diverse interests and translating diverse public views into coherent public policies.

At present, the Solomon Islands has no statutory mechanism for the establishment, operation and development of parties. The country's national Constitution makes only brief reference to parties, under the provision on the protection of freedom of assembly and association. It states that

> Except with his own consent, no person shall be hindered in the enjoyment of his freedom of assembly and association, that is to say, his right to assemble freely and associate with other persons and in particular to form or belong to political parties or to form or belong to trade unions or other associations for the protection of his interests.[18]

While this provides for the freedom to form or belong to parties, it does not provide for the operation and development of parties. Nor does it dictate how parties should participate in the political process. Further, there are no statutory mechanisms that address specific issues such as the definition of political parties (what constitutes a political party?), what qualifies them to register as parties, how members should be disciplined if they change party allegiance after being elected, how parties should participate in the electoral process, how to ensure that there is a shift from elite-based to mass-based parties, and how to strengthen the internal organisation of parties.

Those parties that have been registered are incorporated as charitable trusts under the *Charitable Trusts Act* (Cap. 55). While this enables them to exist and operate as legal entities, it does not provide the kinds of guidelines as outlined above. Parties, therefore, continue to exist and operate in largely the same undisciplined manner as they have since they first came into being in the late 1960s.

The suggestion for the establishment of statutory mechanisms to regulate parties is not new in the Solomon Islands. Many politicians and citizens have expressed similar ideas, although none has provided an elaborate outline of the kinds of political and institutional framework that should be put in place. The Prime Minister, Allan Kemakeza, for example, said that unless there was legislation to prohibit Members of Parliament from switching political alliances, the Solomon Islands would continue to be politically unstable.[19] Kemakeza, however, did not elaborate on what exactly such a piece of legislation would address. It is here that the Solomon Islands could consider, draw on and learn from the experiences of other countries in the Asia-Pacific region, as outlined by Ben Reilly. The Solomon Islands could introduce statutory mechanisms similar to those that Fiji, PNG, Thailand and Indonesia have done in an attempt to create stable, effective and efficient governments.

In politically engineering the development of parties, there are a number of issues that need to be considered. First, while statutory mechanisms for prohibiting 'party-hopping' and regulating party developments within Parliament might produce relatively stable parties, it would not necessarily address the fragility of coalition governments that dominate Solomon Islands' political landscape. PNG, for example, having introduced the *Organic Law on the Integrity of Political Parties and Candidates* (OLIPPC), now has to come to terms with the fragility of coalition governments. This is complicated by the existence of independent Members of Parliament who have no party affiliations and can join a coalition to serve particular interests. In the Solomon Islands (as in PNG), independent members have, in the past, contributed to the instability of coalition governments by shifting their support from one group to another. While the rights of Members of Parliament to represent their constituencies in any way they want is recognised, this is an issue the Solomon Islands must address in any political engineering endeavour. As PNG scholar Henry Okole states,

> there is now ground to fear that Independent candidacy would be greatly abused in the next general election. Something needs to be done before 2007 to address this constitutional right with a view of protecting it. But, at the same time, the integrity of Parliament should not be compromised by free-floating MPs with devious tactics. Independents can unnecessarily sink or change a coalition formation by altering numbers on both sides of Parliament.[20]

Hence, any institutional or political engineering of parties must address the stability of coalitions. Nearly every Solomon Islands government since independence — except for a brief period of PAP rule after the 1989 elections — has been based on coalitions. This is likely to continue given the unlikelihood of a single party gaining power through elections. It is, therefore, pertinent that discussions of party development must also involve discussion about how to strengthen coalitions.

Second, in discussing the engineering of party developments in the Solomon Islands, it is important to note that while prohibiting elected members from 'party-hopping' might positively influence the political behaviour of individual members, it would not necessarily change the internal organisation of parties. How parties are institutionally organised is vital to their development and their ability to attract and maintain mass support as well as the ability to capture and manage power. All the parties in the Solomon Islands, as mentioned above, are thinly organised and often have only nominal existence outside Parliament. The only exception is the PAP, which is the only party that has consciously maintained an organisational structure outside Parliament. Its relative success in the 2001 election (and in leading the current coalition) was attributable to its institutional development.

In Indonesia, Thailand and PNG, there are statutory regulations that require parties to demonstrate a certain level of institutional development before they can participate in elections. In PNG, for example, parties are required to lodge an application for registration to the Registry of Political Parties, the body that approves the registration of parties. This is part of an attempt to force parties to develop institutional structures and to reduce the number of parties.

Fiji, despite changes to the electoral system, does not have such a regulation and this has led to the mushrooming of many small and thinly organised parties that have little (if any) capacity of attracting mass-based support, and gaining and maintaining political power. Even parties such as the Alliance and NFP, which formerly had mass support among indigenous and Indo-Fijian voters respectively, virtually disintegrated in the late 1990s. The Fiji Labour Party has also broken up into two parties: the Fiji Labour Party and the New Labour Unity Party (NLUP), led by Tupeni Baba. This is partly because the 1997 Constitution, while addressing the stability of parties within Parliament, does not dictate how parties are organised and registered outside Parliament.

The Solomon Islands, therefore, might consider putting in place regulatory frameworks that guide the institutional development of parties. This could prevent the mushrooming of many small and thinly organised parties at election times.

Third, parties could also be strengthened through electoral reforms. A form of alternative voting system could be adopted to help strengthen the presence of parties in different parts of the country and force voters to vote along party lines. Fiji's case shows, however, that such changes in the electoral system do not always produce the desired outcome.

Fourth, in attempting to engineer the development of parties, it must be noted that such development and the effective and efficient participation of parties in the governance process cannot be addressed simply by changing statutory frameworks from above. While that is important, we must also note that parties are influenced by the political cultures of the societies in which they operate. Voters' perceptions of the role of parties and the nature of their relationship to Members of Parliament also influence how parties are organised and how politicians relate to parties. Okole notes that in PNG (as in the Solomon Islands) citizens often view the State as a bottomless reservoir of resources and Members of Parliament as 'literal deliverers of anything and at any cost'. This, in turn, dictates how Members of Parliament relate to and use their parties. Similarly, Standish, in discussing the introduction of OLIPPC in PNG, states, 'Observers and advisers on these remain sceptical of political engineering, the notion that the country's entrenched political culture of localized and personalized campaigning and fluid party allegiances can be changed from above — in effect, by constitutional fiat.'[21] Ron May, a senior ANU academic, also states that in PNG clan-based voting will not be easily changed by political engineering at the top.[22]

For parties to function well there is a need to educate citizens about the role of parties and their importance in representative democracy. The development of parties, therefore, depends not only on changes in the party structures, but on parallel improvement in citizens' awareness about parties. As Okole notes, in respect to PNG, there is a need for transformation among the electorates and parliamentary members. This is a long-term issue that will depend on the improvement of the country's formal education system, as well as development in institutions such as mass-media communications. As stated above, the Solomon Islands media is still underdeveloped, making it difficult for parties to reach out to the population. The development of parties in the Solomon Islands will go hand-in-hand with the development of the mass media. This is vital, not only for the purposes of campaigning, but in educating the public (and hopefully changing political culture).

Civil unrest, federalism and political parties

There are two recent events in the Solomon Islands that have important implications for the development of parties. The first was the civil unrest that started on the island of Guadalcanal in late 1998 and resulted in an Australian-led Pacific Islands Forum regional intervention force called the Regional Assistance Mission to Solomon Islands (RAMSI).[23] The civil unrest was described widely by the media and international commentators as an 'ethnic conflict' between the peoples of Malaita and Guadalcanal, because much of the overt violence was between some people from these two islands.

It is interesting, however, that despite the ethnic nature of the conflict, political parties did not become ethnically based. This is unlike the case of Fiji, where parties are generally ethnic-based. It was this (plus the coups of 1987) that led to the introduction of statutory changes, such as the 1997 constitutional reform, that aimed to facilitate the development of multi-party governments. Despite this, parties continued to be founded, and draw support from, the two major ethnic groups — the indigenous Fijian and Indo-Fijian.

In the Solomon Islands, however, the civil unrest did not engender the development of ethnic- or island- or provincial-based parties. Instead, many of the parties continued to revolve around individual big men or Members of Parliament. Parties such as the PAP, which have established formal structures, continue to maintain a multi-ethnic and multi-provincial base.

There are a number of reasons for this. First, the country's enormous ethnic and linguistic diversity[24] makes it difficult for any particular island or ethnic group to capture and maintain political power. Unlike Fiji, where there are two major ethnic groups that can be mobilised to compete for political control, Solomon Islands' ethnic heterogeneity makes it difficult for one or two groups to become dominant.

Second, the civil unrest was primarily between some Guadalcanal and Malaita people, and any parties that are based in these two provinces would not have been able to capture power because collectively they have only 22 Members of Parliament — 14 for Malaita and eight for Guadalcanal — in a 50-member House. Hence, individually, they would not have the numbers to capture power, and it is unlikely that provincial-based parties would be able to attract support from other provinces.

Third, despite the seemingly ethnic nature of the civil unrest, there was widespread recognition, at the community and national parliamentary levels, that the causes of the civil unrest lay in broader socioeconomic and political issues that transcended provincial and ethnic interests. Hence, it could be addressed through collective bipartisan efforts. This is not to say that partisan provincial interests could not be articulated. Of course they could, and this is manifested in the development of social movements such as the Malaita Ma'asina Forum, formed in 2004 with the objective of mobilising Malaitans to develop their province. It is, however, unlikely that such social movements will develop into parties that attempt to capture political power at the national level. This is especially so if the proposed Constitution is adopted. This is because the proposed Federal Constitution states that 'A political party is not eligible for registration if that party is founded purely on religious, linguistic, racial, ethnic, corporatist basis or seeks to engage in propaganda based on those matters.'[25]

Fourth, because parliamentarians tend to gravitate around individuals rather than parties and their policies, it is likely that they will form and maintain parties around individuals rather than ethnic or provincial groups. With individuals, politicians have the freedom to move around and take advantage of the power play more than they would under a provincial-based party.

Although individually each of the above reasons might not have been sufficient to prevent the formation of ethnic or provincial-based parties, collectively they made such parties less attractive as vehicles for capturing and maintaining political power.

The second issue that has important implications for the development of parties in the Solomon Islands is the proposal to change Solomon Islands' system of government from the current unitary system to a federal system.[26] Federalism offers a more decentralised system, which raises three important questions: would parties contest federal and state elections? Would federalism see the emergence of state-based parties? If that happens, would that result in political divisions along island and ethnic groups?

The framework for the proposed federal system is provided for in the draft Federal Constitution that is yet to pass through the National Parliament. Unlike the present Constitution, the draft has a specific provision (Chapter Twenty, Part II, Sections 218–23) that addresses political parties in some detail. It provides for, not only the right to form parties, but guidelines on registration and party discipline. A major provision is that 'A member of Parliament who resigns from the political party that sponsored the member's election or leaves the political party to join another or remains in Parliament as an independent loses his or her seat.' This is similar to the provisions of the 1997 Fiji Constitution.

It seems that under a federal system, while there will be parties that will compete at the federal and state levels, there will be others that will be state-based. It is unlikely that one or two parties will become dominant in the way that the Labor and Liberal Parties have been able to do in Australia, or the Democrats and the Republicans in the US. Whether the emergence of state-based parties will lead to disunity is difficult to say. I suspect, however, that because of the increasing economic interdependence of the provinces (or states-to-be), the existence of state-based parties will not necessarily lead to disunity at the national level.

Conclusion

The development of political parties is vital to advancing stable, effective and efficient government in the Solomon Islands, as well as in other Melanesian countries. Parties play an important role in representative democracy and are central to effective parliamentary governance. This could be done by introducing statutory mechanisms that could regulate the development of party institutions and the nature of their participation in the political process. Several strategies have been employed in the Asia-Pacific region in an attempt to engineer the development of parties, and the Solomon Islands could learn from their experiences.

One thing is obvious: statutory reforms (the top-down approach) cannot, by themselves, produce desired changes at the bottom. The introduction of statutory regulations must accompany awareness programs that will inform citizens of the importance of parties and their role in representative democracy. This means that in attempting to engineer the development of parties we must also be aware of the nature of political culture in the Solomon Islands. This will help us understand the factors that influence the behaviour of politicians and voters, who are both important in the success of parties. Any statutory reform must take into consideration the impact of political culture on party institutions.

It is also important to note that parties will take time to develop in the Solomon Islands. Political engineering could establish the frameworks for party developments. It will, however, take many more years for parties to take root and become part of citizens' political psyche. That will depend on the improvement of political education and mass-media communications.

Footnotes

1   SIBC News, June 29, 2004, available at http://www.sibconline.com.sb (Accessed on November 13, 2004).

2   SIBC News, July 8, 2004, available at http://www.sibconline.com.sb (Accessed on November 2004, 13).

3   SIBC News, July 8, 2004, available at http://www.sibconline.com.sb. SIBC carried this news piece in which the Prime Minister, Allan Kemakeza, denied rumours that there was a rift in his government due to backbenchers' disagreement about the appointment of John Garo.

4   SIBC News, February 12, 2004, available at http://www.sibconline.com.sb (Accessed, November 15, 2004).

5   Steeves, Jeffrey S. 1996. 'Unbounded Politics in the Solomon Islands: Leadership and Party Alignments.' *Pacific Studies*, Vol. 19, No. 1. pp. 115–38, at p. 117.

6   Alasia, Sam. 1997. 'Party politics and government in Solomon Islands.' *State, Society and Governance in Melanesia Project (SSGM) Discussion Paper 97/7.* Canberra: RSPAS-ANU. See also Bennett, Judith. 1987. *Wealth of the Solomons: A History of a Pacific Archipelago, 1800–1978.* Honolulu: University of Hawai'i Press.

7   Ibid.

8   Ibid.

9   Steeves, op. cit.

10   Ulufa'alu, Bartholomew. 1983. 'The Development of Political Parties.' In Peter Larmour and Sue Taura (eds), *Solomon Islands Politics,* Suva: Institute of Pacific Studies, University of the South Pacific. pp. 101–6.

11   Alasia, op. cit.

12   Steeves, op. cit. p. 117.

13   Ibid. p. 123.

14   Ibid.; and Alasia, op. cit.

15   Ibid.

16   Steeves, op. cit. p. 132.

17   Ibid.

18   *Solomon Islands National Constitution*, Section 13 (1).

19   SIBC News, February 9, 2004.

20   Okole, Henry. 2005. 'Dealing with coalition instability'. In *The National* (Commentary), January 5. Available at http://www.thenational.com.pg/0818/focus1.htm (Accessed on January 17, 2005.)

21   Standish, B. 2002. 'Constitutional Engineering in Papua New Guinea's Problematic Democracy.' Paper presented at the Foundation for Development Co-operation Development Research Symposium: South Pacific Futures, Brisbane, July 22–24. Available at http://www.fdc.org.au/files/standish.pdf (Accessed on October 22, 2004.)

22   ABC Radio Australia, Asia Pacific. 2004. Available at http://www.abc.net.au/asiapacific/specials/png/process.htm (Accessed on October 15, 2004.)

23   See Kabutaulaka, Tarcisius Tara. 2001. 'Beyond Ethnicity: The Political Economy of the Guadalcanal Crisis in Solomon Islands.' *SSGM Working Paper* 01/1; Moore, Clive. 2004. *Happy Isles in Crisis: The historical causes for a failing state in Solomon Islands, 1998–2004*. Canberra: Asia Pacific Press; Frankel, Jon. 2004. *The Manipulation of Custom: From Uprising to Intervention in the Solomon Islands*. Wellington: Victoria University Press.

24   The Solomon Islands has a population of about 500,000 people who speak around 87 different languages. There are also identifications along island and provincial lines.

25   Solomon Islands Government. 2004. *Solomon Islands Federal Constitution*. Draft.

26   The demand for federalism has a long history that dates back to the time of independence in 1978, although the current proposal emerged as a result of demands made by Guadalcanal Province during the recent civil unrest. It looks likely that the federal system will be introduced soon. A federal Constitution was drafted and will go before Parliament later in 2005.

THE ORIGINS AND EFFECTS OF PARTY FRAGMENTATION IN VANUATU[1]

Michael G. Morgan

Introduction

This chapter details the origins of Vanuatu's political parties, their policy platforms, parliamentary representation and core constituents, including the particular linguistic, regional and religious biases of each party. In so doing, it charts the progressive fragmentation of Vanuatu's political parties since the late 1980s. At independence in 1980, party politics were polarised largely between the monolithic anglophone Vanua'aku Pati (VP) and an alliance of predominantly francophone opposition groups, the Union of Moderate Parties (UMP). For almost a decade, the VP dominated the Parliament, commanding a nearly two-thirds majority. After 1988, the VP splintered into progressively smaller factions. The subsequent fragmentation of the UMP has created a Parliament of shifting alliances and unstable coalitions. Encouraged by the peculiar political culture of Vanuatu — in which the electoral system and the society in which it operates present few disincentives for factionalisation — this has led to endemic political instability, which has weakened the law-making and oversight functions of Vanuatu's Parliament and made marshalling the numbers to form government the principal task of parliamentary parties. Across the spectrum of Vanuatu's political parties, policy variations have narrowed as the pragmatic considerations of establishing allegiances have brought about the erosion of the distinct party platforms developed during the 1970s. National politicians in Vanuatu now often appear motivated primarily by staying in power.[2]

This has created new challenges for Vanuatu's MPs. Endemic political instability precipitated the Comprehensive Reform Programme (CRP) and countering the consequences of political instability has been the intention of several programs undertaken under the auspices of the CRP. The growing number of foreign advisers undertaking core tasks of the CRP has reignited the issue of Vanuatu's sovereignty and, consequently, support — or otherwise — for the reform agenda has become a major point of differentiation between Vanuatu's political parties.

Drawing these issues together, this chapter examines the coherence of contemporary political groupings, the fragility of government coalitions, the impetuses for party fragmentation, and makes comment on the long-term viability of Vanuatu's current set of parliamentary parties. It includes a review of parliamentary numbers since 1980 and it will provide a prognosis of the single non-transferable vote (SNTV) electoral system in which they operate.

Background

Geographically, the Republic of Vanuatu comprises an archipelago of about 80 islands and reefs, some 70 of which are inhabited. At the time of the 1999 census, its population was 186,678, with almost 80 per cent of that number residing in the rural areas of Torba, Sanma, Penama, Malampa, Shefa and Tafea Provinces.[3] The urban population, however, is expanding rapidly (4 per cent per annum), with more than twenty per cent of the population now residing in Port Vila and Luganville.

Previously known as the New Hebrides, the republic, until 1980, was administered jointly by France and Britain under the Anglo-French Condominium created in 1914, bequeathing Vanuatu bifurcated educational, legal and administrative systems.[4] At independence, Vanuatu declared French, English and Bislama to be the official languages. Given the strong colonial rivalries between the UK and France, the divisions cleaved by colonialism were thought to have been replicated in the Melanesian societies in the New Hebrides,[5] and to have inflected the emergent political culture of the archipelago, rendering political groups — somewhat unproblematically — as anglophone or francophone.[6] Such dichotomies simplify Vanuatu's political landscape and sometimes serve colonialist agendas, which subordinate local motivations in favour of colonial or narrow nationalist purviews.[7]

The point is not to discredit the influence of the colonial powers on political mobilisation entirely, but to recognise the porous and shifting nature of political allegiances in Vanuatu, to problematise 'anglophone' and 'francophone' as absolute political polarities. Most of Vanuatu's political parties share one of two common points of origin, emerging either from the VP or the UMP, although former members of these parties might now be unified in membership of one of Vanuatu's newer parties. Given that the VP came to support a one-language, anglophone education policy in the late 1970s and that much of its elite emerged from Protestant, anglophone education, it has been characterised accurately as an anglophone party. Included in the diverse camp of 'francophone' parties, however, have been several arguably anglophone political groups, opposed ideologically to the centralist, clergy-led nationalists of the VP. Natatok Efate, one such group, was the VP's main opponent on Efate in the inaugural national elections in 1979. The party fielded only anglophone candidates, yet derived much of its electoral support from francophone-dominated areas on the outskirts of Vila, particularly Montmartre and

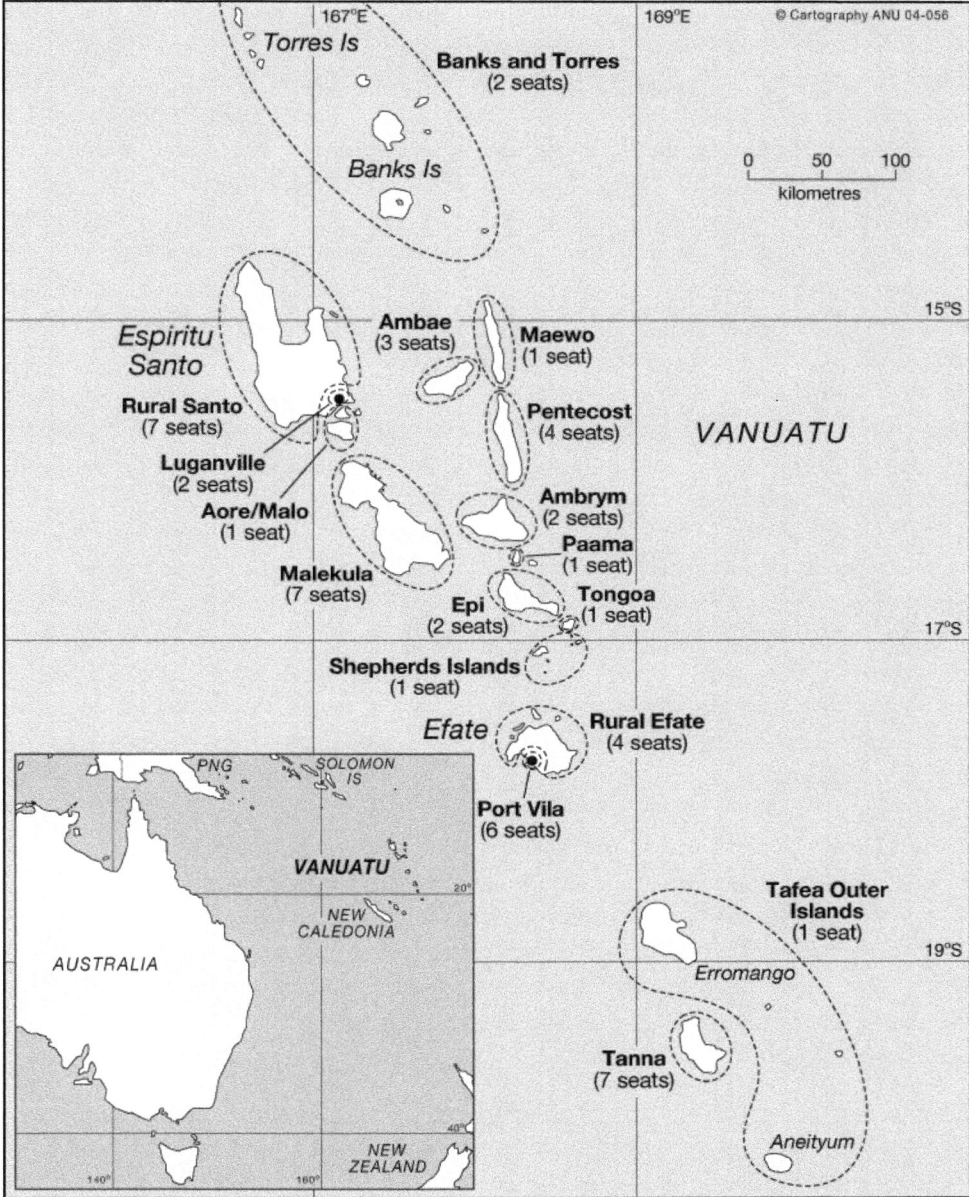

Figure 7.1: Vanuatu: SNTV multi-member constituencies

Erakor.[8] Ideologically, Natatok Efate was closer to the *Modérés* than to the VP. The sweep of French and British influence in Vanuatu should not be underdrawn. Given that the French Administration appeared determined to thwart independence and actively fomented rebellion, most opponents of the nationalist VP have been implicated in the rebellion in one way or another.[9] The perceived intervention of French colonial officers, in particular, raised the ire of the nationalist VP, souring relationships between France and Vanuatu after independence and unfairly tarring all francophone ni-Vanuatu with the brush of sedition.[10] The rebellion — and, to a lesser degree, the polarised political landscape — was more than simply a French and francophone plot. Nagriamel, for example, was multi-ethnic, multilingual and multi-denominational in composition, its eventual cooptation to French and other agenda notwithstanding. Today, anglophone, Protestant communities in Ambae, Pentecost and Maewo support the UMP electorally because of shared histories of involvement in the Nagriamel movement. Beneath the veneer of the candidates and sitting members, it is much harder to delineate clearly between anglophone and francophone camps.

What unified the UMP was its opposition to the VP's rigid centralism. Indeed, despite accepting some level of decentralisation into their platform in the late 1970s (largely at the urging of French Minister for Overseas Territories [DOMTOM], Paul Dijoud[11]), the VP was opposed to incorporating it fully on the grounds that it would make legitimate the agendas of their federalist and secessionist political opponents. Although the VP platform incorporated some level of decentralisation, in practice its policies were geared towards strengthening the central authority of government and party apparatuses. The UMP, in comparison, favoured greater regional autonomy, a policy born out of its fragmented origins, and one that most of its breakaway factions have inherited. For the first decade after independence, therefore, it would be equally meaningful to delineate Vanuatu's political blocs into federalist and centralist camps, in addition to the basic francophone/anglophone divide, recognising also the slippages between these groupings.

The next section provides an overview of past and present parliamentary parties in Vanuatu. Each entry offers historical data on party origins and the particular regional and linguistic affiliations of each group. Where available, the distinct platforms and party structures of the parties are also depicted.

The Vanua'aku Pati (VP), established in 1977 (1971)

Vanuatu's first orthodox political party, the Vanua'aku Pati is also its most successful, having governed for nearly 15 of the past 24 years. Originally named the New Hebrides National Party (NHNP), it was formed in Santo in 1971 by members of the Anglican and Presbyterian clergy, junior British Administration bureaucrats and teachers.[12] In 1977, in line with its nationalist agenda, the NHNP was renamed the Vanua'aku Pati (Our Land Party). Father Walter Lini, a Melanesian Mission priest based in Longana, east Ambae, and teachers Peter Taurokoto and Donald Kalpokas, both Presbyterians, constituted the party's core leadership group.

After its formation, the party pressed for the rapid decolonisation of the New Hebrides through a concerted program of demonstrations and political agitation.[13]

While NHNP leaders often appeared impatient with the colonial powers, they were broadly supportive of the institutions of state; their major grievances with the Condominium stemmed from disagreements over the timetable for decolonisation. Like nationalist parties elsewhere in the decolonising world, the VP was determined to maintain the territorial integrity of the New Hebrides, post-colony, despite the emergence of federalist movements in the southern and northern islands in the 1970s, fomented largely by foreign agents.[14] When the VP won the 1979 national elections, fought over the issue of independence and who would lead the New Hebrides afterwards, these groups attempted open secession. With support from PNG, Australia and New Zealand, the Lini Administration suppressed the rebellion.[15] Because many French *colons* supported the revolts and because the French Metropolitan Government and Colonial Administration were seen to be complicit in the rebellion's planning, the VP adopted an anti-French stance in the early 1980s, culminating in the expulsion of the French Ambassador.[16]

Integral to the VP's original platform was the return of alienated land, the development of Vanuatu and respect for *kastom*. Initially, this was conceived under the rubric of 'Melanesian socialism', derived in part from the writings of African nationalists Julius Nyerere (Tanzania) and Kwame Nkrumah (Ghana), but sharing much with the emerging discourse on 'the Melanesian Way' articulated most clearly by Bernard Narakobi.[17] Its foreign policy was based on its membership of the Non-Aligned Movement (NAM), and involved advocacy for the decolonisation of the remaining Melanesian colonies (West Papua and New Caledonia) and a rejection of Cold War alliances. In practice, this policy allowed it to play off one foreign power against another. In the decade after independence, Australian policy-makers perceived in the growth of relations between Vanuatu, Cuba, Libya and the Soviet Union serious threats to ANZUS policy imperatives in the South-West Pacific, which prompted periodic increases in Australian aid budgets to Vanuatu.[18] Such concerns subsided with the ending of the Cold War. Ever since, VP has gravitated towards centrism.

Like most of Vanuatu's parties, the VP still places a high emphasis on nationalism, the maintenance of traditional culture, customs and national sovereignty. It is the only party with detailed provisions for the empowerment of women built into its party platform.[19] In recent years, recognising Vanuatu's dependency on foreign aid and precipitated by endemic political instability, the VP has become the party of institutional reform, supporting the Asian Development Bank-sponsored CRP. In 2002, this became fixed in the party platform: growing the economy and strengthening public administration.[20] In light of attacks from within the party membership on the CRP as an instrument of foreign domination, VP leaders have proposed a much shorter list of achievable reform priorities and have posited a much greater emphasis on grassroots support.[21]

Parallel with the increasing emphasis on reform was growing disenchantment within the party about its direction and policies. The aspirations of a generation of younger MPs have created splits within the party. Tension culminated in the early months of 2004, when three senior Members of Parliament, including former Prime

Minister Donald Kalpokas, formed a dissident group, termed the Vanua K Group by the Vanuatu Electoral Commission to differentiate it from the other VP factions (see below). Although their position within the party is yet to be determined by the deliberative bodies of the VP, Vanua K members consider themselves to be core members of the VP who maintain support from its rank and file. In terms of electoral returns, however, the split allowed the defeat of senior VP candidates in heartland constituencies such as Tanna and Tafea Outer Islands in the 2004 elections.

The VP is governed by the People's Congress, constituted by delegates from regional subcommittees, island delegates (where there are no subcommittees), members of the commissars' council and members of the National Executive Council. Administrative functions are determined by the Central Administrative Council, which includes the major office-bearers of the party (president, treasurer, secretary et al.), women's and young people's delegates, provincial and municipal councillors and other members as determined by the People's Congress.

The separation between the parliamentary, executive and administrative wings of the party has eroded in recent years. The basic party functionaries are the Commissars (Komisa), who are elected by regional subcommittees for two-year terms and who must be residents of the area they represent. Commissars are responsible for long-term party planning.

The Union of Moderate Parties (UMP), established in 1981 (1973)

The Union of Moderate Parties began its existence at independence as an amalgam of groups opposed to the majority VP. Principal among its constituent groups were the urban Union Communautes des Nouvelles Hebrides (UCNH) and the Mouvement Autonomiste des Nouvelles-Hebrides (MANH), both formed in 1973. The party also attracted support from the Tan Union on Pentecost, Namangki Aute from Malakula, former Nagriamel supporters in Santo, Pentecost, Ambae and Maewo, and from Jon Frum and other social movements in Tanna and the southern islands. Referred to before independence as the *Modérés*, to distance themselves from the 'young radicals' in the VP, the groups renamed themselves the UMP in 1981, arguably to distance themselves from the stigma attached to the rebellion.[22] The UMP draws electoral support from across Vanuatu, concentrated in Sanma, Penama, Tafea and Shefa Provinces. Its support is particularly pronounced in the urban constituencies of Port Vila and Luganville.

Central to the UMP's policy platform is the fostering of economic activity in rural areas through the maintenance of copra and kava prices at levels acceptable to farmers. Under the leadership of Maxime Carlot Korman (1991–95), the UMP advocated the private ownership of land, one of two parties to have done so (the other is Korman's current party, VRP). Currently, this policy has subsided in importance. The party is currently led by Serge Vohor, MP for Santo Rural.

The principal deliberative body of the party is the national congress. Throughout the 1990s, however, severe factional splits emerged within the party and the deliberations of the congress became secondary to political brawling between factional leaders. Decisions taken by the congress were subject to intensive judicial scrutiny.

National United Party (NUP), established in 1991

Former Prime Minister Father Walter Lini and 21 dissident VP members founded the National United Party in 1991, after Lini's ouster from the presidency of the VP. Its former president was Dinh Van Than, a naturalised Vietnamese citizen whose close alliance with Lini precluded any rapprochement with the nationalist VP (who have long considered Than an exploitative foreigner). The ouster of Than as president in favour of Ham Lini, Walter Lini's brother, allowed for its rapprochement with the VP. The party's strongholds are Penama and Torba in northern Vanuatu, but it has won seats in Tanna, Luganville and Port Vila.

Like the VP, the NUP maintains a nationalist platform, seeking to 'promote, to preserve, to revive and to encourage Vanuatu Culture … and … [to encourage] a higher standard of living and status for Ni-Vanuatu'.[23] In recent years, it has campaigned against the continuation of the CRP.

The NUP's party structure is derived in large part from that of the VP, with party authority emanating from the deliberative People's Congress. Similarly, the Central Administrative Council determines administrative functions.

People's Democratic Party (PDP), established in 1994, ceased 1998

Four dissident members of the NUP formed the PDP in 1994 after they questioned the influence of Dinh Van Than over party direction. Led by Pastor Sethy Regenvanu, the MPs defied Lini to accept government positions after the NUP was expelled from a UMP-led coalition government. Three out of the four PDP MPs were voted from office in 1998. Onneyn Tahi, the fourth rebel MP, returned to the VP in 1997.[24] He died in a car crash on Ambae in the lead-up to the 1998 elections. The PDP no longer exists as a parliamentary party.

Tan Union, established in 1977, ceased 2001

According to Vincent Boulekone, a founding member of the party, Tan Union was formed in 1977 to provide an umbrella for all those groups opposed to the VP but broadly supportive of independence.[25] Unlike the VP, Tan Union advocated delayed independence to allow for New Hebrides to develop more. New Hebrides' second Chief Minister, the late Père Gerard Leymang, was a Tan Union member. After the formation of the UMP in 1981, Tan Union formally merged with the new party, with Vincent Boulekone becoming its first president.

Serge Vohor sacked Boulekone from the party in 2000, along with three other senior MPs. The next year, the Tan Union formally merged with the Grin Pati (see below).[26] Boulekone did not contest the 2002 elections. Tan Union no longer exists as a discreet parliamentary party.

Melanesian Progressive Party (MPP), established in 1988

The Melanesian Progressive Party was formed in 1988 after Barak Sope was expelled from the VP and the National Parliament because of his role in inciting the Vila Land Riots, sparked when the Government tried to dismantle the trust fund in which money used to purchase Port Vila from its traditional landowners, including Sope's home community Ifira, was held. Of all the parties, the MPP most closely follows the original platform of the VP, advocating still for the decolonisation of West Papua and championing an autonomist foreign policy. In opposition, the MPP has campaigned against the CRP as a vehicle of neo-colonialism and its members have openly attacked core projects of the CRP and constitutional offices, such as the Ombudsman.[27]

MPP's structure closely resembles that of the VP.

People's Progressive Party (PPP), established in 2001

Sato Kilman, the former Deputy President of the Melanesian Progressive Party, formed the People's Progressive Party after a falling out with Barak Sope in 2001. Although its headquarters are in Malakula, the party has fielded candidates in Torba and Tafea Outer Islands electorates. The PPP emphasises the need for urgent agrarian reform and regional development to encourage regional trade and commerce.[28] It also stresses the need to develop regional centres as hubs for economic activity.

People's Action Party (PAP), established in 2001

Silas Hakwa, a long-standing VP supporter and former Attorney-General, formed the PAP after his breakaway from the VP in 2001. Its major support base is west Ambae in Penama Province.

Fren Melanesia Pati (FMP), established in 1975

Formerly known as Charlemagne, Fren Melanesia Pati was formed by Protestant francophone Pisovuke Albert Ravutia in 1975.[29] Its power base is in the northern islands, particularly in southern Santo Rural constituency, Luganville, Malo/Aore and Malakula. Ravutia was implicated in the rebellion in 1980 and served a term in prison for his involvement.[30] The party is one of the oldest minor parties and has traded well on its small support base, and the popularity of its founder, winning seats in 1983–87 and 1991–2002.

Grin Pati (GP), established in 2000

Formed by the Tan Union's Vincent Boulekone, Paul Telukluk and Père Gerard Leymang in July 2000, the Grin Pati's platform was initially to further sustainable development with respect to custom and the environment, regional autonomy for each of Vanuatu's provinces and free enterprise and social welfare especially for elderly people and under-privileged mothers. Currently, MP for Port Vila Urban, Hon. Moana Carcasses, leads the GP.

Although the party claims membership in the global green movement, in practice it provides a parliamentary umbrella organisation for Ambrymese, Malakulan (Namangki Aute) and Tannese (Jon Frum) social movements. While this is not antithetical to its 'green' policies, its environmental credentials have never been challenged.

The GP adheres to a strict delineation between elected members and party officials. Serving MPs cannot hold offices within the party structure. Also included in the GP structure are provisions for chiefs from the Malvatumauri (National Council of Chiefs) to act as political appointees to government departments.

Jon Frum (JF)

Until the mid-1990s a constituent of the UMP, the parliamentary wing of Jon Frum constituted part of the Alliance for the Development of Vanuatu (ADV) and is now part of the National Community Association (NCA). In the lead-up to independence, members of the Jon Frum movement instigated an uprising in the southern islands, which was suppressed by the British constabulary.[31] In practice, JF MPs have been enduring advocates of community development and religious freedom.[32]

Namangki Aute (NA), established in the 1970s

A breakaway faction of the MANH party, Namangki Aute was formed in the late 1970s by Aimé Maléré and contested Vanuatu's first election in November 1979. Principally a Malakula-based party, NA constitutes part of the Alliance for the Development of Vanuatu (ADV) and is a core group of the GP. Central to its party platform is the development of Malakula as part of a confederation of provinces, a policy that dates to its early resistance to the VP in the 1970s. Included in its policy platform are economic and legislative decentralisation, including the development of urban zones in every province, downsizing the Parliament from 52 to 39 seats (its original number), compulsory voting, recognising the power of chiefs, reinvigorating agricultural cooperatives, alleviating the Value Added Tax's (VAT) effect on the people and recognising and protecting the role of women in society (on the latter issue, the platform does not elaborate further).

Vanuatu Republican Party (VRP), established in 1998

Former Prime Minister Maxime Carlot Korman formed the Vanuatu Republican Party in preparation for the 1998 elections after his toppling as leader of the UMP.[33] Although initially involving only Korman and his personal supporters, the party has since extended its influence throughout the northern islands and now attracts strong electoral support in Malampa Province, particularly Ambrym and Malakula. Although Korman is one of Vanuatu's longest-standing and most prominent ni-Vanuatu francophones, other members of the party, such as Donna Brownie from Malekula, are anglophone. Korman has been an enduring advocate of the private ownership of land

Nagriamel (NGM), established about 1967

Arguably Vanuatu's first political party, the Nagriamel movement emerged on Espiritu Santo in the mid-1960s in retaliation to the widespread alienation of 'dark bush' by French ranchers. Very quickly after its formation, Nagriamel became the vehicle for broad anti-colonial sentiments among local people in the northern New Hebrides and, by the early 1970s, its leadership claimed 10-20,000 adherents spanning from Epi in the central New Hebrides to the Banks and Torres Islands at the archipelago's northerly extension.[34] From the 1960s until the rebellion in 1980, Nagriamel's platform was anti-state, anti-VP and anti-missionary. In the 1970s, the radical liberal ideology of the Phoenix Foundation was incorporated into its ideology.[35]

Nagriamel's influence emanates from Vanafo, north of Luganville, and extends into several northern islands, particularly Pentecost and Ambae, but it is much reduced from its peak in the early 1970s. Ostensibly, the chief's meeting house (*nakamal*) at Vanafo is

Nagriamel's supreme deliberative body. Its ideologies remain rooted in the expectation of 'cargo' arriving from America to emancipate the people. Despite its anti-statist ideologies, Nagriamel has regularly fielded candidates in national elections. It last elected an MP — its leader, Frankie Stephens — to Parliament in 1995. Stephens is the son of the founder of Nagriamel, the late Jimmy Stephens.

Nevsem Nenparata, established in 2004

Nevsem Nenparata was first elected to Parliament in 2004, when Thomas Nentu won the Tafea Outer Islands constituency. The party prioritises local development and national unity and represents a local coalition between several of the federalist parties mentioned above. In Erromangan language, *nevsem nenparata* means 'to come together in peace'.[36] The party incorporates local supporters of the UMP, VRP, the Greens, MPP and PPP, who have pooled their electoral resources. Much of the impetus to form the party came from local chiefs who sought to end political infighting on Erromango and who were dissatisfied with the existing party system and the lack of interaction between MPs and their constituencies. In particular, the impetus for forming the party came from the fear that the Government would potentially squander Erromomango's natural resources, including sandalwood, if there were no Erromangans in Parliament to protect them. The party also benefited fortuitously from the factional split within the VP in the Tafea Outer Island constituency.

Changing party numbers since 1980

Constituted by elections held in November 1979, Vanuatu's first Parliament was dominated by the VP, which commanded 26 of the 39 seats (see Table 7.1). Although the VP is often credited with winning 26 seats, it in fact only won 25. Kalmer Vocor was elected on the Natuitanno ticket, but voted with the Government consistently. Natuitanno was eventually subsumed within the VP. Several members of the *Modérés* elected to Parliament in the November 1979 elections never took their seats. Often considered to have been the trigger for the formal declaration of the Santo and Tanna rebellions, the 1979 elections augured a year of low-level violence, two attempted secessions, the arrest of several MPs, the exile of some of that number and the killing of Jon Frum MP for Tanna, Alexis Yolou. In the aftermath, the VP set about utilising its absolute majority of the House to amend the Constitution and push through whatever legislation it chose.

In the 1983 elections, the VP's majority fell to 24 seats. The VP maintained its dominance of parliamentary proceedings during the second parliament (Table 7.2).

In the 1987 elections, which contested an expanded 46-seat house, the VP won 26 seats (Table 7.3). The UMP, however, consolidated its electoral support, increasing its vote share and consequent representation in the House.[37] In 1987, Walter Lini suffered a stroke in the US. Increasingly under the influence of the Vietnamese-born businessman, Dinh Van Than, Lini lost favour with his VP comrades — in particular, Secretary-General of the VP, Barak Sope — who sought to marginalize him from the day-to-day operation of the party. Several senior MPs, however, had misgivings about the advisability of Sope leading

Table 7.1: First Parliament of Vanuatu, 1979–83.

Party	Seats
VP	25
Pati Federel/UCNH	5
Independent	2
Namangki Aute	2
Natuitanno (VP)	1
MANH (Mod.)	1
Nagriamel (Mod.)	1
Jon Frum	1
Kapiel	1
Total	39

Table 7.2: Second Parliament of Vanuatu, 1983–87.

Party	Seats
VP	24
UMP	12
Nagriamel	1
Namangki Aute	1
Fren Melanesia Pati	1
Total	39

the parliamentary party. The VP was returned to power, but with a reduced majority. By mid-1988, however, these tensions came to a head when the VP Minister of Lands decided to dissolve the Luganville Land Corporation and Vila Urban Land Corporation (VULCAN). The dissolution of the Luganville corporation passed with little protest but in Vila, Barak Sope took the closure of VULCAN to be a reneging on the VP's commitment to customary landowners and an attack on his home community of Ifira (one of the traditional owners of Port Vila land) and on Sope's personal prestige. Sope was eventually demoted from the VP Cabinet. Rather than join the backbenches, he declared his intention to mount a motion of no confidence in Lini, supported by the UMP and four dissident VP members. However, without the support of Sope's faction and with one VP member in the Speaker's chair, the Government had effectively lost control of the Parliament. Sope mounted repeated attacks on Lini as an autocrat and on the VP as a cult of personality.

Trading on his public image as the father of independence, Lini resisted attempts to wrest him of the party leadership and defected to form the NUP in 1991. Donald Kalpokas replaced him as Prime Minister. In the aftermath of the consecutive splits, the VP finally lost power in the 1991 elections. The NUP won 10 seats and formed government with the Korman-led UMP. Barak Sope's MPP absorbed the remainder of the VP's former vote pool and joined the Opposition bloc alongside the remnants of the VP. Throughout the life of the Parliament constituted in 1991, tensions simmered within the governing coalition *and* within the newly formed NUP.

Several members were uncomfortable with the visible hand of Dinh Van Than in NUP party direction and this erupted in 1993 into a public brawl between party members about Than's authority and Lini's capacity to govern. NUP withdrew from the Coalition Government in 1993. Monopolising on the split, the Korman Government offered ministerial posts to the dissident NUP members, who entered government in 1994 as the People's Democratic Party.

From the outset, the Parliament constituted in the 1995 elections was unstable (see Table 7.4). Although the main parties each claimed that they would be able to constitute

Table 7.3: Third Parliament of Vanuatu,
1987–91.

Party	Seats
VP	26
UMP	19
Independent	1
Total	**46**

Table 7.4: Fourth Parliament of Vanuatu,
1991–95.

Party	Seats
UMP	19
VP	12
NUP	10
MPP	4
Fren Melanesia Party	1
Total	**46**

Table 7.5: Fifth Parliament of Vanuatu,
1995–98.

Party		Seats
Unity Front		
VP	13	
Tan Union	5	}20
Melanesian Progressive Party	2	
UMP		17
National United Pati		9
Independents		2
Nagriamel		1
Fren Melanesia Pati		1
Total		**50**

Table 7.6: Sixth Parliament of Vanuatu,
1998–2002.

Party	Seats
VP	19
National United Party	13
UMP	8
Melanesian Progressive Pati	4
Vanuatu Republican Pati	2
Fren Melanesia Pati	2
Grin Pati	2
Jon Frum	2
Total	**52**

government in their own right, the elections for the extended 50-seat Parliament resulted in no clear majority. The party with the largest number of seats, the Unity Front, did not form government, deferring that right to the next largest bloc, the UMP. The term of Parliament was notable for the split that emerged within the UMP, with both factions claiming to represent the party rank and file. The strength of the feud became clear after the elections when the two UMP factions negotiated separately to form government. One faction attempted to form government with the NUP. The other attempted to form government with the Unity Front. The factional leaders of the UMP vied for the position of Prime Minister. The ramifications were profound. The disintegration of the largest party (UMP) within a Parliament in which no party could claim a majority in its own right meant that even a minor shift in allegiance could — and did — effect a change in government. Between 1995 and 1997, the Government changed three times via votes of no confidence and there were eight major coalition changes.[38] The period was notable for the inactivity of government ministers: Minister of Finance, Barak Sope, failed to table an Appropriation Bill for 1996–97. In 1996, frustrated by the failure of the

Government to pay their salaries and allowances, the Vanuatu Mobile Force (VMF) abducted the President to further their claims. In early 1997, government coffers were empty, forcing the Vohor Government to accept the offer of a tied loan from the Asian Development Bank (ADB), which paved the way for the CRP. In January 1998, disgruntled former employees of the VNPF, supported by urban unemployed people, rioted after an Ombudsman's report implicated senior government officials in a preferential loans deal. After three years of endemic political instability, Vanuatu appeared to be on the brink of a serious breakdown of law and order.

Vanuatu underwent its sixth national election in March 1998 (see Table 7.5), in the middle of the parliamentary term. Again, the size of Parliament was extended to 52 seats. Called on the request of Prime Minister Serge Vohor in favour of facing a motion of no confidence from within his own party, the elections resulted in a coalition government between the VP and one of its breakaway factions, the National United Pati (NUP) of Father Walter Lini. Running on a platform of government renewal and accountability, the coalition sought to reverse the political fragmentation of the previous years. It adopted, moreover, the rhetoric of institutional reform. Prime Minister Donald Kalpokas stated:

> The people of Vanuatu ... no longer trust the government ... to provide the services that they need ... Investors and workers have lost confidence that it can implement its policies to ensure that the economy grows and in the end raise the standards of living of the people.[39]

While the VP/NUP Government raised hopes of a rapprochement between former comrades, it was undermined eventually by the same problems of previous coalitions governments — internal manoeuvring.

The implementation of the CRP dominated government business. On taking office, it inherited many of the problems of the Vohor Government — particularly, a deficit estimated to be four billion vatu ($A44 million). Vohor was reported to have provided tax concessions to UMP allies and weak tax-enforcement capabilities. The Kalpokas Government accepted a $A28.6 million tied loan from the ADB, earmarked for the reduction of the bureaucracy and the implementation of guidelines for public servants. Kalpokas, however, was criticised for the slow pace of reform and the lack of visible indicators of economic growth. Rural constituents were concerned by the introduction of the VAT, which they felt benefited urban dwellers and Chinese (*sinois*) merchants more than them.

Opposition spokesmen criticised Kalpokas for being beholden to foreign interests (see below) and, facing a motion of no confidence, he resigned, allowing Barak Sope to take power. Despite commanding only four votes in the National Parliament, Sope was able to take office because of a peculiarity of the Standing Orders of the Vanuatu Parliament: rather than being the leader of the majority party, the Prime Minister must be elected by all Members of Parliament.[40]

Between his accession in 1999 and his ouster in April 2001, Sope undertook several perilous financial deals in the hope of pulling Vanuatu quickly from the brink of financial disaster, rather than the lengthier and politically unpopular process of institutional reform. The most prominent involved Amerendra Nath Ghosh, who arrived in Port Vila in February 2000 with what was described as 'possibly the world's largest ruby', which he intended to 'donate' to the people of Vanuatu. Ghosh promised to initiate a project to seal the road around Efate, build a walled complex for the Council of Ministers and negotiate with foreign consortia to build a new international airport.[41] In return for the ruby, it was reported that Ghosh was to receive $A388 million in bearer bonds from the Reserve Bank, equal to 140 per cent of Vanuatu's gross domestic product. Had Sope issued the bonds, Vanuatu's total debt would have quadrupled.[42] His record of financial management was the trigger for a motion of no confidence in March 2001.[43]

Edward Natapei, the leader of the VP, then came to power as leader of a VP/UMP government coalition, committed to following through with its reform agenda. The continued survival of the VP/UMP Government Coalition brought respite from the entrenched political instability of the 1990s, but key obstacles remained, principally poor public opinion of the CRP. By following this course, Natapei signalled his intention to stamp out the form of maverick leadership that Sope embodied, and hopefully to lessen the potential for the economic mismanagement and corruption that Vanuatu had witnessed in the past decade. Natapei's Government included several MPs who had been closely involved with financial scams and had poor records of economic management, but the exigencies of Vanuatu's Parliament meant that he had to ally with one of the larger parties. UMP spokespeople reiterated their allegiance to the VP forcefully and publicly, but key UMP MPs, including the Deputy Prime Minister, had been targeted by the Ombudsman and police for investigation.[44]

Table 7.7: Seventh Parliament of Vanuatu, 2002–06.

Party	No.
UMP	15
VP	14
National United Party	8
Independents	6 [45]
Melanesian Progressive Party	4
Vanuatu Republican Party	3
Grin Pati	2
Total	52

Table 7.8: Eighth Parliament of Vanuatu, 2004–.[47]

Party	Seats
NUP	10
UMP	8
VP	8
Independents	8
VRP	4
PPP	4
Grin Pati	3
MPP	3
National Community Association (NCA)	2
PAP	1
Namangki Aute	1
Total	52

The 2002 elections were fought over the continuance of the ADB-sponsored CRP.[46] The NUP and MPP campaigned against the program, stating that it was neo-colonial and designed to benefit Western powers to the detriment of grassroots ni-Vanuatu. The VP regained power in Vanuatu's seventh Parliament. Despite placing second to the UMP in terms of members elected to Parliament, the VP was able to claim the leadership in government by attracting two independents to join it before constituting the Coalition Government with the UMP. One of that number was Jackleen Reuben Titeck, a VP member disendorsed as a candidate by his local committee, who had won his seat nonetheless.

The VP/UMP Coalition governed until November 2003, when, citing poor attendance at Cabinet meetings and possible collusion with the Opposition, the UMP was dumped. Key UMP MPs were also alleged to have misappropriated funds, although no further action was taken. The UMP was replaced with the NUP, the People's Progressive Party and elements of the ADV, including former Prime Minister Maxime Carlot Korman and Moana Carcasses.

Throughout the term, the Government was criticised for its poor record of local development. Projects were seen to stagnate as the Government prioritised stability and financial accountability, resulting in pressure being exerted on government MPs for more rural development projects. In early 2004, a factional split emerged within the VP, prompted by the leadership aspirations of junior party members. The tension culminated in the temporary split from the party elite of senior members Donald Kalpokas, Sela Molisa, Joe Natuman and Jackleen Reuben Titeck. The term was ended prematurely after the Speaker dissolved Parliament to pave the way for fresh elections. This was prompted by the annulment of the candidacy for President of Alfred Maseng on the grounds that he had a criminal record. Maseng won the Electoral College votes against the Government-favoured candidate, triggering moves towards a motion of no confidence in Prime Minister Natapei, supported by the dissident members of his own government.

Constituted by snap elections called in 2004 after the dissolution of Parliament by the Speaker, the 2004 elections resulted in one of Vanuatu's most fragmented Parliaments. Several senior parliamentarians — including several ministers and former Prime Minister, Donald Kalpokas — were voted from office. In all, 23 sitting members lost their seats. Despite the recognition of the dangers of political instability by the major parties, the 2004 elections demonstrated the progressive Balkanisation of National Parliaments and the possible death of big-issue politics, as voters appeared to favour locally credible social movements, minor parties and independents.

The elections were called to end political instability, but the major parties suffered severe losses. As Table 7.8 demonstrates, parliamentary power is spread relatively evenly between three medium-sized blocs, one with 10 members (NUP) and two with eight members (VP and UMP). Independents or minor parties hold 26 seats in the Parliament: a simple majority. The Parliament will therefore be less stable than any of its predecessors. The Coalition Government formed by Serge Vohor is an unwieldy coalition, incorporating five independents and 23 members of five parties.[48] Although the Coalition maintains a 28-seat majority at present, its sustainability is limited by its incredible fragmentation. A minor shift in the balance of power could result in the NUP, the UMP or several smaller parties being dispensed with in favour of the VP.

A (more-or-less) stable Cabinet was formed in August 2004, referred to misleadingly as a 'government of national unity'. Despite threats from the Prime Minister, Serge Vohor, that he would call a 'state of emergency', negotiations remained peaceful. Much of the impetus for instability in the preceding few months had come from the elections for President. In August, that position was filled by one of the frontrunners in the earlier collegial run-offs, Kalkot Matas Kelekele, a member of the original independence movement and a former VP and NUP stalwart.

Earlier that month, NUP had joined UMP in government, giving it two major blocs of eight members each, and commensurate shares of Cabinet portfolios. The remainder were divided between the minor members of the Coalition. Included in the Cabinet was breakaway VP member for Tanna, Joe Natuman, a Vanua K MP, who holds the Ministry of Education portfolio.[49] Former Prime Minister Barak Sope was granted the Ministry of Foreign Affairs, possibly signalling a volte-face in Vanuatu's diplomatic relations with the regional powers, Australia and New Zealand. Accepting large soft loans from the People's Republic of China, the Vohor Government has become comfortable resisting Australian policy imperatives, the good governance agenda and core programs undertaken under the CRP, including strengthening Vanuatu's legal frameworks. Indeed, almost immediately after taking power, Vohor's Cabinet mounted attacks on the high number of foreign advisors in Vanuatu — prompting rebukes from the opposition VP — and criticised Australia as racist for its resistance to Melanesian labourers working in Australia.[50] In the past few years, gaining access to the Australian labour market has become popular political rhetoric. In early September 2004, the Government terminated the appointments of two senior AusAID consultant lawyers working in the State Law Office (Attorney-General's Department) and expelled Australian Federal Police liaison officers, although it later rescinded both decisions.

The SNTV electoral system

Vanuatu's legislature consists of a unicameral Parliament containing 52 seats,[51] elected every four years, using a single non-transferable vote (SNTV) electoral system.[52] Members of Parliament are elected on the basis of universal suffrage through an electoral system that includes multi-member, SNTV constituencies to 'ensure fair representation of different political groups and opinions'.[53]

Constituencies vary in size depending on their social make-up, although there are significant discrepancies between the number of people represented and the number of seats in each constituency. At the time of the 2002 elections, constituencies varied in size from seven-member to single-member constituencies. Generally speaking, representation is geared in favour of rural constituencies. The largest constituency, Port Vila (with 18,978 registered voters) elects six members to Parliament. The three seven-member constituencies are Tanna (17,212 registered voters), Malakula (15,789) and Santo Rural (14,411). Rural Efate (15,556) elects only four members to Parliament despite being larger than Santo Rural and only marginally smaller than Malakula. In comparison,

Pentecost also elects four members to Parliament, despite having only 9,440 registered voters. The smallest constituency is the Shepherds Group of Islands, with 940 registered voters, who elect one member (see Figure 7.1).

The Anglo-French Condominium introduced the SNTV electoral system in preparation for the 1975 elections for the National Representative Assembly (NRA), the precursor to Vanuatu's National Parliament. It allowed the colonial powers to avoid the involved and politically contentious process of setting up electoral wards and it kept the electoral system as straightforward as possible, which was considered crucial to allow for democracy to operate in a society with apparently limited literacy levels.[54] Arguably, the system was also devised with the intention of dispersing the absolute electoral dominance of the VP in the lead-up to independence, ensuring some level of representation for the VP's diverse, but minority opposition and hopefully lessening the impetus for rebellion, which was prevalent in the 1970s.[55] It failed on both counts. The VP won the 1979 elections resoundingly, claiming an absolute majority in the National Parliament. Sparked by their losses in the election, sections of the *Modérés* attempted secession.

In practice, the element of proportional representation contained in the SNTV system cemented the dominance of the majority parties (the VP and UMP) for the first decade after independence while simultaneously allowing representation for smaller parties, especially in larger multi-member constituencies. According to the Vanuatu Electoral Commission, SNTV limits the incentive for party fragmentation contained in other proportional representation systems.[56] The benefits under the system for large parties with concentrated voter support are that they are able to receive a substantial seat bonus, such as the VP received between 1979 and 1987.[57] Nonetheless, since the late 1980s, the majority parties have splintered and there has been an upsurge in the number of independent candidates running for — and winning — office.

The system has inbuilt restrictions on overstocking electorates with candidates from the one party. In multi-member constituencies, SNTV requires party organisers to educate their electors to avoid popular candidates attracting overwhelming majorities, while their less popular stablemates are unsuccessful, as occurred in the Malakula constituency in 2002. Four UMP candidates attracted a total of 1,078 votes in the Malakula electorate but none was elected, whereas Namangki Aute — the Malakulan social movement — ran two candidates, who polled 978 votes collectively; both won seats in the National Parliament. Enacting strategies to avoid such vote-splitting has become a major preoccupation of Vanuatu's political planners.

According to Howard van Trease, a major benefit of the system is that it 'allows minority cultures to be represented in the most culturally diverse country — with 100 languages for 200,000 people — in the world'.[58] A consequence of this aspect of SNTV is that levels of representation, quantified in terms of numbers of successful votes cast, are decreasing.[59] In turn, this allows members to be elected with minority shares of the vote. For example, in 1998, UMP's Henri Taga, one of the six MPs elected from the Port Vila constituency, polled just 352 votes out of the nine thousand or so votes cast.[60]

Once the dominance of the major parties was broken in the 1990s, the propensity of the SNTV system to reward smaller parties became obvious. Small parties with concentrated localised voter bases stand to beat large parties with dispersed voter bases, allowing Vanuatu's provincial social movements such as the Jon Frum movement significant advantages within the confines of its Tanna electorate given its large support base and limited pool of eligible candidates. Small, locally credible parties that can mobilise concentrated support have an excellent chance of electoral victory. Thus, while the VP, NUP and UMP are able to command votes on a national scale, the increasing number of candidates contesting each seat means that electoral results are increasingly difficult to predict and the smallest of shifts in voter support can effect major changes in the number of members elected to Parliament and the success or failure of the more established political parties.

Bearing in mind these aspects of the SNTV system, the major parties have tailored their electoral strategies accordingly, monitoring closely the number of candidates preselected by their respective national committees in preparation for elections to avoid overstocking electorates. Nonetheless, no strategies have been able to counter the tendency for national elections to result in a high turnover of candidates. In the 2004 national elections, for example, 23 of the 52 Members of Parliament were not returned. The VP, beset by internal struggles, lost six seats, not taking into account the eventual political allegiances of the dissident Vanua K MPs.

The major victors were the smaller regionally based parties. The system has allowed for the proliferation of candidates, which propels political instability and is exacerbated by it. As I argue below, given the high incidence of factional splits in Vanuatu, the predisposition of the system to reward small groups makes unwieldy coalitions a necessity for forming government.

At present, little political will is directed towards reforming the electoral system. The major parties, however, recognise that the system allows for the election of minor parties relatively easily. Given the increasing swings against the major parties, it is likely that some measures will be taken to secure governments in office, such as the organic law reforms undertaken in PNG, or an alteration in the ways in which the Executive is constituted; that is, reform to the SNTV electoral system.

Growing disenchantment

Another feature of Vanuatu's electoral politics is the increasing disenchantment with the system by local people. Since independence in 1980, voter turnout has declined steadily. In 1979, 90.32 per cent of eligible voters went to the polls.[61] In 1991, this number had dropped to 71.3 per cent.[62] In the 2002 elections, the overall turnout had stabilised at 63 per cent, although by-elections have attracted much lower turnouts: in the February 2001 by-election in Malekula, voter turnout was just 40 per cent of registered voters.[63]

These trends suggest widespread disenchantment with the electoral system. Although civic education programs have targeted rural communities explicitly to educate voters on the roles of Members of Parliament and public servants,[64] significant confusion about the role of parliamentarians exists in both rural and urban areas. Officers of the Vanuatu Electoral Commission and its support organisations are abused routinely in rural areas because they are confused with party campaigners. No continuing voter education programs have been implemented and neither the Electoral Commission nor the Parliament have the resources to support them.

Key local leaders have argued that democratic government is leading Melanesian people inexorably to calamity. The apparent creation of divisions through politics — voiced in Bislama as *politik* — is seen by many ni-Vanuatu to augur the societal violence witnessed in the Solomon Islands or PNG. A former member of the National Parliament in Vanuatu and now a regional non-governmental organisation director, Hilda Lini, attempted to capitalise on this belief when she called for the endorsement of a new, more thoroughly indigenous form of governance in Vanuatu: 'This outdated Western system of democracy will continue to corrupt Melanesia, resulting in the continuous uncontrolled crime, violence and poverty [and] ongoing crisis.'[65] An enduring irony of Vanuatu politics is that while public criticisms of the fragmented National Parliament and the apparent inertia of governments are commonplace, voters have discarded the major parties in favour of locally credible independent candidates or members of smaller parties. And it is the increasing presence of independents and smaller parties that motors political instability.

It is to the effects of the progressive disintegration of Vanuatu's political parties in the past eight national elections that we now turn.

The implications of political fragmentation

Historically, the major precipitants of party fragmentation have been leadership challenges within the major parties, prompted by the highly personalised nature of Vanuatu politics, in which MPs vie for factional and, ultimately, party dominance as a matter of routine. The losers of such contests often form their own parties, attracting factional supporters to their new banners and temporarily reducing the influence of the original party. Such dynamics precipitated the factional splits within the VP in 1988 and 1991 and are a continuing irritant to party leaders. The VP's increasing problems of membership fidelity are impelled by the aspirations of younger politicians whose patience for the party's old guard — many of whom were architects of the independence movement — has waned. Among these elder statesmen, there is the perception that the younger aspirant MPs lack the ideological coherence of Vanuatu's first generation of political leaders. The thwarted ambitions of individual politicians seeking advancement within party structures have provided the impetus for party splits.

Political fragmentation is also often motivated at the grassroots level. Dissatisfaction with the performance of political parties or the fear that politicians are subverting a community's interests to opportunistic ends motivates community leaders to break away from larger political parties. Local community leaders (such as chiefs and pastors) play a crucial role in the initial selection and endorsement of candidates and they continue to exert influence throughout the incumbency of a member. This relationship is less pronounced in senior politicians, but few are entrenched enough to completely ignore their constituency lest their support be removed. The significant grassroots contribution to these processes makes remedying the situation more difficult. Given that grassroots ni-Vanuatu consider the establishment of new political parties to be a marker of leadership skills, there are few visible institutional or social disincentives for politicians to maintain party coherence rather than breakaway or stand as independents. This situation has created several parties whose platforms are very similar but whose leaders routinely appear to be opposed, such as the VP, the MPP and NUP.

Coalitions

Coalitions have been a regular, albeit transitory, feature of Vanuatu politics since the formation of the *Modérés* grouping — the precursor to the UMP — in the mid-1970s. After the fragmentation of the VP, coalitions became necessary vehicles for the formation of government. Indeed, each government since the 1991 elections has been a coalition. Such coalitions, however, have often proved precarious, being plagued by fierce infighting and competition over ministerial posts. Coalition member parties engage in frenetic efforts to progress upwardly within governments, mostly with the intention of claiming the prized post of Prime Minister or one of the other preferred portfolios. A particular responsibility of the Prime Minister since the late 1990s has been to mediate these tensions; to ensure his position and the position of his party at the apex of the State — and thereby ensure access to the resources and networks of distribution for their constituents — with workable and more-or-less stable coalitions. These tensions must be mediated through inducements (ministerial portfolios, the appointment of political adherents and *wantoks* to party and bureaucratic positions) and sanctions (censure, expulsion), the latter an absolute last resort because of its tendency to result in further fragmentation. Largely, opposition members are denied access to government resources, motoring their often-frantic attempts to rejoin the Government ranks. Fragile coalition governments are often forced to 'horse-trade' to maintain their hold on power and opposition parties readily accept ministerial posts, parliamentary committee positions or parliamentary offices (such as Speaker) as inducements. Indeed, one of the major tasks of opposition parties is to find their way into government, however they choose.

Increasingly, opposition parties have also formed coalitions to present unified fronts to incumbent administrations, although they have generally been short-lived. The first major opposition coalition to be formed post-independence was the Unity Front — incorporating the VP, Melanesian Progressive Party, Tan Union and Nagriamel — created in 1995.[66] The Unity Front was formally disbanded in mid-August 1996, when a new grouping known as MTF,[67] combining the Melanesian Progressive Party, Vincent Bulekone's Tan Union and the Fren Melanesia Pati of Albert Ravutia, emerged and joined forces with a UMP faction and the NUP to topple the Korman Government. Some coalitions are incredibly short-lived: the Opposition Tokemau Federation, comprising the UMP, NUP, VRP and the MPP, existed only from April to May 2002.

These tendencies necessarily propel political centrifugalism within the parliamentary parties and, therefore, within the National Parliament. A situation has arisen in which opposition and government coalitions are intrinsically frail. Failure to provide desirable positions to coalition members can result in loss of government. Even the slightest shift in power in Parliament can initiate a complete reorganisation of ruling coalitions, such as occurred between 1995 and 1997, and present almost insurmountable obstacles to policy-making and implementation.[68]

The reform agenda

The major casualties of national political manoeuvring during the 1990s were parliamentary oversight, law-making and durable policy formation and implementation, especially with relation to macro-economic policy.[69] In periods of intense political instability, policy formulation, even at its most fundamental level, was subordinated to horse-trading. For example, between his inauguration as Minister of Finance in February 1996 and his eventual dismissal from Cabinet in mid-1997, Barak Sope had failed to provide a development budget or an annual budget for the previous two years.[70] More recently, it has become apparent that the regular incapacitation of parliamentary sessions in the 1990s contributed to the dominance of the Legislature by an unaccountable Executive.[71] With public scrutiny diverted by a succession of political dramas, several short-lived governments stripped state coffers and sold off state assets, often to themselves as private citizens.[72] During the mid-1990s, corruption became a primary means of advancement for government MPs, particularly those who sought to augment their own wealth with resources misappropriated from the State.

In early 1997, Vanuatu was virtually bankrupted and Serge Vohor — then UMP Prime Minister — began the implementation of the CRP, supported by the ADB and other foreign aid donors, citing the need for government renewal and the overhaul of Vanuatu's social, political and economic structures. According to its authors, the CRP was the blueprint by which the 'poor performance of the institutions of government' would be rectified through the strengthening of the Office of the Ombudsman and the enactment of a leadership code.[73]

The impact of the CRP on party policies has been indirect but nonetheless significant. Fuelled by reports of the negative impact of structural adjustment programs in PNG and the widespread pessimism about Westminster democracy in Vanuatu mentioned above, the fear that the CRP might endanger the sovereignty of ni-Vanuatu has been an enduring theme in political rhetoric since 1997. Increasingly, support or otherwise for the CRP has been a point of differentiation between the parties. Barak Sope, the leader of the MPP, has stated that the CRP would cause suffering to the people of Vanuatu and 'serves the interests of Australia and New Zealand', although in office he has been forced to grant the project tacit support.[74] Conversely, the VP has supported the program openly.

Reforms enacted under the CRP have encouraged some level of political stability by drawing attention to the weak state of Vanuatu's economy and the potentially disastrous effects of unaccountable governance. Furthermore, the ADB has started an institutional strengthening project in the National Parliament to improve the support mechanisms available to MPs and thereby foster improved national leadership.

Gender

Another casualty of political instability has been the inclusion of women in public decision-making.[75] Despite the involvement of several women in the early nationalist movements and continuing programs supported by the UN to support women's election to public office, only four women have ever been elected to Vanuatu's National

Parliament.[76] In addition to their poor representation in the National Parliament, women represent only 9 per cent of the 300 or so decision-making positions in the country's 30 key government and private institutions, a situation that worsened during the political instability of the 1990s when women were actively marginalised from decision-making bodies.[77] These statistics reflect broader issues of gender imbalance in Vanuatu, where women's roles in the public sphere are limited by significant cultural and institutional constraints.[78] Women's right to participate in decision-making positions has often been challenged by conservative institutions such as the Malvatumauri. In an environment where references to *kastom* — practices believed by local people to be indigenous — are prevalent in public life, women's empowerment is often cast on the side of Western, and therefore divisive, influences.

The UN Fund for Women (UNIFEM) supported the creation of the Vanuatu Women in Politics (VANWIP) Project in 1995 to encourage women to run for public office. In the 1995 and 1998 elections, the major parties were forced to deploy women members to actively campaign against VANWIP candidates in their electorates. While VANWIP was unsuccessful, each of the major parties consequently incorporated some level of gender recognition into their respective platforms, recognising potential pay-offs in the form of electoral support. The effects of this platform shift were limited. Only the VP incorporated detailed strategies for women's empowerment in its party platform in a detailed manner, although most parties now have women representatives on their executives or support their election in principle. One effect of women's poor representation in Parliament is the relative ease with which male MPs derail legislation, such as the *Family Protection Bill* (proposed anti-domestic violence legislation). The *Family Protection Bill* was cleared by the VP/NUP Cabinet for tabling in Parliament in 1999 and again by the VP/NUP Government in 2004, but was delayed by political instability or withdrawn by less-sympathetic regimes such as Barak Sope's Coalition (1999–2001). However, the UMP led Government of Serge Vohor briefly championed the bill, recognising that the VP failed to get it past the council of ministers. Vohor's Government fell in 2004. The Malvatumauri remains opposed to the involvement of women in public decision-making, meaning that often, while paying lip service to gender empowerment, political parties opt to incorporate chiefly representatives into their platforms — almost a mandatory strategy to legitimate electoral support — and marginalise women further.

Given the efforts of UNIFEM and VANWIP mentioned above, it is ironic that the two current serving women MPs — Isabelle Donald (VP) and Leinavao Tasso (independent), both from Epi — won their seats on their longstanding commitment to voluntary community service through local church organisations, rather than through the networks of the VNCW, a major stakeholder in VANWIP. VNCW officials are often considered by local women's groups to be overpaid and inefficient, beset by the same internal squabbling as the major political parties.

While they have had little success in winning election, from a gender perspective, the preparedness of women to run for office is heartening. Whether they are more or less susceptible to the centrifugal forces that their male counterparts are subjected to in office remains to be seen.

Conclusions and projections

Given the fragmentation of the VP and the further erosion of the major parties' electoral support in the snap election of 2004, it is likely that Vanuatu will undergo further political instability in the coming parliamentary term. In an environment of such instability, the formulation of policy will be subjected to further strains as the political manoeuvring in Parliament is intensified by the reliance on numerous parties to form government, a situation only intensified by the turn against the major parties.

Should local stakeholders seek to arrest these developments, reform to the electoral system will be necessary; removing the tendency of the SNTV system to reward smaller local parties will remove *one* of the impetuses for political fragmentation. Already, local strategies to combat political instability, based on local leadership, are increasingly visible. The formation of the Nevsem Nenparata alliance offers a case in point. At the movement's foundation, its organiser, Chief Mike Yori, stated:

> before Independence, the chiefs held power and everything worked correctly. Immediately after Independence it was the VP which rules [sic]. Then the government split and everything deteriorated. Unity doesn't any longer seem possible with politics. Now we must go back to the chiefs and enable them to sort out how we can again find the pathway to unity.[79]

Indeed, inspired by widespread disillusionment with the Westminster-style system of government, such sentiments will only rise with further political instability. Local strategies such as Nevsem Nenparata, however, are unlikely to stabilise the National Parliament. Given the geographic, ethnic and cultural diversity of Vanuatu, an increasing emphasis on local networks and local knowledge will in all likelihood create an equally diverse Parliament with *no* unifying ideologies, the implausibility of Vanuatu's major political parties disappearing overnight notwithstanding.

Vanuatu's political culture offers some of the greatest obstacles to political stability. Electoral results since 1980 demonstrate the subordination of national concerns to local ones in Vanuatu politics and imply the shift from issues of national significance driving politics (decolonisation, non-alignment) to issues of more local importance (local development, responsive local representation, access to development funds), exemplified by the increasing support for locally credible — perhaps parochial — candidates whose major platforms are local development above all else. No MP can afford to ignore entirely local demands in favour of the abstract principles of national development and good governance. Unfulfilled promises to constituencies carry with them the threat of electoral defeat for any MP. Nonetheless, little consideration is given in regional communities to the relationship between national political instability and support for local independent candidates or those from minor parties. Arguably, it is the focus on local concerns that propels political instability, as the power of the established political parties is eroded by increasing numbers of independents and minor parties in the National Parliament. It is not simply that the SNTV system erodes the support bases of the established parties. Their electoral attrition implies also their failure to satisfy local demands for reciprocity;

local independents and minor local parties are seen to be less prone to the dictates of centralised party executives and are plausibly more responsive to local demands. There are several paradoxes contained within Vanuatu's contemporary political culture. Larger parties, less receptive to specific local demands, are nonetheless more likely to foster a greater degree of political stability in the National Parliament simply because they can sidestep the politically risky issue of maintaining a simple majority in Parliament by allying themselves with a handful of independents and minor parties, whose allegiance goes to the highest bidder. At present, however, electoral returns appear to favour smaller parties and independents, and their presence in the Parliament will be a continuing source of political instability. Vanuatu can ill afford to be subjected to renewed political instability such as it experienced during the 1990s.

Footnotes

1   I thank Roland Rich, Eric Wittersheim, Bob Makin and Gordon Haines for their comments on drafts of this chapter. All mistakes are my own.

2   See Ambrose, David. 1996. 'A Coup That Failed? Recent Political Events in Vanuatu.' *Discussion Paper 96/03*. State, Society and Governance in Melanesia Project (SSGM). p. 1.

3   National Statistics Office, Vanuatu. 1999. *The 1999 Vanuatu National Population and Housing Census*. Port Vila: National Statistics Office. p. 15.

4   MacClancy, Jeremy. 1980. *To Kill a Bird with Two Stones*. Port Vila: Vanuatu Cultural Centre; MacClancy, Jeremy. 1981. 'Current Developments in the Pacific: From New Hebrides to Vanuatu, 1979–80.' *Journal of Pacific History*, Vol. 16, No. 2. pp. 92–104; van Trease, Howard. 1987. *The Politics of Land in Vanuatu: From Colony to Independence*. Suva: University of the South Pacific (USP).

5   Miles, William F. 1994. 'Francophonie in Post-Colonial Vanuatu.' *Journal of Pacific History*, Vol. 29, No. 1; Forster, R. A. S. 1980. 'Vanuatu: The End of an Episode of Schizophrenic Colonialism.' *Round Table*, 280.

6   Miles, William. F. 1994, op. cit. pp. 49–50; see also Miles, William. 1998. *Bridging Mental Boundaries in a Postcolonial Microcosm: Identity and Development in Vanuatu*. Honolulu: University of Hawai'i Press; Molisa, Grace, Nikenike Vurobaravu and Howard van Trease. 1982. 'Vanuatu — Overcoming Pandemonium.' In *Politics in Melanesia*, Suva: Institute of Pacific Studies (ISP), USP. pp. 83–115; van Trease, Howard (ed.) 1995. *Melanesian Politics: Stael Bong Vanuatu*. Suva: ISP-USP.

7   Morgan, Michael G. 2003. 'Politik Is Poison: The Politics of Memory Among the Churches of Christ in Northern Vanuatu.' PhD, The Australian National University (ANU). pp. 206–21.

8   Tatangis, Amos. 1995. 'Efate.' In Howard van Trease (ed.), op. cit. pp. 352–3.

9   See e.g., transcript of Jimmy Stephens' trial, cited in *Voice of Vanuatu*, November 27, 1980; Beasant, John. 1984. *The Santo Rebellion, an Imperial Reckoning*. Honolulu: University of Hawai'i Press. pp. 142–3; MacClancy, Jeremy, 1981 and 1980 op. cit.; Shears, Richard. 1980. *The Coconut War: Crisis on Espiritu Santo*. Melbourne: Cassell; Miles, William F., 1998, op. cit.; Molisa, Grace et al. op. cit.

10   See e.g., Virelala, Jean Paul. 1995. 'To be Francophone in Vanuatu.' In Howard van Trease (ed.) op. cit.

11   Ghai, Yash. 1988. *Law, Government and Politics in the Pacific Island States*. Suva: ISP-USP. p. 16.

12   Plant, Chris (ed.) 1977. *New Hebrides, the Road to Independence*. Suva: ISP-USP and South Pacific Social Sciences Association. pp. 25–6.

13   MacClancy, Jeremy, 1981 and 1980, op. cit.

14   Beasant, John. op. cit.

15 McQueen, Norman. 1988. 'Beyond Tok Win: The Papua New Guinea Intervention in Vanuatu, 1980.' *Pacific Affairs,* Vol. 61, No. 2; Morgan, Michael G., 2003. op. cit.; Rodman, William. 2000. 'Outlaw Memories: Biography and the Construction of Meaning in Postcolonial Vanuatu.' In Pamela J. Stewart and Andrew Strathern (eds), *Identity Work: Constructing Pacific Lives.*

16 Beasant, John. op. cit.; Leder, Jean. 1981. *Les Cent Jours Du Bout Du Monde: Autopsie D'une Tragedie.* Noumea.

17 Otto, Ton. 1997. 'After the "Tidal Wave": Bernard Narakobi and the Creation of the Melanesian Way.' In Ton Otto and Nicholas Thomas (eds), *Narratives of Nation in the South Pacific, Studies in Anthropology and History,* Amsterdam: Harwood Academic Publishers. Cf. Nkrumah, Kwame. 1963. *Africa Must Unite* London: Heinemann; Otto, Ton. 1991. 'The Politics of Tradition in Baluan Social Change and The Construction of the Past in a Manus Society.' PhD, ANU; Owusu, Maxwell. 1979. 'Evolution in the Revolution: Nkrumah, Ghana and African Socialism.' *Africa Today,* Vol. 26, No. 2.

18 Albinski, Henry. 1995. 'The Security Perspective.' In Fyodor Mediansky (ed.), *Strategic Cooperation and Competition in the Pacific Islands,* , Sydney: Centre for South Pacific Studies, University of New South Wales and Australia-New Zealand Studies Center, Penn. State. p. 128.

19 VP. 2002. 'Vanua'aku Pati Platfom.' Port Vila.

20 *Trading Post,* April 25, 2002. p. 3.

21 *Trading Post,* August 25, 2001.

22 Boulekone, Vincent. 1995. 'The Politics of Tan Union.' In Howard van Trease (ed.), op. cit. p. 203.

23 National United Party (NUP). *Constitution.* Section 4(a).

24 *Vanuatu Weekly,* June 14, 1997.

25 Boulekone, Vincent. op. cit. pp. 199–201.

26 *Port Vila Presse,* April 6, 2002. p. 3.

27 Morgan, Michael G. 1998. 'Political Chronicles 1995–1998.' *Journal of Pacific History,* Vol. 33, No. 3.

28 *Trading Post* August 18, 2001. p.1

29 Plant, Chris. op. cit. pp. 10, 50.

30 *Radio Vanuatu News Bulletin,* December 7, 1982.

31 Calvert, Ken C. 1980. 'Martyrs and Mercenaries.' *Pacific Islands Monthly.* p. 31.

32 E.g. *Trading Post,* November 24, 2001. p. 2.

33 Morgan, Michael G. 1998. *op cit.*"

34 Jackson, A. L. 1972. 'Current Developments in the Pacific: Towards Political Awareness in the New Hebrides.' *Journal of Pacific History,* Vol. 7. p. 177; cf. Plant, Chris. op. cit.

35 Doorn, Robert. 1979. *A Blueprint for a New Nation: The Structure of the Nagriamel Federation.* New York: Exposition Press; Stephens, Jimmy, in Plant, Chris, op. cit. p. 40.

36 *Port Presse Online,* May 28, 2004.

37 Howard van Trease (ed.), op. cit. pp. 73–118.

38 Morgan, Michael G, 1998. op. cit.

39 *Trading Post,* February 18, 1998. p. 4.

40 *Standing Orders of Parliament/Reglement Interieur Du Parlement,* (January 1, 1982), s.8 (1–4).

41 *Nasara,* April 14, 2001.

42 *Australian Financial Review,* February 26, 2001.

43 Morgan, Michael G. 2003. 'Converging on the Arc of Instability? The Fall of Barak Sope and the Spectre of a Coup in Vanuatu.' In R. J. May (ed.), *Arc of Instability? Melanesia in the Early 2000s,* Canberra and Christchurch: SSGM, ANU and the Macmillan Brown Centre for Pacific Studies.

44 *Trading Post,* May 19, 2001.

45 Of these, two were affiliated closely with the VP.

46 See *Port Vila Presse,* April 20, 2002. p. 1.

47 CPOD, *Election Tracker Overview* [web site] (Centre for Public Opinion and Democracy, ca2004 [cited September 7, 2004]); available from http://www.cpod.ubc.ca/admin/collateral/pdfs/tracker/Vanuatu_2002_Parl.pdf.

48 *Vanuatu Daily Post,* July 9, 2004. p. 2.

49 *The Independent,* August 7, 2004. p. 2. Fellow Vanua K supporter, Sela Molisa, remained a member of the opposition VP backbench. Former Foreign Minister Moana Carcasses became the Minister of

Finance. Tannese UMP MP Judah Isaac became the Minister of Health. The Vanuatu Republican Party's Pipite Marcellino took responsibility for the Minister of the Comprehensive Reform Program. Pierre Tore, VRP Port Vila, became the Minister for Youth and Sports.

50 *Vanuatu Daily Post,* August 11, 2004. p. 2. Vohor stated: 'If ni-Vanuatu were white skinned like the Samoans or the Cook Islanders, perhaps the Australians would not be reluctant in relaxing the immigration laws to accommodate unskilled labourers to Australia.'

51 Since 1980, the number of seats in Parliament has been raised from 39 to 52.

52 *Representation of the People Act [Cap 146],* No. 1 of 1987 (June 28, 1982). Republic of Vanuatu. *Constitution.* (1980), s.17.

53 Vanuatu. *Constitution.* s.17–19.

54 Howard van Trease (ed.) op. cit. p. 145.

55 Vanuatu Electoral Commission. 2002. *6th General Elections Report.* Port Vila: Vanuatu Electoral Commission. p. 8; Howard van Trease (ed.), op. cit.

56 Vanuatu Electoral Commission, op. cit. pp. 7–9.

57 Ibid. p. 8.

58 *The Independent,* July 24, 2004. p. 2.

59 van Trease, Howard. 2004. 'Vanuatu's National Elections, July 2004: Continuity and Change.' In *SSGM Seminar Series,* Canberra: State, Society and Governance in Melanesia Project.

60 Vanuatu Electoral Commission, op. cit. Fig. 15; *Port Vila Presse,* April 6, 2002. p. 3.

61 *Nabanga,* November 21, 1979. pp. 4–5.

62 CDP, *Vanuatu Election Results, 1991* [web site] (Centre for Democratic Performance, March 6, 2002, ca2004 [cited May 2004]).

63 Vanuatu Electoral Commission, op. cit. p. 32.

64 Bolenga, Jeanette. 1998. *A Report on Wan Smol Bag Theatre's Voting Rights Play During the 1998 General Elections in Vanuatu.* Port Vila: Vanuatu Electoral Office.

65 *Port Vila Presse,* October 27, 2001. p. 1.

66 *Pacnews,* November 15, 1994.

67 The coalition took its name from the first initials of its constituent parties: (M)elanesian Progressive Party, (T)an Union and (F)ren Melanesia Pati.

68 Morgan, Michael G. 1998. op. cit. p. 287.

69 ADB. *Annual Report 1997.* Singapore: Asian Development Bank, 1998; ADB, 2003, *Priorities of the People: Hardship in Vanuatu.* Manila: Asian Development Bank; ADB. 2001. *Vanuatu 2001 Economic Report: Strengthening Development Policies.*

70 *Vanuatu Weekly,* August 10, 1996. p. 2.

71 UNDP. 2001. *Integrating Reform: Legislative Needs Assessment, Republic of Vanuatu.* Suva: UNDP-GOLD. Cited online at http://www.undp.org.fj/gold/docs/vanuatul.pdf

72 Vanuatu Office of the Ombudsman. 1995. *First Annual Report to Parliament by the Ombudsman of the Republic of Vanuatu.*

73 Vanuatu. 1997. *Comprehensive Reform Programme, Draft Endorsed by the National Level Task Team for Presentation to the Council of Ministers and National Summit.* Port Vila: Office of the Prime Minister. p. 4.

74 *Trading Post,* May 19, 2001; *Trading Post* September 17, 1997.

75 Molisa, Grace Mera. 2001. *The Vanuatu Governance and Accountability Project Output 1.2 Van/97/001 Vanwip Component Project Completion General Report.* Port Vila: Vanuatu National Council of Women; Molisa, Grace Mera. 2002. *Women and Good Governance.* Port Vila: Blackstone Publishing.

76 Maria Crowby was elected UMP MP for Port Vila in 1987. Hilda Lini was elected as a VP MP for Port Vila in 1987 and then served as NUP MP, 1991–98. Isabelle Donald was elected VP MP for Epi for 2002–04, and 2004–. An Epi independent, Leinavao Tasso, was elected to parliament in 2004.

77 Molisa, Grace Mera, 2002. op. cit.

78 See e.g., McLeod, Abby. 2004. *Women, Peace and Security: An Examination of the Role of Women in the Prevention and Resolution of Conflict in Vanuatu.* Suva: UNIFEM.

79 *Port Vila Presse Online.* May 28, 2004.

PARTIES AND THE NEW POLITICAL LOGIC IN NEW CALEDONIA

Alaine Chanter

Introduction

New Caledonia has more than 50 years' experience with party politics yet finds itself today in a situation of party fragmentation that some consider disconcertingly similar to that of neighbouring states with far less experience in party politics and Western political institutions. The reason for this disarray is, at first blush, paradoxical. The two main political groupings that either coalesced or were forged around the issue of independence are now being destabilised by this very issue, at a time when both claim success in relation to it. The anti-independence Rassemblement pour la Calédonie dans la République (RPCR) and the pro-independence coalition Front de Liberation National Kanak et Socialiste (FLNKS) both argue that the 1998 Noumea Accord — brokered between them by the French State — set in train processes conducive to the realisation of their vision for the future political status of New Caledonia. The RPCR seeks to maintain New Caledonia in the French Republic while the FLNKS has long argued for New Caledonian independence. The agreement indeed offers both possibilities. It progressively transfers political powers to a New Caledonian government but stops short of complete sovereignty pending one or more referenda on independence to be held between 2013 and 2018. The RPCR's wager is that greatly increased autonomy will undercut the impetus for independence, while the FLNKS considers that a positive experience of autonomy will render the next step of full independence relatively uncontroversial. Meanwhile, electoral support for both groups has slumped, suggesting the difficulty of selling these interpretations. Doing well is the relatively new and more centrist anti-independence party, L'Avenir Ensemble, as well as the more radical pro-independence

Partie le Liberation Kanak (Palika). These successes tell us something of the shifting ideological landscape in New Caledonia. They also reveal how party and movement structures are increasingly unable to negotiate in a context where new issues have come to the fore while the question of independence is once again on hold. Doumenge's observations on the late 1970s, that a fragmentation of politics resulted from 'the incapacity of traditional formations to deal with the problems of the moment', might well hold true today.[1] The reasons for this incapacity, and the consequent emergence of new political forces, are discussed in this chapter.

The Matignon Accords

The Noumea Accord is not the first compromise agreement between the RPCR, the FLNKS and the French State. In 1988, the Matignon Accords were signed on the heels of several years of insurrectionary activity between pro- and anti-independence militants that culminated in the Ouvéa crisis, in which four gendarmes and 19 Kanaks were killed. The scale of this violence shocked all communities in the French territory and precipitated crisis talks between the FLNKS, the RPCR and the newly elected French Socialist Government under Prime Minister Michel Rocard. The agreement to emerge out of these talks committed all parties to peaceful coexistence while the French State engaged in a 10-year program of economic development, particularly in the relatively undeveloped rural regions of the north and the Loyalty Islands, where the population is primarily Melanesian. This strategy, coined a 'rebalancing' of development, acknowledged the far greater affluence of Noumea and its surrounding municipalities, where most Europeans live, compared with that of the rest of the territory. The differential development plan was attractive to FLNKS negotiators because it proposed strategies to pump prime investment in Kanak regions,[2] and was accompanied by new political structures, in particular the dividing of the territory into three provinces — those of the South, North and Loyalty Islands — which would ensure that Kanaks would have a significant measure of political and economic control over the regions where they dominated. Also crucial to their acceptance by FLNKS negotiators was the promise of a referendum on independence in 10 years. Demands for a referendum had been a key pillar of the FLNKS' political strategy during the 1980s, bolstered by the reinsertion of New Caledonia on the UN's list of territories to be decolonised. At this time, the FLNKS demanded an immediate referendum on independence. To the surprise of many, a delay of 10 years was agreed to 'with the understanding that it would enable a peaceful ten-year transition to a successful vote for independence'.[3] A key to this calculation was the agreement that the electoral roll for voting in a referendum would be limited to those who were resident in the territory in 1988, and their voting-age descendants. This acknowledged an important factor in electoral politics in New Caledonia: although a majority of Melanesians supported independence, Melanesians had become a minority in the territory in the 1960s[4] as a result of migration by metropolitan French and other Pacific Islanders, attracted by an economic boom in the territory brought on by strong world demand for nickel. New Caledonia has the world's third-largest deposits of nickel and it is its major export. Restricting the electoral roll would limit the political impact of further migration to the territory and shift the electoral demographics in favour of independence due to the higher birth rate among Melanesians. The decision to agree to a referendum in 10 years was therefore a strategic response to the reality that an immediate referendum would have resulted in a majority vote against independence.

In spite of this formula, the Matignon Accords met with considerable hostility among Kanaks, many of whom viewed them as a sell-out of the hard-won political impetus gained from years of insurrectionary struggle. A year after the signing of the accords by FLNKS leader Jean-Marie Tjibaou, he and his deputy, Yeiwene Yeiwene, were assassinated by a militant Kanak. For its part, the anti-independence community was less than enamoured by the inclusion of a prospective referendum, evident in the fact that 67 per cent of voters in Noumea rejected acceptance of the accord.[5]

Much effort went into 'selling' the accord to RPCR and FLNKS constituencies, a process that was actively engaged in by the local mainstream media.[6] The wager was that greater economic development for Kanak communities would reduce demands for independence and produce more moderate Kanak leaders who were concerned with issues of economic development rather than independence.[7]

Despite French promises during the Matignon years to pursue strategies to restrict the electoral roll, as well as to promote local employment and encourage repatriation of metropolitan French public servants,[8] the proportion of Melanesians in the population continued to decrease in relation to other communities, with the prospect for success in a referendum becoming ever more diminished.[9] By the mid-1990s, the prospect of an imminent referendum was thrown further into doubt. RPCR leader, Jacques Lafleur, had, in 1991, called for a postponement of the referendum for 30 years to allow the territory to attain a level of economic development and political self-sufficiency that would enable a proper decision on its political future.[10] Although initially rejected by the FLNKS, it was not long before FLNKS President, François Burck, himself began to publicly broach the prospect of another prolongation of a referendum.[11] A major reason why the FLNKS entertained such a prospect was that a vote, were it to happen, would invariably result in a majority vote against independence. Despite the FLNKS' earlier calculation that a period of demonstrating responsible economic management would show that the Kanak community was ready to assume full responsibility, the anti-independence community had not been persuaded. Pushing the issue to a vote would only further divide and polarise the community and result in the possibility of renewed violence and political turmoil. By the mid-1990s, therefore, the major political parties had agreed to a deferment of the referendum and instead accepted a negotiated settlement, which would culminate in a vote on independence, this time in 15 to 20 years.[12]

Alban Bensa and Eric Wittersheim write that in the immediate aftermath of the signing of the Noumea Accord there was general relief that a new pact would bring the promise of 15 to 20 more years of relative peace. But this first reaction was also paradoxical, in that it was based on quite different convictions about the possible outcome of the process. Anti-independence groups were generally pleased with the apparent softening of pro-independence demands during the Matignon decade. They envisaged a further cooption of the Kanak political bourgeoisie with an outcome of independence in association with France — a state of considerably devolved autonomy but without complete sovereignty.[13] This softening was evident in defections from the FLNKS, particularly to the centrist Fédération des Comités de Co-ordination des Indépendantistes (FCCI), established by once radical advocates for independence, and the alignment of the FCCI with the RPCR in a 'spirit of dialogue'. It was also apparent in the agreement of the FLNKS to countenance a further prolongation of a referendum on independence. On the other hand, pro-independence groups thought 'that the road towards independence [was] finally open'.[14]

This chapter argues that, on current reckoning, the anti-independence scenario is most likely to eventuate, a fact reflected in writers now describing the current state of affairs as one of decolonisation without any necessary prospect of independence.[15] For this to be a scenario acceptable to hitherto advocates of independence, there would need to be the prospect of a genuine sharing of political power in the country between Kanak and loyalist political parties. There would have to be, in other words, a situation of considerably devolved autonomy in which all the major political groupings could demonstrate an active and influential involvement in determinate political processes. It is for this reason that the Noumea Accord established a collegial form of government elected by proportional representation. The intention was that, within this structure, there would emerge a multi-party Cabinet[16] to ensure genuine power-sharing. Until very recently, RPCR domination of New Caledonian politics has made a mockery of this notion of collegiality, and has led pro-independence leaders to describe the accord as being 'hijacked' by the RPCR.[17] Bensa and Wittersheim query whether the new institutional structures 'allow the different communities to together build a nation'.[18] The major stumbling block to this outcome is the entrenched adversarial position of the RPCR, as well as its custom of manipulating the levers of power through its dominant personalities and their grip on the New Caledonian political economy. Ironically, while the Matignon and Noumea Accords bear the imprint of RPCR demands, albeit in compromise form, they establish expectations for a more consensual political culture to which the RPCR is ill equipped to respond. History might not always be destiny, but in the case of the RPCR it is a powerful factor in signalling the limits of RPCR capabilities.

The RPCR in historical, sociological and political context

Local politics in New Caledonia has always been enacted in the context of a strong French State that has maintained control over political and economic activity in the territory until very recently.[19] This notion of control needs some explanation. In New Caledonia as elsewhere in the colonial world, control over local activity was largely vested in the Governor of the colony, and later the High Commissioner, but also in a local comprador class that has acquired considerable wealth and influence throughout the more than 150 years of French presence. This class has existed as the political bastion of French power, but it has also had its squabbles with France. Indeed, early politics in the colony was characterised by strident disagreements between local settlers who railed against the power of the Governor and sought the establishment of democratic institutions, including a free press, to counter this power, which was often exercised arbitrarily.[20]

Moreover, as local settlers developed the economy, some became wealthy and found themselves in competition with metropolitan economic interests in the colony. This was particularly the case with the local mine owners, who today are among the richest families in New Caledonia — the so-called 50 families[21] — and who from the outset complained about the French company Le Nickel's domination of nickel mining and smelting. While this comprador class generally understood that its dominance was secured by its relationship with France, disagreements were often expressed through demands for France to lessen its hold over local politics and the economy. They became translated in the post-war period into calls for greater political autonomy.[22]

This at times ambivalent attitude towards France and the exercise of colonial power was also manifest in the waxing and waning of relationships between French and local political parties and movements. Early settlers looked to political processes and institutions in metropolitan France to guide their demands for greater political freedoms from France but, as Dornoy observed, conservative politicians have generally 'always resented the influence of metropolitan parties'.[23] This resentment was part of the colonial experience of subordination, as well as recognition of the increasing cultural and sociological differences that characterised New Caledonia from France. The view expressed by prominent conservative politician Pierre Frogier in 1977,[24] that metropolitan parties 'did not suit the mentality of Caledonians',[25] has dogged the relationship until this day. The formation of the RPCR in 1978 out of existing fractured conservative parties might have occurred at the behest of then Mayor of Paris Jacques Chirac during a visit to the territory, but it was also very much a local initiative to unite disparate conservative parties in the face of a formidable enemy — the official call by Melanesian politicians for independence.

Relationships between metropolitan political parties and local politics might be described as somewhat opportunistic. During World War II, when the first political parties were being conceived in New Caledonia, the local settler population rallied behind De Gaulle's Free France movement and the colony became an important staging post for the US's Pacific campaign. The strength of Gaullist influence was evident in postwar politics, with De Gaulle consolidating ties with New Caledonian conservatives when he visited the territory in 1956.[26] As a result, local elections in 1958 witnessed the emergence of a new conservative political force, the Rassemblement Calédonien, headed by wealthy mine owner Henri Lafleur, which won 11 of 30 seats in the Territorial Assembly.[27] A year later, Lafleur was elected to the French Senate and supported the metropolitan push to withdraw political powers from New Caledonia. By the late 1960s, however, the Rassemblement Calédonien had changed its tune, turning against De Gaulle to seek greater autonomy.[28] Even the creation in 1977 of a local version of the metropolitan French Rassemblement pour la Republique (RPR) and its decision to go into alliance with other conservative groups reflected an ambivalence 'necessary to keep New Caledonia within France while retaining its personality'.[29]

Dornoy is correct when she writes that the main aim of conservative politics in New Caledonia has been to conserve,[30] although she might add that what is being conserved is the relative privilege of the wealthy, along with a perception of relative privilege among others, such as non-French migrants and resettled metropolitan French (*Metros*), who view greater autonomy or independence as threatening their prospects in the society. What is at play in this notion of conservation is a complex and ever shifting analysis of benefit and loss from the range of factors that impinge on local politics and the economy. These include: changing metropolitan French policies toward New Caledonia and their relative support from metropolitan political parties; the strength of local agitation for change to the status quo by oppositional groups (in later years, the pro-independence movement); and internal rivalries within the comprador class, which have often led to a fracturing of conservative political energies.

There is also the reality of considerable class and ethnic difference within the conservative movement. While the European community is in general aware of its relative privilege, when compared with most Kanaks, there are great and palpable dispar-ities in levels of wealth, status and class within the European community. New Caledonia is unusual for having a white urban proletariat that is largely working class and works for wealthy European-owned businesses, some of which are owned by locals.[31] It also has relatively poor rural Europeans — known as *broussards* — who work the land on holdings that are small compared with those of wealthy absentee landlords. *Broussards* 'have felt marginalized socially, economically, and politically by the RPCR's Noumean bias'.[32] There is always therefore the possibility of dissatisfaction and a need to keep this tension under wraps. This has generally been facilitated by the fact that these poor Europeans are often reliant on patronage from wealthy businessmen for their livelihoods.

The formation of the RPCR in the year that Kanaks called officially for independ-ence meant that the party's aim was always primarily to oppose the increasingly strident moves made by pro-independence Kanaks, many of which took the Territory to the brink of civil war, particularly in the period from 1984 to 1988. Before the RPCR's formation, the dominant political party in the territory was the Union Calédonien (UC), which, since the time of its formation in 1951, had advocated for greater autonomy for the territory.[33] The UC's slogan, 'two colours, one people', expressed its pluri-ethnic emphasis and its incorporation of Kanak demands for greater political recognition and social justice. By the mid-1970s, however, ferment in the UC over the question of whether autonomy was sufficient for the realisation of Kanak aspirations, and the ultimate call by the UC for a pluri-ethnic independence, led to a break-up of the party and a mass exodus of Europeans, who eschewed the prospect of independence. Most aligned themselves with the RPCR.

From 1978 to 2004, Jacques Lafleur was president of the RPCR and New Caledonia's Deputy in the French National Assembly. Lafleur is a member of one of New Caledonia's '50 families', the members of whom

> not only live affluently but also hold key positions in the territory's economy and administration, as well as important posts in the RPCR, forming a plutocracy of considerable influence. They are popularly perceived as having traditionally held a monopoly on New Caledonia's socio-economic power.[34]

As the main political grouping advocating the maintenance of New Caledonia in the French Republic, the RPCR has garnered about 40 to 50 per cent of the total vote in territorial elections until 1989,[35] with the majority of its support in Noumea and the surrounding municipalities.[36] Its support base is dominated by Caledonians of European descent and more recently arrived *Metros*, but it has also been the party most adhered to by the range of migrant communities in the territory, including Wallisians and Futunians, Polynesians, Indonesians, Vietnamese and ni-Vanuatu, who have felt threatened by the prospect of a Kanak socialist independence. The RPCR also draws sizeable Melanesian support. For example, in the 1989 provincial elections, the RPCR gained 33.9 per cent of the overall vote in the Loyalty Islands,[37] and a small number of Melanesians have gained considerable influence in the party. This composition enables the RPCR to claim the status of multiracial or 'pluri-ethnic' party — indeed, the bearer of the UC's legacy of 'two colours, one people'.

As mentioned earlier, the European constituency incorporates a wide range of occupational and class groupings. This has been a source of friction within the party at various times. In particular, the Noumea focus of the party has led to considerable resentment from *broussards* who have been at the front-line of rural insurrectionary activity and have felt abandoned by the party at various moments.[38] Infamous spats have occurred between party members. For example, when RPCR member of the Territorial Congress Justin Guillemard spoke out about *broussard* feelings of personal insecurity, describing RPCR leaders as 'Noumean racketeers', he was expelled for his outburst.[39] Guillemard maintained the rage, describing the Matignon Accords as sharing 'out political and economic power between the politico-racketeers on the one hand, and the terrorist assassins on the other hand, supposedly for ten years, a time lapse that will allow you to carry out some good and juicy deals'.[40] Resentment of the RPCR has also fermented in Noumea, particularly among small business owners who 'at times harbor resentment about the RPCR leaders' control of Noumea's economy', and from the urban proletariat who find their job options at times circumscribed by their divergence from the RPCR line.[41] These sociological and politico-economic factors behind RPCR malaise have been exacerbated by some RPCR decisions, in particular Lafleur's signing of the Matignon Accords.

Voting statistics provide an indication of levels of support for RPCR policies. In addition, the occasional public dispute between RPCR members delineates fault lines in its constituency. But generally, the internal workings of the party remain secret, and this might be explained by the relatively undemocratic nature of a party that has relied on internal patronage for party mobility. This contrasts quite significantly with the modus operandi of most pro-independence parties, which have generally held annual congresses where decisions are taken by majority vote, if not consensus. It is difficult to know therefore what the policy debates are within the RPCR, or the extent to which policy options are discussed openly within it. There is evidence that Lafleur had to work hard to steer his party towards acceptance of the Matignon Accords.[42] Later dissent within the RPCR after Lafleur's signing of the Noumea Accord crystallised around claims of a lack of democracy within the party and the inordinate power of Lafleur (see section on centrist politics below). There are strong reasons to believe that these have been central characteristics of party operations for a very long time.

Disagreement within the RPCR has precipitated the establishment of more right-wing loyalist pressure groups and parties, in particular the Front Calédonien (FC) and the New Caledonian chapter of the Front National (FN[NC]). The FC, formed in 1982, primarily gathered together disaffected *broussards*, and French migrants from other French colonies, such as Algerian *pieds-noirs*. Its members were more likely to initiate direct action in pursuit of its loyalist objectives. Infamously, the FC organised a 'picnic' in the southern town of Thio in 1985, resulting in armed clashes with FLNKS militants and considerable publicity for the party, even in metropolitan France.[43] The FC lost its only two seats in the 1989 provincial elections, gaining only 4.1 per cent of the vote in the south, the only region where it stood candidates.[44] The FC's vote appears to have transferred largely to the FN(NC), which has increased its electoral strength considerably since its formation in 1984. The FN(NC) is a subsidiary of the metropolitan Front National and reports directly to it. The intimacy of this relationship was experienced early in the party's history when metropolitan FN leader, Jean-Marie Le Pen, circulated a letter questioning the presence of a Melanesian, François Neoere, at the head of the party, forcing his resignation in early 1986.[45] The Front National's appeal in New Caledonia is its consistent and strident refusal to engage in negotiations about the question of independence, a stance that obviously makes it distinct from the RPCR. The FN(NC) described the Matignon Accords as an abdication to the 'murderous folly of the FLNKS',[46] and called for the abrogation of the accords after the high 'no' vote in the referendum in the greater Noumea region. A reduction in its number of seats in the 1989 provincial elections led McCallum to suggest that the FN(NC)'s influence as a loyalist force was waning.[47] In the 1999 provincial elections, however, the party regained its two lost seats in Congress, giving it a total of four, a position it retained in the 2004 provincial elections. The electoral balance in the Southern Province now affords the FN(NC) the balance of power, which it is more likely to exercise in alliance with the RPCR if required, rather than with the more reconciliatory Avenir Ensemble.[48] Its influence is therefore becoming stronger and reflects the fact that a small[49] but resolute proportion of the population in the south rejects countenancing any compromise over the question of independence.

Another leakage from the RPCR has been from its Wallisian constituency. Wallisians are the third-largest ethnic group in New Caledonia, comprising about 10 per cent of the population on the main island.[50] The community has tended to align itself with the RPCR against calls for a Kanak socialist independence from which they fear they will be excluded. During the 1980s, the RPCR employed a small group of Wallisian bodyguards who made their presence felt at anti-independence demonstrations and engaged in street fighting with independence supporters, activities that generated much hostility towards this community from Kanaks.[51] By the late 1980s, however, Wallisians began to shift away from the RPCR. In 1989 Kalepo Muliava formed the Union Oceanien (UO), criticising the RPCR for its opportunistic attitude towards Wallisians and claiming that, under the RPCR, the Wallisian community 'hasn't advanced an inch in ten years. We are as marginalised as the Kanaks'.[52] Moreover, Muliava held out an olive branch to Kanaks, acknowledging Wallisian 'cultural cousinage with Kanaks'.[53] By 1994, a new islander party, the Rassemblement Démocratique Océanien (RDO), was formed under the leadership of Aloisio Sako. It declared support for an independent, democratic and multiracial nation.[54] The RDO was accepted into the FLNKS in 1998 and Sako was elected to Congress on the FLNKS ticket in 1999 and again in 2004.[55] Although most Wallisians continue to vote for the RPCR, the significance of the RDO cannot be underestimated. The results of any referendum on independence could be determined by the extent to which it is able to attract the Wallisian vote. Relations between Kanaks and Wallisians remain rocky in some communities and are getting worse in others. In late 2001, armed conflict erupted between Kanaks and Wallisians in the St Louis community in Mont-Dore near Noumea, resulting in three dead and several wounded.[56] In addition, RDO President Sako expressed frustration at the slowness of assistance to Wallisian communities under the terms of the Noumea Accords, stating: 'We have contributed to the wealth of this country, we have worked hard … Yet today most of the aid measures and re-balancing benefits Kanak not us.'[57] There are clearly sizeable obstacles in the way of the further alignment of Wallisians to the pro-independence cause.

After the 2004 RPCR election slump, Lafleur resigned from the position of president, signalling the possibility that a new political emphasis might emerge within the party. It is difficult to see, however, where the party can move, with the more conciliatory ground now being occupied by Avenir Ensemble and the intransigent position by the FN(NC). It will maintain its symbolic status as signatory to the accords but might see its political status further wane as a result of the new logic of compromise that it introduced into the political equation in New Caledonia by the very act of signing the accords.

Pro-independence political parties

Universal suffrage came to Melanesians only in 1957,[58] however, a decision by the French National Assembly in 1951 had conferred voting rights on almost half of eligible Melanesians, marking the genesis of their political mobilisation within party structures.[59]

Until recently, the main pro-independence party in New Caledonia has been the Union Calédonien (UC), and all but one FLNKS leader has been from the UC.[60] It has been widely accepted that the impetus behind the formation of the UC in the early 1950s came from the Protestant and Catholic Churches in the territory.[61] More recently, work by the New Caledonian historian Ismet Kurtovich has uncovered the extent to which this agitation from the churches was itself a response to the popularity of the communist movement within Melanesian communities. This movement was the first to champion indigenous and migrant rights as central to the political project. The presence among the organising group of two Melanesian chiefs encouraged other Melanesians to identify with the sentiments expressed by this movement. Alarmed by its popularity, the churches quickly agitated to set up alternative political structures that would redirect this political impetus towards more contained ambitions.[62] These efforts ultimately resulted in the official formation in 1956 of the UC, which had existed successfully since 1951 as a movement and had attained considerable electoral success, with the election of its leader, Maurice Lenormand, as Deputy to the French Assembly in 1951,[63] and by gaining a majority of seats in territorial elections in 1953, including its first Melanesian members.[64] Its slogan, 'two colours, one people' and program reflected the extent to which indigenous advancement was at the core of the movement's mission, although, as Henningham notes, its style was somewhat paternalistic.[65]

By the mid-1950s, the UC had strengthened its social agenda and increased its following among trade unions.[66] This generated deep hostility from conservative forces, which accused Lenormand of communist sympathies and of being anti-French. This criticism continued despite Lenormand campaigning for the maintenance of New Caledonia in the French Republic at the referendum of September 1958, initiated by De Gaulle in all the overseas dependencies and giving each the possibility of independence.[67] A further manifesto drawn up in 1967 once again rejected independence and requested instead 'a statute of self-government to implement decolonization in New Caledonia'[68] — a position that seems similar to that adopted by the UC today.

Considerable radicalisation occurred among young Melanesians during the 1970s, in part as a result of the participation of some in radical student politics in France during the 1960s as well as because of the more general push for recognition of indigenous rights in international forums. This radicalisation led to severe problems for the UC, which opposed the option of independence. The first breakaway political group was the Union Multiraciale de Nouvelle-Calédonie (UMNC), which split from the UC in 1970, and which led calls for independence. It was the UMNC's leader, Yann Celene Uregei, who had returned home from an official visit to France to demand independence in the Territorial Assembly for the first time. As a result of pressures from outside and within the party, the UC Congress of 1977 adopted a position for independence. Speakers at this congress once again voiced positions that are uncannily prescient today, particularly the idea that internal self-government was the best way to move towards independence.[69] Despite the mass exodus of European members, the UC has nonetheless remained the largest pro-independence party in New Caledonia, with membership from Catholic and Protestant communities spread across its regions. Henningham estimates that the UC is supported by some 55 to 60 per cent of pro-independence Kanaks,[70] a number that has probably reduced as a result of the rise in popularity of Palika (discussed below). Henningham's description of the UC as 'pragmatic' and social democratic[71] generally holds today. These characteristics have led the UC and the FLNKS to agree to the Matignon and Noumea Accords, decisions that, as mentioned above, have resulted in considerable alienation from the UC's constituency given the prospect of independence is once again distant.

Another more radical pro-independence party, the Union Progressiste Multiraciale (UPM), was formed in 1974 as a breakaway party of the UMNC (which became the Front Uni de Liberation Kanak [FULK] in 1977), with the main aims of land reform and the economic development of Melanesians.[72] The party changed its name to the Union Progressiste Melanesien (UPM) in 1977[73] and continues to the present. This party has been concerned primarily with land reform and was at the forefront of land occupations in the 1980s.[74] Although in its early iterations it employed radical rhetoric and had links with the French Trotskyist Ligue Communiste Revolutionnaire,[75] in more recent years it has tended to align with the UC on policy matters, putting into contention Henningham's description of the party as 'radical' and 'Marxist'.[76]

In 1976, the Parti Socialiste Calédonien (PSC) was formed with the socialist principles of the nationalisation of territorial resources, particularly nickel mining, and the advancement of working-class interests. Importantly, the PSC did not at this time support independence, arguing that New Caledonia was too small a state to consider such an option. Instead it supported greater autonomy.[77] The party shifted to supporting independence in the 1980s and is the only pro-independence party to include a predominantly European membership, most of whom are trade unionists.[78] Finally, in 1976, various radical movements coalesced in the formation of the Parti de Liberation Kanak (Palika), which advocated the demise of colonialism in New Caledonia through 'revolutionary Kanak Socialist Independence'.[79] Although Palika advocated revolutionary struggle to overthrow colonialism, it nonetheless participated in the 1977 territorial elections, with a significant showing in each of the electoral regions, particularly the Loyalties and the east.[80] Palika argued that social reforms could be achieved via this means and that parliamentary salaries would help the party progress its platform.[81]

This issue of parliamentary participation has been a dilemma within pro-independence political parties. The boycotting of elections has been a key strategy in parties' armoury, yet there have also been times when they have contested elections individually or collectively as part of a united movement. The decision to forge the type of alliances that would ultimately result in the creation of the FLNKS was driven by new electoral laws initiated in the late 1970s by conservatives in the French Parliament.[82] These established a minimum bar of 7.5 per cent of votes in order to gain a seat in the Territorial Assembly.[83] These measures were intended to thwart participation by the smaller pro-independence groups but instead precipitated their fusion in the Front Independentiste (FI),[84] which successfully contested the 1979 elections, gaining 14 seats compared with the RPCR's 15, with a centrist FNSC holding the balance of power with seven seats.[85]

In 1981, after generally positive comments from the Socialist Party on the issue of self-determination, the FI supported the Socialist candidate, François Mitterrand, in the second round of the election. Nonetheless, the FI was suspicious of the Socialists, a view that was borne out when no strong support for independence ensued from Mitterand's victory.[86] However, a generally reformist climate and the knowledge of increased support for Kanak aspirations within government in France led to pressure for political reform in New Caledonia and to the circumstances in which the FI, in alliance with the centrist FNSC, gained power, with UC leader, Jean-Marie Tjibaou, leading the Government.[87] By this stage, Palika had excluded itself from the FI and therefore any chance of parliamentary participation. This followed an internal split, which resulted in the formation of a new political party based primarily in the Loyalty Islands, the Liberation Kanak Socialiste (LKS).[88] Internal tensions between FI parties led to leakages in various electoral contests.[89] Increasing disenchantment of pro-independence parties towards the policies of the Socialist Government, particularly the Lemoine Statute, which eschewed immediate independence in favour of greater autonomy and a referendum on independence in 1989, produced increasing tensions, riots and direct action waged by Palika militants — in other words, considerable instability. Meanwhile, the UC drew up its own timetable for independence, which determined that a referendum in 1984 would result in independence in 1985. Importantly, this plan presupposed electoral reforms that limited voters to Kanaks and residents who had one parent born in the territory.[90] The 'pragmatic' UC had for a long time known that a successful vote on independence could occur only through limiting the electoral franchise.

All these tensions came to ahead in the 1984 territorial elections, which were boycotted and obstructed by the FI (the LKS participated). The FI also withdrew all members from government institutions and planned the establishment of the provisional government of Kanaky, renaming itself the FLNKS. As Connell writes, through this radicalisation, the FI 'was coming much closer into line with the more militant and socialist Palika, which had long argued that … independence will not fall from the sky through the good will of Mitterrand, other Pacific countries, the United Nations or the good God; it can only be achieved through the struggles of Kanaks and exploited workers. Without a struggle there will be no independence.'[91] The first Congress of the FLNKS was attended by all pro-independence parties (the UC, Palika, UPM, PSK, FULK), barring the LKS. Palika attended because it saw that the FLNKS had moved towards its own more radical position in support of militancy and direct action.[92]

In the face of this crisis, a new plan was developed by a special envoy to the territory, Edgard Pisani, which advocated the solution of independence in association with France, with a referendum in July 1985 and the possibility of independence in association on January 1, 1986. Importantly, voting would be restricted to those who had lived in the territory for at least three years. The FLNKS rejected this solution as neo-colonial, with one FLNKS leader describing it as a 'mutilated' form of independence.[93] Continued insurgency resulted in the development of a new plan by the French Prime Minister, Laurent Fabius (herein after 'the Fabius Plan"), which introduced one of the key components of subsequent political compromises, the division of New Caledonia into political regions, in this case four — the North, East, South and Loyalty regions — and the devolution of powers to these regions. A referendum on self-determination was proposed for 1987. This outcome was ultimately endorsed by the FLNKS at its 1985 Congress, albeit in a lukewarm manner.[94] Significantly, the outcome of the elections was a victory for the FLNKS in all regions bar the South, and it was UC militants who acquired the role of President in the North, East and Loyalties.[95] UC pre-eminence reflected the numerical strength of the UC vis-à-vis other pro-independence parties, but also the lead that the UC had taken in much of the militancy of 1984 and 1985. The UC has paid a disproportionate price for this militancy with the assassination of a string of leaders: first, UC Secretary-General Pierre Declercq in 1982, then UC leader Eloi Machoro in 1985, followed by Jean-Marie Tjibaou and Yeiwene Yeiwene in 1989.

The election of a conservative government in France in March 1986 produced a blocking of funds to the regions and the development of a new statute, termed the Pons Statute, which conceived of a division of the territory into four new regions, with the north divided according to an east and west axis, a division that had been long opposed by the FLNKS.[96] An acute level of frustration at the retraction of the meagre gains constituted by the Fabius Plan led to the FLNKS boycotting the 1987 referendum and the April 1988 regional elections.[97] These boycotts were, for the first time, adhered to by all pro-independence groups — the LKS had joined the FLNKS in the face of the deteriorating political circumstances. The political crisis served to focus energies on communal goals and smooth over differences. This provisional solidarity was always going to be sorely tested in less polarised political circumstances.

These indeed existed in the 1990s. As UC leader Roch Wamytan said in 1991, 'Three years ago it was easy to be cohesive in the face of the active campaign against the French; now the FLNKS needs to adjust to a new situation.'[98] Internal tensions erupted after the assassination of Tjibaou and Yeiwene by a militant pro-independence Kanak. Much finger-pointing and recrimination ensued. At the same time the FLNKS had to comport itself as a relatively united and responsible signatory to the Matignon Accords, a juggling act that required much deft handling of discord.[99]

Since the signing of the Matignon Accords, compromise has continued to be the Realpolitik of FLNKS policy, and this has led to further dissension among those who perceive that little of substance has been done to improve Kanak economic and political opportunities, let alone signal the possibility of independence. This has led the UC to lose electoral support in favour of the less compromised Palika. Palika's reputation as a more militant party was strengthened in the 1990s as a result of tensions in the FLNKS between UC leaders and the then FLNKS President, Palika's Paul Neoutyne, who consistently asserted demands for Kanak socialist independence in the face of equivocal comments on the issue by UC leaders. In what amounted to an acknowledgment that such comments had harmed the party, UC leader and Vice-President of the FLNKS, Roch Wamytan, said that the party would channel its energies into winning support from other pro-independence parties, rather than becoming chummy with the RPCR.[100] By 1995, relations between Palika and the UC were not much better. After the Matignon Accords, senior members of the UC broke away from the party and formed the Fédération des Comités de Coordination d'Indépendence (FCCI).[101] The FCCI claims to 'cut across old divisions'[102] in its support of the accords, but its poor showing in the 2004 provincial elections supports Connell's earlier view that they are 'perceived as having lost the support of their constituencies' and have joined 'the line awaiting Lafleur's powerful patronage'.[103]

Faced with the seeming obsequiousness of senior sections of the UC in the 1990s and a Kanak electorate already suspicious of the Matignon Accords, the UC's reputation as leading party of the pro-independence cause has been seriously undermined. As one Kanak commented in relation to the FLNKS, but also by implication the UC, 'Challenge and distrust in the leadership come from the grassroots level, especially young Kanak militants who have always felt betrayed by the signing of the Matignon Accords in 1988, sweeping away their dream to see a liberated Kanaky which many have died for during the armed struggle against the French establishment in the early 1980s.'[104]

No unified FLNKS list could be agreed to in the lead up to the 1999 provincial elections with various groupings contesting the three provinces. Fragmentation was even more acute for the 2004 provincial elections, with 14 pro-independence lists in the

Southern Province, nine in the north and eight in the Loyalty Islands.[105] As a result, in the Southern Province, no list received over the 5 per cent benchmark with the result that six pro-independence seats were lost. The absence of any pro-independence voice in the Southern Province creates a de facto form of partition in New Caledonia, which is, as Maclellan notes, 'in stark contrast to the spirit of partnership and "working together" that the Noumea Accords encourages'.[106] Fragmentation has led to voter support for pro-independence parties (40 per cent) not being translated into seats in Congress (less than one-third).[107]

Connell asks whether the unprecedented level of discord within the FLNKS suggests that 'FLNKS actually represents nothing more than an "imagined community"'.[108] Insofar as the independence imagination is fading within it, this might indeed be the case. French Government policy has been very successful in reorienting independence energies towards more pragmatic questions of economic and social development, with the result that the rage is no longer being maintained in many FLNKS quarters. But there is a community that once belonged to the FLNKS that still imagines independence, and Palika appears to be one of its rising stars.[109]

Another is the militant Union Syndicalist des Travailleurs Kanak et Exploité (USTKE). The USTKE was a founding member of the FLNKS and celebrated its 20th anniversary in 2001, reaffirming 'its goal of building a multiracial, independent Kanaky'.[110] It has been strongly critical of the Noumea Accord, in spite of being a party to its negotiations.[111] It is also the sole voice to demand an immediate accession to independence on the grounds that any devolved process would result only in a country dominated by loyalists.[112] Perhaps because of its radicalism, the USTKE has been very successful in the past 15 years in dominating unionism in New Caledonia. It has not been shy about using confrontational strike action, winning significant gains for workers in the process. This has further enhanced its appeal to workers of European, Melanesian and, most importantly, Wallisian ethnicities, making it a genuinely multiracial organisation.[113] The USTKE's fusion of independence demands with militant unionism signals a maturation of New Caledonian civil society. It recognises that colonial patronage has not just affected the continuing political status of New Caledonia but has resulted in endemic discriminatory economic relationships. Fighting for workers' rights therefore achieves not only purely economic goals but addresses underlying political inequities.[114] Its multiracialism is also considered progressive in a context where race has often been the fault-line of political divisiveness.

Centrist politics

Until recently, centrist politics have struggled to get a hold in New Caledonia. The reasons for this are in part suggested by the analysis already undertaken: Kanak demands for independence led to a polarisation of opinion and a political and ideological climate that was far from conducive to moderation. This is not to say that attempts did not occur, but the most successful of these were in the period before the eruption of widespread violence in 1984 and subsequent to the enactment of the Matignon Accords, which elevated moderation and compromise as a central dynamic of the political process.

But there is another reason why centrist politics has had difficulty germinating. This relates to the active efforts by conservative forces in the territory to stymie moderate voices, be these political figures or the occasional forays into the media of centrist political groups.[115] The vilification throughout the 1960s of UC leader Maurice Lenormand is a case in point. Despite his generally moderate views on promoting greater autonomy in the territory, and his continued insistence that New Caledonia remain part of France, he was subject to accusations of being a communist, to judicial prosecution on trumped-up charges of being responsible for a bombing at the UC newspaper's headquarters, as well as having his house burnt.[116] More generally, the UC's political moderation before their 1977 call for independence received little acknowledgment, let alone affirmation, from conservative political groups.

One notable if short-lived exception was the prominence of the centrist FNSC group, which did well in the 1979 territorial elections, gaining seven seats to the RPCR's 15 and the FI's 14, and therefore holding the balance of power.[117] FNSC members had primarily been supporters of the UC in the period before its advocacy of independence. They went into coalition with the FI in 1982 out of opposition to 'the RPCR's inflexible response to the political demands of the FI'[118] — a move that served only to discredit them in the eyes of their supporters, with the result that the party collapsed in 1984 and most supporters moved to the RPCR or even to the FN(NC). The FNSC had tried to propagate more centrist views by establishing in 1981 a daily newspaper, *La Presse Calédonienne*, in competition with the monopoly daily, *Les Nouvelles Calédoniennes*, but the paper did not attract advertising revenue, largely as a result of pressure from RPCR stalwarts on potential advertisers.[119] This was not the first time that such pressure tactics had been employed. Such practices are consistent with Chappell's observation that 'Less respectful critics refer to Lafleur's powerful political and economic patronage system as a "mafia"'.[120]

The lack of success until recently of centrist political parties belies the fact that centrist positions have a long heritage in New Caledonia and are rooted in important sociological foundations. During the FNSC's tenure, a conference organised by the Socialist Government between the FI, the RPCR and the FNSC and held in France acknowledged the place of Europeans of New Caledonian heritage, arguing that their interests had often been forgotten in the polarisation around issues of independence, and referring to this group as 'victims of history'.[121] These people have a long experience of living alongside Melanesians, and their lifestyles evince considerable hybridity. In addition, there is noticeable *metissage* within this community. They identify primarily as Caledonian before being French, and have acquired the name *Caldoche* in recent years. Although racism has tarnished their interactions with Melanesians, they are increasingly aware of the need for mutual accommodation. Often they are people of modest means who have difficulty identifying with the elitist politics of RPCR leaders. Their interests were initially represented by the UC, which, as discussed above, advocated pluri-ethnicity and championed various economic and social rights. The UC's support for political autonomy was consistent with this reformist agenda, but it was then always a form of autonomy in association with France.

It is the historical resonance of this position that enabled the Socialist Government of François Mitterrand to propose in 1985 a compromise solution for the territory that entailed a form of independence in association with France. While the proposal was considered scandalous by pro- and anti-independence groups alike for giving away too little or too much, it in fact advocated a position that had dominated postwar politics. Doumenge notes that between 1953 and 1972, a majority of the electorate had favoured 'internal autonomy'.[122] Indeed, in the 1953 election for the Territorial Assembly, the UC had advocated a form of autonomy with France retaining control only of foreign affairs, defence and finance,[123] a proposal that was uncannily similar to Pisani's independence in association. The UC again pushed for a similar statute in 1967.[124]

There is, therefore, considerable precedence to current decolonisation policies enacted through the Matignon and Noumea Accords. Indeed, aside from the period of acute polarisation over independence, all major political persuasions have at various times called for a phased introduction of degrees of self-government in recognition of the need to establish political institutions capable of assuming new responsibilities. Thus, the UC's reversion to a more centrist position in the 1990s is not only an acknowledgment of its limited ability to continue an insurrectionary struggle, but also a reflection of genuine ideological positions held within the party, particularly by its older leaders.

In addition to this historical resonance, the political impetus towards consensus and conciliation promoted by the signing of the Matignon and Noumea Accords, as discussed above, has undermined the ability of its signatories to assert extreme positions. In the case of the FLNKS and the RPCR, the accords have largely undermined their raison d'être. This is the context in which centrist political groups have acquired prominence in the past 10 years. Their leaders in this period have been a handful of well-known personalities in New Caledonia, foremost among them the businessman and former Employers Federation head Didier Leroux. Leroux's party, Une Nouvelle-Calédonie Pour Tous (UNCT), formed in 1995, surprised most observers by winning seven seats in the Southern Province and two in the Northern Province in elections held that year. The UNCT's success resulted in the RPCR losing its majority in the Territorial Congress for the first time and precipitated new 'unholy' political alliances between FLNKS members and the RPCR.[125] In its election publicity, the UNCT voiced positions that have come to characterise more centrist anti-independence politics. In particular, the theme of promoting peace and toleration contrasted strongly with Lafleur's well-known assertion that the path towards peace was not through concessions to the demands of the different communities in the territory but rather through maintaining the strength of the European community in the face of these demands. Rather, the UNCT considered New Caledonian 'pluralism' a positive characteristic not "synonymous with division but … rather the expression of democracy'.[126] Elsewhere Leroux spoke of his desire for a society 'where it is good to live together, and not in a peace where the winner imposes itself on the loser'.[127] In a direct swipe at Lafleur, the UNCT called for more ethics in public life through avoiding 'elected representatives using their mandate in order to favour businesses in which they have interests in order to enrich themselves personally'.[128] At its first congress, the UNCT called for New

Caledonia to remain linked to France through institutional, judicial and financial means, but nonetheless advocated a large degree of political autonomy similar to that afforded French Polynesia.[129] By 2004, when Leroux was re-elected to Congress on the Avenir Ensemble ticket, these political premises had permutated somewhat into a 'deep conviction that Caledonia can only remain in the Republic if it is able to construct a more just and tolerant society' through reducing 'the political and social fractures that divide it'.[130]

Evidence that this desire was widespread came in the 2004 elections when Avenir Ensemble gained a majority of seats in the Southern Province, displacing for the first time the RPCR's majority (19 to the RPCR's 16). This resulted in Avenir Ensemble's Harold Martin replacing Jacques Lafleur as President. Martin had been one of several prominent RPCR members (including Sonia Lagarde, Marie-Noëlle Thermereau and Philippe Gomes) who had openly rebelled against Lafleur's authority in the party during the 2001 municipal elections by calling for greater democratisation and a greater adherence to the consensual spirit of the Noumea Accords. Announcing his 2004 alliance with Leroux, Martin stated that the goal of a 'common destiny' was not being pursued by the RPCR, adding, 'This agreement is supposed to help us build a common destiny, whatever our political, ethnic differences are ... But it certainly doesn't look that way.'[131]

Martin was joined by Lagarde, Thermereau and Gomes on the Avenir Ensemble ticket, and Thermereau was ultimately elected as President of the Government of New Caledonia, signalling the demise of RPCR political authority and the emergence, as one commentator put it, of a new form of stability in which 'change has ceased to frighten'.[132] When Themereau had resigned from the RPCR in 2001, she had done so denouncing Lafleur's 'impressive drift towards greater and greater personal power'.[133] Her election was greeted with cheers from a packed gallery. Analogies were drawn with the fall of the Berlin Wall and comments were made that people could now express themselves freely without fear of reprisals, indicating how strong Lafleur's personal power had been.[134] But Themereaux's election was not just a beginning; it also signified a fruition of changes that had been occurring during the 1990s. In the decade after the signing of the Matignon Accords, various forums broached the issue of a New Caledonian identity that was not racially delineated. Work done by scholars at the French University of the Pacific, as well as by writers and journalists, has taken impetus from the sentiments of the accords to advance a view of New Caledonian identity that dared speak in reconciliatory terms.[135] Avenir Ensemble's ascendancy in part reflects this work. FLNKS leader Roch Wamytan was indeed correct when he commented that the Noumea Accord showed 'mentalities had evolved'.[136] This evolution might result in a greater acknowledgment of the necessity, and perhaps the benefits, of coexistence, but it suggests the need for independence.

The extent to which the political question has now shifted away from that of independence per se to one of coexistence is evident in the changing political discourse of hitherto more radical politicians. Palika's Déwé Gorodé was elected as Government Vice-President in the 2004 elections. In a subsequent radio interview, she interpreted the new citizenship called for in the Noumea Accord as involving Kanak acceptance of 'those who arrived in our country after us, to build the nation together'. Reflecting on the process leading up to the Noumea Accord, she added, 'It meant we had to talk with them, we had to work with them, and then we signed an agreement with them. We must convince each other and work together to build this country.'[137] Such conciliatory discourse is a far cry from the radicalism of calls for Kanak socialist independence. It suggests that pro-independence politics is also working to win over the expanding middle ground.[138]

Conclusion

It is broadly accepted that some of New Caledonia's longstanding political structures — particularly the RPCR and the FLNKS — are in disarray. These signatory parties to the Matignon and Noumea Accords bear the responsibility for reorienting politics away from acute physical confrontation towards more conciliatory processes. Perhaps ironically, however, they have both demonstrated an inability to reorient their own modus operandi towards this new political logic.

I have argued that this political atmosphere has drawn out sentiments that have always existed as undercurrents in New Caledonian society. These include acute racism, divisive French policies towards the colony, a powerful comprador class that has stymied equitable development and a period of heightened political tension precipitated by demands for independence that banished any moderation from the political lexicon for a very long time. The RPCR and the FLNKS signed up to the accords because, essentially, they had little choice given the level of insurgency and the possibility of civil war. Perhaps it is now fitting that the baton should be handed on to new, or fundamentally reworked, political forces, which can bring a fresher eye to the formidable tasks ahead. For many, this still involves achieving independence for New Caledonia. Loyalist politics have come quite a way in countenancing this possibility, just as pro-independence politics have muted the more radical calls for an independence determined by Kanaks alone. But the centrist forces emerging at the moment are unlikely to trip the wire and support independence in nine years. This will result in ever increasing numbers of disenfranchised Kanaks, and perhaps Wallisians, who cannot look to a future in which their interests come to the fore. Lest we forget the lessons of the 1960s and 1970s, this is the stuff from which radicalism is born.

Footnotes

1   Doumenge, Jean-Pierre. 1995. 'L'Enracinement des mouvements politiques en Nouvelle-Calédonie: Faits et Prospective'. Unpublished paper. p. 3.

2   The French Government is required to allocate three-quarters of its civil capital investment funds and project subsidies to the northern and Islands Provinces. High Commission of the Republic in New Caledonia. 1977. *New Caledonia: The Matignon Accords, 1991 Progress Report*. Noumea: Pacific Compos. p. 8.

3   Wamytan Roch cited in Connell, John. 2003. 'New Caledonia: An Infinite Pause in Decolonization?' *The Round Table*, Vol. 368. pp. 125–43, at p. 130.

4   Connell, John. 1987. 'New Caledonia or Kanaky? The political history of a French colony.' *Pacific Research Monograph*, No. 16, Canberra: National Development Studies Centre, ANU. p. 97.

5   McCallum, Wayne. 1992. 'European Loyalist and Polynesian Political Dissent in New Caledonia: The Other Challenge to RPCR Orthodoxy.' *Pacific Studies*, Vol. 15, No. 3. pp. 39–40.

6   Chanter, Alaine. 2002. 'Postcolonial Politics and Colonial Media Representations in New Caledonia.' *Pacific Studies*, Vol. 25, No. 3. pp. 17–36, at pp. 26–7.

7   Connell, 2003, op. cit. p. 128.

8   Maclellan, Nic. 1999. 'The Noumea Accord and Decolonisation in New Caledonia.' *The Journal of Pacific History*, Vol. 34, No. 3. pp. 245–52, at p. 249.

9   The population of Melanesians fell from 44.8 per cent in 1988 to 44.1 per cent in 1998. Maclellan, ibid. p. 5.

10   *Pacific Report*, June 25, 1992.

11   Ibid.

12   Connell, 2003, op. cit. p. 130.

13   Bensa, Alban and Eric Wittersheim. 1998. 'A la recherché d'un destin commun en Nouvelle-Calédonie.' *Le Monde Diplomatique*. Available at http://www.monde-diplomatique.fr/1998/07/BENSA/10658.html,

14   Ibid.

15   Chappell, David A. 1999. 'The Noumea Accord: Decolonization Without Independence in New Caledonia?' *Pacific Affairs*, Vol. 72, No. 2. pp. 373–91.

16   Maclellan, Nic. 2004. 'From Eloi to Europe: Interactions with the ballot box in New Caledonia.' Unpublished paper. p. 11.

17   Ibid. p. 12.

18   Bensa and Wittersheim, op. cit.

19   Chesneaux, Jean. 1988. 'Kanak Political Culture and French Political Practice: Some Background Reflections on the New Caledonian Crisis'. In Michael Spencer, Alan Ward and John Connell (eds), *New Caledonia: Essays in Nationalism and Dependency*, St Lucia: Queensland University Press. pp. 56–80, at p. 68.

20   Chanter, Alaine. 1999. 'Will There Be a Morning After? The Colonial History of the Media in New Caledonia.' *The Journal of Pacific History*, Vol. 34, No. 1. pp. 91–108, at pp. 94–6.

21   McCallum, op. cit. p. 33.

22   Henningham, Stephen. 1992. *France and the South Pacific: A Contemporary History*. North Sydney: Allen & Unwin. p. 55.

23   Dornoy, Miriam. 1984. *Politics in New Caledonia*. Sydney: Sydney University Press. p. 197.

24   Frogier was elected President of New Caledonia's Government Council in 2001. Chappell, David A. 2002. 'New Caledonia — Political Review.' *The Contemporary Pacific*, Vol. 14, No. 2. pp. 446–55, at 448–9.

25   Dornoy, op. cit. p. 159.

26   Connell, 1987, op. cit. p. 248.

27   Ibid. pp. 249–50.

28   Ibid. p. 254.

29   Dornoy, op. cit. p. 199.

30   Ibid. pp. 260–1.

31   Henningham, op. cit. pp. 64–5.

32   McCallum, op. cit. p. 33.

33   Henningham, op. cit. pp. 49–56; Connell, 1987, op. cit. pp. 243–8.

34   McCallum, op. cit. p. 33.

35   Ibid. pp. 29–32; Doumenge, op. cit. p. 19.

36   McCallum, op. cit. pp. 28–9.

37   Ibid. p. 56.

38   Ibid. p. 33.

39   Ibid. p. 35.

40   Ibid. p. 39.

41   Ibid. p. 38.

42   Chanter, 2002, op. cit. pp. 26–7.

43   McCallum, op. cit. pp. 46–7.

44   Henningham, op. cit. p. 107.

45   McCallum, op. cit. p. 41.

46   Ibid. 44.

47   Ibid.

48   McCallum, ibid. pp. 43–4, notes that the FN(NC) has, on a couple of occasions, engaged in electoral alliance with the RPCR in order to maximise the loyalist vote.

49   Ibid. pp. 44–5.

50   Chappell, 2002, op. cit. p. 449.

51   Connell, 2003, op. cit. p. 135.

52   McCallum, op. cit. p. 51.

53   Ibid.

54   Maclellan, 1999, op. cit. p. 248; Chappell, 1999, op. cit. p. 380.

55   Maclellan, ibid. p. 248.

56   Chappell, 2002, op. cit. pp. 449, 455.

57   Ibid. p. 455.

58   Dornoy, op. cit. pp. 166–167.

59   Ibid. p. 160.

60   The exception is Paul Neoutyne of Palika, who was FLNKS President in the mid-1990s.

61   Henningham, op. cit. pp. 49–50.

62   Kurtovich, Ismet. 2000. 'A Communist Party in New Caledonia (1941–1948).' *The Journal of Pacific History*, Vol. 35, No. 2. pp. 163–79.

63   Dornoy, op. cit. p. 161.

64   Ibid. p. 164.

65   Henningham, op. cit. pp. 53–4.

66   Dornoy, op. cit. p. 165.

67   Ibid. p. 168.

68   Cited in Dornoy, Ibid. p. 170.

69   Connell, 1987, op. cit. pp. 262–8; Dornoy, op. cit. p. 177.

70   Henningham, op. cit. p. 77.

71   Ibid.

72   Connell, 1987, op. cit. pp. 262–8.

73   Dornoy, op. cit. p. 185.

74   Henningham, op. cit. p. 79.

75   Ibid.

76   Ibid.

77   Dornoy, op. cit. p. 187.

78   Ibid. p. 79.

79   Henningham, op. cit. p. 79.

80   Dornoy, op. cit. p. 249.

81   Ibid. p. 210.

82   Connell, 1987, op. cit. p. 278.

83   Ibid.

84   The FI consisted of the UC, Palika, FULK, UPM and the PSC (Connell, 1987, op cit. p. 278).

85   Ibid.

86   Connell, 1987, op. cit. pp. 286–8.

87   Ibid. pp. 299–304.

88   Ibid. p. 305.

89   Ibid. pp. 310–11.

90   Ibid. p. 311.

91   Cited in ibid. p. 316.

92   The founding parties of the FLNKS were the UC, Palika, UPM, PSK, FULK, the USTKE and the Groupe des Femmes Kanakes Exloitées en Lutte (GFKEL).

93   Hnalaine Uregei cited in Connell, 1987, op. cit. p. 339.

94   Connell, 1987, op. cit. p. 352.
95   Henningham, op. cit. pp. 99–102.
96   Ibid. pp. 100–1.
97   Ibid. p. 102.
98   *Pacific Report*, November 21, 1991.
99   There were suspicions that FULK had played a role in the plan to assassinate Tjibaou and Yeiwene.
100 *Pacific Report*, November 22, 1993.
101 Maclellan, 1999, op. cit. p. 247.
102 Connell, 2003, op. cit. p. 132.
103 Ibid. p. 132.
104 Cited in ibid. p.133.
105 Macllellan, 2004, op. cit. p. 11.
106 Ibid.
107 Ibid.
108 Connell, 2003, op. cit. p. 140.
109 Chappell, 2002, op. cit. p. 451.
110 Ibid. p. 454.
111 *Pacific Report*, February 28, 1998.
112 Bensa and Wittersheim, op. cit.
113 Chappell, 1999, op. cit. p. 381.
114 Hnalaine Uregei, personal correspondence, 1994.
115 Chanter, 1999, op. cit.
116 Henningham, op. cit. pp. 59–60.
117 Connell, 1987, op. cit. p. 279.
118 McCallum, op. cit. p. 36.
119 Chanter, 1999, op. cit. p. 101.
120 Chappell, 2002, op. cit. p. 452.
121 Henningham, op. cit. pp. 74–5; Barbançon, Louis-José. 1992. *Le Pays du Non-Dit*. Nouméa: Offset Cinq Edition, p. 62.
122 Doumenge, op. cit. p. 1.
123 Connell, 1998, op. cit. p. 245.
124 Connell, 1987, op. cit. p. 253.
125 *Pacific Report*, July 31, 1995.
126 *UNCT online*. 1996. Available at www.UNCT@geocities.com,
127 *L'Humanité online*, October 26, 1996.
128 UNCT online, op. cit.
129 *Pacific Report*, November 1, 1996; *L'Humanité online*, op. cit.
130 *Gouvernement de la Nouvelle-Calédonie online*. 2003.
131 'Anti-independence block gain seats in New Caledonia's Congress", *Pacnews online*, May 10, 2004. Available at http://www.hellopacific.com/news/general/news/2004/05/10/10reg7.html
132 Ibid.
133 Ibid.
134 'Political Quakes Shake French Pacific: The End of an Era?' *Oceania Flash online*, June 7, 2004. Available at http://www.asiapac.org.fj/cafepacific/resources/aspac/tahiti070604.html
135 Coulon, Marc (ed.) 1996. *Être Caldoche aujourd'hui*. Lifou: Ile de Lumière.
136 'Le oui l'emporte au référendum sur la Nouvelle-Calédonie.' *TF1 online*, November 8, 1998.
137 'Building the nation in New Caledonia — Program Three Opinion by Déwé Gorodé.' *ABC online*, 2004. Available at http://abc.net.au/timetotalk/english/opinion/TimeToTalkOpinion_440057.htm
138 Gorodé's election means that the two highest positions in government are held by women. These were the first provincial elections in which a new law required equal representation of women and men on party tickets. The law came into effect in the French Pacific in 2000 and requires that 'On each list, the difference between the number of candidates of each sex can be no greater than one. Each list must be composed alternatively [sic] by a candidate of each sex.' Cited in Maclellan, 2004, op. cit. p. 4.

FIJI: PARTY POLITICS IN THE POST INDEPENDENCE PERIOD

Alumita L. Durutalo

Introduction

The Fiji Group consists of more than 300 islands, which were colonised by the British in 1874, a period concurrent with the expansive phase of industrial capitalist development and commercial growth in Europe. Through colonisation, Fiji was absorbed into the capitalist world economy, joining Africa, Asia and the Caribbean. Before colonisation, indigenous Fijians believed that they had lived in Fiji since 'time immemorial', translated in Fijian as '*e na dua na gauna makawa sara*'. The latest archaeological evidence of human settlement in Fiji, estimated to be 3,000 years old, was discovered recently on the island of Moturiki in the Lomaiviti Group.[1]

Indigenous Fijian sociopolitical and economic organisation in the pre-European era was organised along relationships that emanated from sociopolitical structures such as the '*itokatoka*' (extended family), '*mataqali*' (sub-clans), '*yavusa*' (clans), '*vanua*' and '*matanitu*' which were both political constructs. Outside Fiji, regular contacts were maintained with nearby neighbours, Tonga to the east and Samoa to the north-east. In this context, and also because of its geographical location, Fiji has always been classified by anthropologists and other scholars as comprising Polynesian and Melanesian characteristics in terms of the physical features of the people as well as culture.

After colonisation on October 10, 1874, the Colonial Administration established a complex system of indirect rule through the Native (later Fijian) Administration. Similar to the model of a 'state within a state', the institution was to govern Fijians through their chiefs.[2] The institution, although restructured over the years, has been maintained ever since. The arrival of Indian indentured labourers in 1879 and other later immigrants did not affect the operation of the system of indirect rule. While later immigrants were governed directly by the Colonial State, Fijians were administered through the Native Administration.

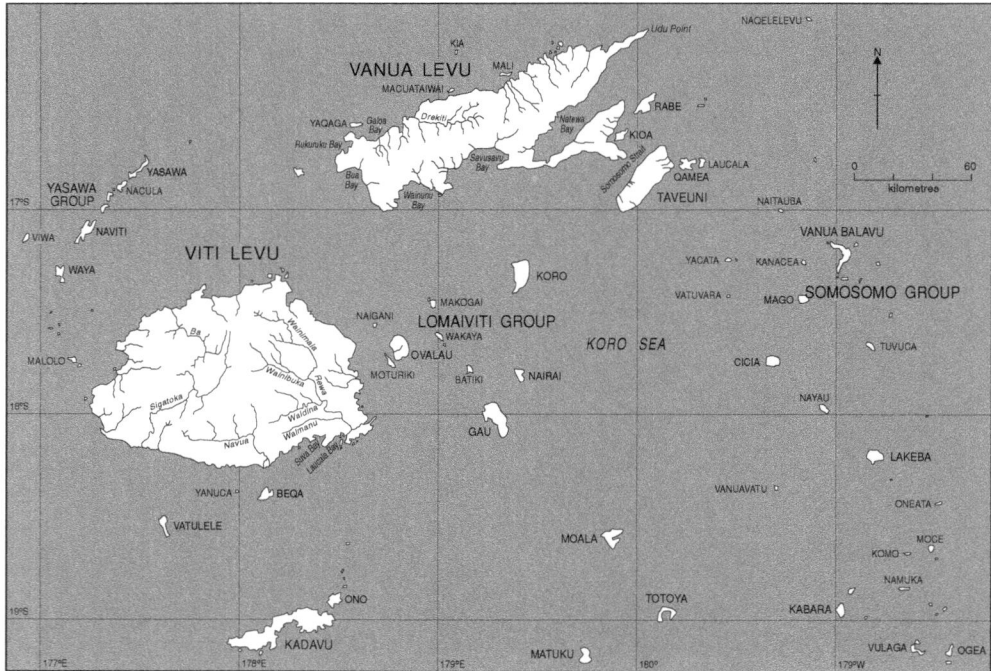

Figure 9.1: Fijian Islands

Party politics was introduced to Fiji in the 1960s, before political independence in 1970. It continued the Colonial Government's system of representation through the Executive and Legislative Councils. The membership system in the Legislative Council was organised along ethnic lines according to the major ethnic groups in Fiji, namely Fijians, Indo-Fijians and Europeans. This system of representation reflected colonial compartmentalisation of races in Fiji. It was an administrative leadership strategy of divide and rule, which was characteristic of leadership in the colonies of the British Empire. The specifics of such political leadership depended on the nature of the society in which colonisation was imposed.

I have identified three major periods of active party formation in Fiji between 1970 and 2005. These are 1970 to 1987; 1990 to 2000; and 2001 and beyond. The period between 1987 and 1990 saw military rule in Fiji after the execution of two military coup d'etats by Major General Sitiveni Rabuka. These periods have also seen three different constitutions: the 1970 Independence Constitution, the 1990 (post-1987 coups) Constitution, and the 1997 Constitution. Fiji's Independence Constitution introduced a bicameral system of government based on the Westminster model, consisting of an Upper and Lower House, or Senate and House of Representatives respectively. The Upper House consisted of 22 nominated members, and the Lower House 52 elected members.[3] The 1990 Constitution saw the Westminster bicameral system of government continue, however, the allocation of seats in the Upper and Lower Houses changed to 34 and 70 members respectively.[4] This altered again after the 1997 Constitution, whereby the Senate had 32 nominated members, and the House of Representatives 71 elected members.[5]

Two different electoral systems were adopted under the three constitutions in Fiji. The 'first-past-the-post' system was used from the first elections in 1963 until the elections of 1994 and the 'alternative-vote system', which was adopted from the Australian electoral system for use in 1999, remains in place to this day. Since the beginning of party politics in the 1960s, Fiji has had an ethnic voting system whereby citizens vote under the three major ethnic categories, namely Fijian,[6] Indo-Fijian[7] and general voters.[8] The constitutionalisation of this ethnic voting system in 1970 re-enforced ethnic politics in Fiji.

Considering Fiji's colonial background, it was inevitable that the ethnic nature of political parties in Fiji emerged and prospered. In this sense, Fiji's pioneering political parties in the post-independent period reflected ethnic cleavages and formed a 'natural' extension of the different political demands during the period of colonisation, as Ali makes clear:

> As rulers, British officials had to satisfy simultaneously three divergent requests: to safeguard Fijian paramountcy, to preserve the privileges of the European minority resentful of any attempt to erode their special position, and to grant Indians political rights which did not emphasize inequality and discrimination against them.[9]

In 1929, after the granting of franchise to Indians along racial lines, Vishnu Deo, the Indian Member for the Southern Constituency, made further demands. He introduced a motion into the Legislative Council that common franchise be granted to Indians similar to that granted to other British subjects in the colony, as the communal franchise was regarded by Indians as a direct contradiction of the Colonial Government's undertaking that Indians would be treated equally with other races in Fiji.[10]

Fijians by this time had not been granted the franchise. Their representatives to the Legislative Council were nominated by the Governor through the Council of Chiefs. Demands by Vishnu Deo for common franchise for Indians were interpreted by European and Fijian members of the Legislative Council as an infringement of the supremacy of Fijian rights in the Deed of Cession Charter. Furthermore, for Fijians, like Europeans, a common roll implied Indian dominance so the proposal was rejected on these grounds. Specifically, the Indian political demand for a common franchise threatened the European politico-economic dominance in Fiji.[11]

By the 1950s, when the demand for a common roll had still not been granted, Indo-Fijian leaders nevertheless pressed for a political system that enabled greater participation in decision-making by local people. Self-government rather than government by colonial bureaucracy would have enabled greater participation and integration of Indo-Fijians, they argued. This would have facilitated their acquisition of an indispensable position in the colony.[12]

Fijian demands were influenced by the changes that were introduced mostly through colonisation. According to Ali:

> The realization that a community descended from immigrant labourers was likely to outnumber them, perhaps permanently in their native land aroused deep emotions of future uncertainty.[13]

By 1960, 10 years before political independence, Fiji had emerged as a colony that was beset by compartmentalised interests. No common ground had been forged by the three major races as a basis for establishing the foundation of a nation-state. Different demands emerged and shaped the nature of Fiji's political parties in the period immediately before and after political independence.

Party politics in Fiji: a brief history

The practice of party politics among the different ethnic groups in Fiji was clearly influenced by the historical experiences of each group. For indigenous Fijians, the first and perhaps foremost influence was their culture. Specifically, traditional relations within sociopolitical constructs such as the '*itokatoka*', '*mataqali*', '*yavusa*', '*vanua*' and '*matanitu*'[14] influenced the structure and nature of Fijian political parties. In modern Fiji, relations within these constructs are utilised to either solicit support or extend competition, rivalry and dissent. Internal competition for power among the different *vanua* and *matanitu* throughout Fiji explains regional cleavages in the formation of Fijian political parties. In the first general elections in 1963, for instance, the two regions in Fiji in which political parties were formed were eastern and western Viti Levu. In eastern Viti Levu, the Fijian Association was dominated by eastern Fijian chiefs and elites, and it would go on to become the Fijian arm of the Alliance Party (AP) when it formed in 1966, the other two arms being the Indian Alliance and the General Electors. The Fijian Association was formed in 1955 by high chiefs in the Fijian Affairs Board, the ruling body of the Fijian Administration. To counter the formation of this chiefly organisation in eastern Fiji, in western Viti Levu, two different parties came to prominence, namely the Western Democratic Party (WDP) and the Fijian National Party (FNP), both of which were formed by key Fijian political figures, Apisai Tora and Isikeli Nadalo respectively.

Founder of the WDP, Apisai Tora, hails from the village of Natalau in the province of Ba in western Viti Levu. His political career in Fiji has spanned a period of more than four decades and he continues to serve as a Fijian Senator to this day. Along with the WDP, he has been directly involved in the formation of three other Fijian political parties in western Fiji, an accomplishment unmatched in the history of party politics in Fiji.

Similarly, the founder of the FNP, the late Isikeli Nadalo, came from the western Viti Levu province of Nadroga/Navosa and was involved in Fiji's party politics for more than 20 years. Nadalo and Tora joined the Indian-dominated National Federation Party (NFP) for a long period. Tora, however, joined the eastern Fijian-dominated AP in 1981 and remained in it until after the general elections of April 1987, when the AP lost to the Fiji Labour Party (FLP)/NFP Coalition.

Such regional cleavage in the formation of Fijian political parties demonstrates the complexity of power relations within Fijian society, as there was no overall Fijian chief before colonisation by the British.

Even though Fijians have formed different political parties over the years, a second major factor and common, uniting thread in this process has been the shared experience of Fijians through colonisation, i.e., the threat of being politically marginalised by new immigrants in their native land. Major Fijian political parties that have formed to promote and defend the supremacy of Fijian rights in Fiji include the Fiji Independent Party (FIP), the Fijian Nationalist Party (FNP), the Soqosoqo ni Vakavulewa ni Taukei (SVT) Party and the Soqosoqo Duavata ni Lewenivanua (SDL) Party.

FIP was formed in 1971 and contested only the first post-independence general election of 1972. Its first and only President was Viliame Savu. Most of its members were active in the formation of the Fijian Chamber of Commerce before political independence, and many of them went on to join Sakeasi Butadroka's[15] FNP, which was formed in 1974 and shared much of FIP's political ideology, namely the promotion of indigenous Fijian rights over other ethnic groups in Fiji.[16]

The SVT Party was formed with the sanction of the 'Bose Levu Vakaturaga' or Council of Chiefs after the 1987 military coups and the promulgation of the 1990 Constitution. Its aim was to replace the Fijian Association arm of the AP as the mainstream Fijian political party. The SDL Party was formed in 2001 as a consequence of George Speight's coup in 2000. Like AP and the SVT Party, it emerged as an eastern Fijian mainstream political party, aiming, perhaps, to capture the political power base of both of its predecessors. It promotes the rights of indigenous Fijians and Rotumans through its policies on affirmative action.

In essence, then, since the two military coups of 1987 and the re-enforcement of ethnic politics through the 1990 Constitution, newly formed Fijian political parties have tended towards an emphasis on ethnicity as the most important criterion in the formation of Fijian political parties. A promise to serve Fijian interests has been the most common platform among Fijian political parties. While some parties, such as AP, have attempted to present a broad platform for all Fijians, others, because of their regional or ideological confinement, inevitably narrow their platform to their 'home' regions or to certain groups of Fijians. Examples of regionally based political parties are the Party of National Unity (PANU), the Bai Kei Viti (BKV) in western Viti Levu and the Matanitu Vanua (MV) in Vanua Levu and northern Tailevu. Ideologically confined parties include the Veitokani ni Lewenivanua Vakarisito (VLV) or Christian Democrats[17] and the Nationalist Vanua Tako-Lavo Party (NVTLP).

Among Indo-Fijians, the major influence in the formation of political parties reflected the nature of the economic exploitation they encountered during the colonial era. On the one hand, were the demands of those who came to Fiji as indentured labourers for the Australian-owned Colonial Sugar Refining (CSR) Company. On the other, were the demands of those who had immigrated to Fiji as free settlers and established their own businesses. Political demands initially reflected the different classes of Indian immigrants. The political issues that arose from the core of the Indian middle class expressed a demand for equality with European settlers in terms of the adoption of a common roll electoral system. Further demands emerged in the mid-1930s on issues relating to farmers' leases after the abolition of the indenture system. In response to these political demands, the Colonial Government attempted to encourage moderate leadership among militant Indo-Fijians.[18]

Demands for a common roll were further kept at bay by the Colonial Administration with consistent evocation of the Deed of Cession Charter, which stated that its foremost task was to safeguard the paramountcy of Fijian interests. Indians were seen by Europeans and Fijians as a threat to their interests. For Europeans, political equality implied a challenge to their political and economic monopoly in Fiji. For Fijians, it was a direct challenge to their sociopolitical and economic rights as the indigenous people of Fiji.[19] If European colonisation was bad enough, being dominated by Indians in their native land after colonisation was seen as even worse. The fear resulting from Indo-Fijian political demands thus shaped the nature of party politics in Fiji.

Indo-Fijian political parties on the whole evolved through the contest for leadership between those who lived in the cane-growing areas, especially in western Viti Levu, and the urban middle class who lived mostly in Suva, in south-eastern Viti Levu. The more militant leaders of the farmers' unions in western Viti Levu went on to form the NFP in 1966 and the moderates in Suva formed the Indo-Fijian arm of Ratu Sir Kamisese Mara's AP in 1966.[20]

Party politics between 1970 and 1987

The AP formed in 1966[21] and was multiracial, including members from all three major ethnic groups — the Fijian Association, the Indian Alliance and the General Electors.[22] Each party member joined the AP through one of the ethnic components of the party. In this context, although AP was multiracial, it was dictated by the requirements of ethnicity. Like a government within a government, each of the three arms of the party was a separate entity within a whole. In reality, the party's constitution and its manifestos were interpreted in three different ways by AP members. An understanding of the party and what it meant to members was viewed through an ethnic lens.

Members of the Fijian Association arm viewed the AP from the perspective of the eastern Fijian sociopolitical hierarchy since the party was founded by eastern Fijian high chiefs in the Fijian Administration, such as Ratu Sir Edward Cakobau and Ratu Sir Penaia Ganilau. The political power base of the Fijian Association was derived from grassroots village Fijians in the 14 provinces. This support was gained mainly out of respect for chiefs in party politics. An understanding of the party and its complexities was derived through its elite leadership. Leadership within the Fijian Association arm of the AP followed traditional hierarchy and protocol.[23] In this context, although the AP was multiracial, its Fijian Association members regarded the party as the only party that safeguarded the paramountcy of Fijian interests and should promote such interests first and foremost. As such, being founded on a basis of unity of race and class, the AP was a fragile political organisation. Durutalo makes the point that:

> The composition of the party was politically volatile because ethnic Fijian grass root [sic] unity was used to support class interests.[24]

This further demonstrated that the multiracial union within the AP was inevitably an 'unbalanced and an unequal one'. During the 1982 voter registration, out of a total of 14,304 registered AP voters, 10,503 (73 per cent) were Fijians, 2,104 (14.71 per cent) were Indo-Fijians and 1,697 (11.86 per cent) were general electors.[25] These figures demonstrate the dominance of the Fijian Association arm in the 'multiracial' AP.

Likewise, the other political parties that were formed by other ethnic groups were dominated by those ethnic groups. The NFP, for instance, was almost a wholly Indo-Fijian party, as seen in the results of voter registration before the 1982 general elections. Out of a total of 9,799 registered voters, the NFP registered 9,406 Indo-Fijian (96 per cent), 356 Fijians (3.6 per cent), and 37 General Electors (0.36 per cent).[26]

Unity among members of the Fijian Association arm of the AP was maintained through patron-clientelism whereby the patrons or the political leaders maintained the allegiance of their clients (voters) in a number of ways. Perhaps, first and foremost, was the traditional allegiance of the clients to the patrons and vice versa. Most of the political leaders in the Fijian Association were eastern Fijian chiefs so their traditional status was used in a modern context to demarcate power bases.[27] Before the beginning of party politics, Fijians had never participated in modern elections in which they had to vote for their leaders as individuals. Fijian membership of the Legislative Council until 1963 was by way of the Governor's nomination through the Council of Chiefs.

The first general election after independence was in 1972. By this time, it was clear that two major political parties dominated Fiji's party politics. These were the AP and the NFP. The general electors, who were the 'non-Fijians' and 'non-Indo-Fijians', in general had always voted with the AP.

Under the 1970 Constitution, there were 52 seats in Fiji's House of Representatives for which voting was conducted according to a 'first-past-the-post' system. Fiji was demarcated into three different electoral boundaries to cater for the three ethnic voting categories of Fijians, Indo-Fijians and the general electors, which were further divided into communal and national seats. The results of the 1972 general election, as shown in the table below, reflect the polarity of Fiji's party politics and the general tendency of each ethnic category to vote for its own party — Fijians for the AP and Indo-Fijians for the NFP. General electors tended to vote with the AP throughout its 17 years of existence between 1970 and 1987.

Table 9.1: Results of the 1972 General Elections.

Seats	Alliance Party	National Federation Party
Fijian communal	12	0
Indo-Fijian communal	0	12
General communal	3	0
Fijian national	7	3
Indo-Fijian national	7	3
General national	4	1
Total seats	33	19

(Source: Howard, M. C. 1991. p. 82.)

The dissenting tradition in Fijian party politics (1970–87)

Between the two major ethnic groups, Fijians and Indo-Fijians, the latter tended to subscribe to the NFP, at least before the formation of the Fiji Labour Party (FLP) in

1985. Fijians, on the other hand, have always formed alternative political parties since party politics began in the 1960s.

Apart from the two major political parties — the AP and the NFP — a minor Fijian political party that also contested the elections in 1972 was Viliame Savu's Fiji Independent Party (FIP). The FIP was formed by a group of Fijians who were dissatisfied with the Fijian Association and also with the terms of Fiji's Independence Constitution. In my interview with Savu in 2002, he indicated that the chiefs who had negotiated Fiji's Independence Constitution had not done enough to secure a special place for indigenous Fijians; in particular, they did not do enough to help Fijians in setting up businesses. Their dissent was finally expressed in the formation of an alternative Fijian political party.[28] Fijian political parties in this perspective became an avenue for expressing dissent within Fijian society. This opportunity was not open during the period of colonisation when all citizens were united under the Colonial State and there were limited avenues for redressing problems.[29]

There were other Fijians who joined non-Fijian political parties such as the NFP. These included Apisai Tora and Isikeli Nadalo of western Viti Levu, Ratu Julian Toganivalu, a chief of Bau, and Ratu Mosese Tuisawau, a high chief of Rewa. Tora and Nadalo formed their political parties, the Western Democratic Party and the Fijian National Party respectively, in the 1960s. They joined the NFP in 1972. In 1975, Sakeasi Butadroka of Rewa joined the ranks of dissenting Fijians when he formed the FNP. As discussed earlier, supporters of FIP supported Butadroka's FNP after its formation. Butadroka extended the FIP's 'Fijian marginalisation' claim by accusing the AP Government of not doing enough to help indigenous Fijians. He blamed Fijian economic marginalisation on the prosperity of non-Fijians. Butadroka's solution for this problem was the repatriation of Indo-Fijians to India. His racial outburst in Parliament cost him his AP parliamentary seat when he was dismissed by former AP Prime Minister, Ratu Sir Kamisese Mara.

Not all dissenting Fijians subscribed to Butadroka's solution to Fijian economic marginalisation. Each dissenting group from different regions of Fiji continued to form their own parties or joined other political parties such as the NFP. Ratu Soso Katonivere, a high chief from the Pprovince of Macuata in Vanua Levu, joined other dissenting Fijians in the NFP. During the first elections of April 1977, Ratu Osea Gavidi of Nadroga in western Viti Levu stood as an independent candidate at the request of the Nadroga/Navosa chiefs and people. He won a seat in Parliament. Gavidi championed the plight of the pine landowners in his province who were marginalised by the AP Government's policy on the development of the pine industry.[30]

Dissent among indigenous Fijians caused the first defeat of the AP at the polls in April 1977. Butadroka's FNP managed to gain 25 per cent of indigenous Fijian votes. The FNP undercut the AP political power base, causing a victory for the rival NFP. Other Fijians who stood as independents or joined other political parties such as the NFP also won seats in Parliament. However, a leadership rift within the NFP after the April 1977 general elections delayed their choice of a Prime Minister. This resulted in the nomination of former AP Prime Minister, Ratu Sir Kamisese Mara, by the Governor-

General, Ratu Sir George Cakobau, to lead a care taker government until elections were held again in September 1977, which the AP won.[31]

The AP's return to power created more challenges. By 1981, a new Fijian political party, based in western Viti Levu, Ratu Osea Gavidi's 'Western United Front' (WUF), was formed. With the backing of western pine landowners, Gavidi won his seat in 1977 as an independent candidate. The pine landowners' longstanding grievance against the AP finally culminated in another Fijian political party. Lal explains that:

> Western Fijians have long complained of regional discrimination and step-brotherly treatment. In the 1960s and early 1970s, several attempts were made to re-assert a distinct western identity, but the separatist tendencies were contained through traditional reconciliation ceremonies. The WUF is the latest and probably the most ambitious attempt to articulate western grievances in some coherent political fashion.[32]

During the 1982 general elections, the AP managed to win 28 of the 52 seats in Parliament, with the WUF winning two and the NFP 22.[33] Opposition to AP rule continued and, in 1985, the formation of the Fiji Labour Party (FLP) posed the ultimate challenge to the long reign of AP.

The Fiji Labour Party and the 1987 military coups

The most formidable opposition to the AP between 1970 and 1987 occurred with the formation of the FLP in 1985. While Fiji's political parties have always tended to be ethnic in orientation, the FLP was the first attempt to form a large political party through the trade unions. As I made clear in 2000,[34]

> The formation of the party posed a long term challenge to ethnic politics in Fiji, especially in an era of increasing globalisation. The specific impetus behind the formation of the party lay in the IMF-required austerity measures in 1984-85 which recommended deregulation of the labour market, reduction in the size of government, a freeze on the expansion of the civil service posts, a wage freeze, privatization of parastatals, and removal of price controls and subsidies.

The door for political competition was opened wide after the formation of the FLP. The party was not only well organised and supported locally by workers across the ethnic divide, it had its international affiliations through global labour and trade union organisations. The FLP's multi-ethnic structure threatened a number of interests in Fiji, not least the AP. While the AP was viewed broadly as an elite multiracial party, the FLP did not have its ethnic compartmentalisation and people could become direct members. The leadership of the FLP by Dr Timoci Bavadra, an indigenous western Fijian, posed a direct threat to eastern Fijian chiefly elites who had assumed the leadership role in Fiji since independence in 1970. The party also challenged class interests within Fiji's political economy.[35] FLP's coalition with the NFP finally sealed the fate of the AP in the general elections of 1987, ending its 17-year rule. Exactly one month after Dr Bavadra's FLP/NFP Coalition Government formed, however, the first 1987 military coup d'etat was executed by Major General Sitiveni Rabuka. The coup overthrew Fiji's 1970 Constitution together with its elected government.

Party politics under the 1990 Constitution (1990–2000)

Between the two coups of 1987 and 1990, Fiji was ruled by an interim military government under the leadership of former AP Prime Minister, Ratu Sir Kamisese Mara. It was during this period that the Fijian establishment through the Council of Chiefs attempted to introduce a number of things. First was the promulgation of a new constitution for Fiji in 1990. The Constitution and its electoral provisions were regarded as racist by non-Fijians and also some Fijians. Second, in 1991, a new Fijian political party was launched to replace the Alliance Party. The 'Soqosoqo ni Vakavulewa ni Taukei' (SVT) Party was formed with the blessing of the Council of Chiefs. Its new leader was coup chief, Major General Sitiveni Rabuka. The Fijian establishment generally assumed that all indigenous Fijians would rally behind the new constitution and the SVT Party. This did not happen, however, as indigenous Fijians started forming alternative political parties even before the launching of the SVT Party. Apisai Tora, for example, formed the All National Congress (ANC) with other former AP members in the west in his home village in Natalau, Sabeto, in 1991.

Since the electoral provisions were drastically altered in the 1990 Constitution, allowing for wider communal voting, it was inevitable that the SVT Party would win. Thirty-two out of the 37 Fijian seats were derived from the 14 provinces and only five seats were allocated to the urban dwellers.[36] The SVT Party formed the first government under the 1990 Constitution.

The FLP and the NFP contested the 1992 general elections separately. On the whole, Fijian support for the FLP declined after the 1987 coup. Such political crises tend to polarise people's choices into ethnic categories.

The failure of the 1993 Budget led to another general election in 1994. Conflicts leading to the failure of the SVT Government's Budget emerged from within the ranks of the SVT Party itself. Josevata Kamikamica led a breakaway group from the SVT Party and formed a new Fijian political party called the Fijian Association Party (FAP). This party was one of the six Fijian political parties that took part in the 1994 general elections. Another group of Fijians stood as independents and another as candidates of the FLP. The table below shows the percentage of votes polled by each of the eight political parties in the Fijian provincial and urban constituencies during the 1994 general elections.

Seven political parties competed in the 1994 elections: the 'Soqosoqo ni Vakavulewa ni Taukei' (SVT); the Fijian Association Party (FAP); the Fijian Nationalist Party (FNP); the All National Congress (ANC); the Fiji Labour Party (FLP); the 'Soqosoqo ni Taukei ni Vanua' (STV); the National Democratic Party (NDP); along with independent candidates (IND). The STV was another regional-based party, formed by landowners in the Province of Nadroga/Navosa who were dissatisfied with the SVT as a mainstream Fijian political party. The table generally indicates that while the SVT Party emerged to replace the AP as a mainstream Fijian political party, it did not, however,

Table 9.2: Votes Polled by Fijian Political Parties in the 1994 General Elections.

Fijian Provincial Constituencies	Valid votes	SVT %	FAP %	FNP %	ANC %	FLP %	STV %	NDP %	IND %
Ba	11,769	55.8	2.8	1.1	40.3	-	-	-	-
Bua	4,428	88.2	2.8	1.2	-	-	-	-	7.8
Cakaudrove	10,550	93.3	6.7	-	-	-	-	-	-
Kadavu	3,855	96.9	2.2	0.9	-	-	-	-	-
Lau	4,957	41.9	57.8	0.4	-	-	-	-	-
Lomaiviti	4,815	84.6	2.8	4.1	-	-	-	-	8.5
Macuata	5,283	91.2	6.2	2.5	-	-	-	-	-
Nadroga/Navosa	8,719	48.5	-	-	13.9	-	37.5	-	-
Naitasiri	6,866	40.0	52.8	7.2	-	-	-	-	-
Namosi	1,650	80.2	-	17.4	-	-	-	-	2.3
Ra	5,392	24.9	2.6	18.2	-	-	2.4	-	51.9
Serua	2,250	58.3	-	25.7	10.7	-	-	0.97	4.3
Tailevu	9,879	48.1	29.1	18.9	0.8	-	-	-	3.1
Fijian Urban Constituencies									
Suva city	8,085	72.1	21.6	3.9	2.4				
Serua/Rewa west	3,441	68.0	23.9	4.0	2.6	-	-	-	1.4
Tailevu/Naitasiri	9,977	69.9	25.1	-	4.9	-	-	-	-
Western urban	6,008	61.7	12.0	5.8	8.6	5.1	-	-	6.9
Total	27,511	68.5	21.1	2.9	4.7	1.1	-	-	1.7
Grand Total	**111,540**	**63.4**	**15.3**	**6.3**	**8.0**	**0.2**	**2.8**	**0.02**	**4.0**

(Source: Electoral Commission Report for January 1, 1994–December 31, 1996.)

deter the formation of alternative Fijian political parties in different regions. The move by the Council of Chiefs and the Fijian establishment to unite Fijians under one political party did not prevent the formation of specific regional parties such as the ANC, STV and NDP.

Regionalism in Fijian party politics was again demonstrated clearly in the results of the 1999 general elections as shown in the next table. By 1999, the FNP had changed its name to the Nationalist Vanua Tako-Lavo Party (NVTLP), and three new political parties were formed before the 1999 elections. These were the 'Veitokani ni Lewenivanua Vakarisito' (VLV), the Coalition of Independent Nationals (COIN) and the Party of National Unity (PANU). The VLV was formed by a faction of the Methodist Church of Fiji and COIN was formed by a group in the Province of Bua on Fiji's second-largest island of Vanua Levu. PANU was formed by the Ba Provincial Council in western Viti Levu and continued the tradition of party formation in the western region of Fiji.

Table 9.3: Votes Polled by Fijian Political parties in the 1999 General Elections.

Fijian Provincial Constituencies	Valid votes	SVT %	FAP %	NVTLP %	VLV %	PANU %	FLP %	COIN %	IND %
Bua	5,330	20.09	-	4.38	54.37	-	-	20.77	-
Kadavu	4,987	83.40	9.81	-	6.80	-	-	-	-
Lau	5,927	47.51	-	-	50.82	-	-	-	-
Lomaiviti	6,361	22.0	-	-	-	-	23.4	-	54.6
Macuata	7,926	46.29	-	-	53.71	-	-	-	-
Nadroga/Navosa	13,071	41.05	50.65	-	-	-	-	-	-
Naitasiri	8,992	-	71.21	28.79	-	-	-	-	-
Namosi	2,315	43.41	56.54	-	-	-	-	-	-
Ra	7,811	-	-	47.02	-	52.98	-	-	-
Rewa	5,193	-	59.70	40.30	-	-	-	-	-
Serua	3,345	37.28	-	62.72	-	-	-	-	-
Ba East	8,398	34.9	-	5.66	6.88	52.55	-	-	-
Ba West	10,052	34.47	-	-	-	63.53	-	-	-
Tailevu North	7,449	53.63	46.36	-	-	-	-	-	-
Tailevu South	7,110	40.38	53.59	6.03	-	-	-	-	-
Cakaudrove East	6,582	78.01	-	-	16.70				
Cakaudrove West	7,920	68.94	6.94	-	24.1	-	-	-	-
No. of seats won		4	5	1	3	3	-	-	1
Fijian Urban Constituencies									
North East	10,182	68.94	6.94	-	24.1	-	-	-	-
North West	12,342	32.77	-	-	-	67.23			
South West	9,475	43.24	56.76	-	-	-	-	-	-
Suva city	9,191	42.22	57.78	-	-	-	-	-	-
Tamavua/Laucala	10,014	45.19	54.81	-	-	-	-	-	-
Nasinu	9,096	49.57	50.42	-	-	-	-	-	-
No. of seats won		1	4	-	-	1	-	-	-
Total No. of seats won		5	9	1	3	4	-	-	1

(Source: *Fiji Times*, May 20, 1999)

The table shows that, by 1999, Fijians no longer favoured the Council of Chiefs and Fijian establishment party, the SVT. The main reason for the drastic decline in support for the party was Prime Minister Rabuka's decision to review the 1990 Constitution, which was formed as result of his two military coups in 1987. Rabuka's 'political eclipse' did not augur well with the majority of indigenous Fijians who had enabled the success of his coups through their support.[37] The SVT's rival, FAP, won more Fijian seats in the 1999 elections, which were won by the FLP, which then formed a coalition with FAP, PANU and VLV.

The formation of a coalition to form a multi-party Cabinet is a provision in the 1997 Constitution. Specifically, the 1997 Constitution states that the Prime Minister must form a multi-party Cabinet according to the relevant requirements of the Constitution, which includes an obligation to the fair representation of all parties with members in the House of Representatives. Such political parties are to be included in Cabinet according to the proportion of their numbers in the House. If a party with more than 10 per cent membership in the House of Representatives declines the offer from the Prime Minister to join the Cabinet, then the seats allocated to it can be offered to another party in proportion to its respective entitlement. In the case where all other parties have declined the invitation to the coalition, the Prime Minister can look to his own party or at a coalition of parties to fill the places in Cabinet. In selecting members from other political parties for Cabinet positions under the 1997 Constitution, the Prime Minister is required to consult with the leaders of the respective parties before making appointments.[38] In the case of the People's Coalition Government, the invitation that was extended to the SVT after the 1999 general elections was rejected by the FLP because of the conditions the SVT wanted the FLP to fulfil.

On May 19, 2000, exactly a year into the rule of the FLP People's Coalition Government, Fiji underwent more political turmoil when George Speight attempted another coup. Although the coup was unsuccessful, the FLP People's Coalition Government was not returned to power.[39] An interim government under the leadership of Laisenia Qarase took over the reigns until fresh elections were held in April 2001.

Party Politics: 2001 and beyond

Before the 2001 elections, yet again a number of new Fijian political parties were formed. These included Laisenia Qarase's 'Soqosoqo Duavata ni Lewenivanua' (SDL) and the Matanitu Vanua (MV) Party. On the main island of Viti Levu, MV was formed by supporters of the George Speight destabilisers of May 2000. In Vanua Levu, where the idea of a new Fijian political party was first mooted, MV was formed to replace Rabuka's Council of Chiefs-sponsored SVT Party. The idea of a Matanitu Vanua party emerged out of the Fijian political thought of founding a government out of the unity and consensus of the *vanua* as a geopolitical entity. This party emerged initially from the grassroots in the various *vanua* within the provinces of Cakaudrove, Bua and Macuata.[40]

During the 2001 general elections, the MV Party won all four Fijian communal seats in the provinces of Cakaudrove, Bua and Macuata. The fifth Parliamentary seat for the MV was won in George Speight's stronghold of Tailevu North Fijian provincial constituency on the island of Viti Levu. The spontaneous formation and success of the MV has continued a long trend of dissent and alternative party formation within Fijian society since the 1960s. It has partially demonstrated the dynamic nature of Fijian party politics as it is interwoven with traditional politics. Fijian sociopolitical constructs such as *vanua* and *matanitu* are entrenched permanently as bases of unity under political parties. This feature of Fijian party politics evolves from the diverse and complex nature of tradi-tional Fijian society itself. It also explains the constant rise and demise of Fijian political parties and the difficult attempt to unite all Fijians under one party. The table below shows the number of Fijian political parties that contested the 2001 elections and the percentage of votes polled by the parties.

Table 9.4: Percentage of Votes Polled by Fijian Political Parties in the 2001 General Elections.

Fijian Provincial Constituencies	Valid votes	BKV %	FAP %	NVTLP %	VLV %	PANU %	FLP %	MV %	DN T %	NFP %	NLUP %	POTT %	SDL %	SVT %	IND %
Bua	5,264							61.08					38.92		
Kadavu	4,326												55.39	44.61	
Lau	5,705						1.33						91.48	4.31	2.87
Lomaiviti	6,247										11.11		72.31	13.06	3.52
Macuata	6,640							61.34					38.66		
Nadroga/ Navosa	11,719	9.13	20.21				12.94	4.51					53.22		
Naitasiri	8,603							24.39					75.61		
Namosi	2,224			1.12			1.35	12.05					85.48		
Ra	7,613	16.59						32.17					51.23		
Rewa	5,133		2.1					33.96					51.35	10.44	2.14
Serua	3,054		6.88	7.76				13.98					62.61	8.78	
Ba East	7,846					41.35							58.65		
Ba West	9,155	39.88											60.12		
Tailevu North	6,791							51.38			5.27		36		7.35
Tailevu South	7,212		10.34					32.63					50.21		6.82
Cakaudrove East	5,844							56.09					14.1	29.81	
Cakaudrove West	7,066							67.79							32.21
No. of seats won								5					12		
Fijian Urban Constituencies															
North-East	9,854							21.53			10.23		53.76	14.47	
North-West	10,730												68.4	31.6	
South-West	9,125		2.36	1.39				16.52	1.22		7.47		61.82	9.23	
Suva city	8,742			1.44				10.42	0.88		12.67		55.75	18.14	0.69
Tamavua/ Laucala	9,495			2.94	2.36		3.77	12.56			10.42		61.16	6.79	
Nasinu	8,329		1.39		1.36			14.85			7.26	2.64	65.73	5.11	1.66
No. of seats won													6		

(Source: UNDP Project Fiji Elections 2001 web site: http://www.undp.org.fj/elections/ Accessed February 14, 2002.)

During the 2001 elections, the Council of Chiefs sponsored-SVT Party was totally defeated. The demise of its charismatic leader, former Prime Minister Sitiveni, Rabuka spelled the end of the party. In its place emerged the SDL as the new mainstream Fijian political party. The rise and demise of Fijian political parties in general demonstrates internal rivalries, dissent and shifting alliances, common characteristics of traditional Fijian politics.

The ruling SDL and MV Coalition still has to contend with rival Fijian political parties in the elections of 2006. These will include those that competed in the 2001 general elections and those that were formed after the last elections in preparation for the 2006 elections. Filipe Bole's Fiji Democratic Party (FDP) was formed in 2002[41] and Ratu Epeli Ganilau's National Alliance Party was registered on January 18, 2005.[42] These two new parties have merged as one under the banner of the National Alliance, aiming to strengthen multiracialism from a Fijian perspective. Their attempt to strengthen multiracialism through party politics is similar to the attempt by political parties such as Dr Timoci Bavadra's FLP, which was formed in 1985. While the FLP had Fiji's trade unions as its power base, the National Alliance Party still has to identify and secure its power base.

With the formation of yet new political parties in the period after the 2001 elections, the trend indicates that party formation will be a long-term trend within Fijian society. For Indo-Fijians and general voters, under the United People's Party (UPP), stability in terms of supporting one or two political parties has been a long-term trend since party politics started. This trend is likely to continue.

The future of Fiji's party politics

After four decades of party politics in Fiji, a number of outstanding features have emerged. Firstly, political parties have reflected the nature of pre-colonial and colonial societies in Fiji. For indigenous Fijians, modern political parties have been more than organisations for political representation in government; they have also been a means of expressing dissent and independence, reflecting the nature of pre-colonial society. Despite the attempt by the Fijian establishment to impose unity through party politics, diversity has continuously been expressed through the formation of alternative political parties in different regions since the 1960s. The military coups of 1987 exacerbated party formation, fully exposing the diversity and complexity of Fijian culture and society.

Another outstanding characteristic of party formation in Fiji, which is generally observable between 1970 and 2005, is the tendency for indigenous Fijians to be actively involved in alternative party formation. Throughout the three major periods of active party formation already identified, alternative Fijian political parties have emerged to compete with the major and mainstream political parties such as the Alliance, the SVT and currently the SDL Party. Furthermore, in the same period, dissenting Fijians have also joined and won parliamentary seats in non-Fijian political parties. Two prominent western Fijian pioneering politicians, Apisai Tora and Isikeli Nadalo, joined the NFP in 1972. Other eastern and northern chiefs, including Ratu Mosese Tuisawau, Ratu Soso Katonivere, Ratu Julian Toganivalu and Ro Asesela Logavatu, joined later. While dissenting Fijians who refused to join mainstream political parties such as the AP and later the SVT were easily dismissed by mainstream Fijian society as 'rebels' or at times 'communists', what has been overlooked by critics is that Fijians were never united politically before colonisation and the introduction of party politics. Such unity was realised partially for the first time after colonisation and the establishment of the Colonial State. This did not, however, eradicate the influence and authority of traditional institutions. The coexistence of 'traditional legitimacy' and 'legal rational legitimacy' makes modern party politics a complex issue indeed.

Since the military coups of 1987 and the demise of the AP, parties that emerged to fill the vacuum, such as the SVT in 1991 and the SDL since 2001, have introduced platforms that appear to capture the interest of Fijian voters first and foremost. The ruling SDL, for instance, has included a Fijian 'blueprint' in their policy for the development of indigenous Fijians and Rotumans. What the FIP initiated and the FNP followed with regarding specific provisions for indigenous Fijians and Rotumans, the SDL is currently turning into specific policies. With the 2006 elections approaching, Fijian voters might once again be drawn to pragmatic politics as demonstrated by the SDL's blueprint.

With globalisation and the strengthening of the 'good governance' agenda by international lending agencies, Fiji too is caught in such philosophy and rhetoric. In such a situation the governing SDL/MV is caught in a complex internal dilemma. On one hand, the Government is pursuing good governance, while on the other, it directly implicates loyal supporters who took part in the 2000 coup and its ensuing mutiny. Trials of those who were implicated in the 2000 crisis have continued, resulting in the imprisonment of a number of high chiefs from eastern and north-eastern Fiji. Bau high chief and Deputy Vice-President of Fiji, Ratu Jope Seniloli, along with Natewa high chief and former Deputy Speaker of the House of Representatives, Ratu Rakuita Vakalalabure were imprisoned in 2004. Seniloli has since been released on medical grounds to serve his sentence outside prison. Naitasiri high chief, the '*Qaranivalu*', Ratu Inoke Takiveikata, is still in prison for his role in the 2000 mutiny. Other high chiefs, including the '*Tui Cakau*' and high chief of the '*Matanitu Tovata*', Ratu Naiqama Lalabalavu, Ratu Josefa Dimuri, a high chief of Macuata, and two high chiefs from Cakaudrove, have also received prison terms.[43] Lalabalavu and Dimuri have been released to serve their terms outside prison as well.

The 2000 coup has already had widespread consequences on Fijian society and party politics. The fate of the ruling government therefore depends on its handling of the crisis, given that its political power base is centred on the traditional areas of chiefs who were implicated in the coup. This does not, however, imply that opposition Fijian parties such as the National Alliance Party will automatically be voted into Parliament by Fijians; for the crisis of 2000 might have been read by a number of indigenous Fijian voters in a different light than the legal rational reasoning applied by the modern judiciary system. Such circumstances throw up the complexity of modern party politics as it blends with continuing ancient Fijian rivalries.

Between 1960 and 2005, allegiance to one or two political parties has been common among Indo-Fijians and members of other ethnic groups. For these groups, party formation and choice has been consistent and stable in the four decades of party politics. This can be explained partially through their common historical experience. For Indo-Fijians, the NFP has been the longest existing party in Fiji since its formation in 1965. Its stability might also be explained in other ways. Firstly was the common experience of the majority of party members through the indenture system or through their business activities, for those who migrated specifically to establish businesses. In this case, economic experience necessitated the founding of a common platform. Secondly, the party acts as a unifying force in an adopted country and has been successful in fulfilling its objectives among its members through the requirements of a modern party system — objectives such as the desire to attain political and economic rights. On the whole, the success of a party depends on its members and what they make of it.

The results of the 2006 elections for non-Fijian political parties are predictable according to the long-term trend of party politics in Fiji. The triple overthrow of the FLP has made the party resilient to political destabilisation. Hard-core supporters of the party from across the ethnic spectrum remain committed. Added to this has been the support of Indo-Fijians who, since the formation of the party in 1985, have regarded the FLP as the best alternative to the NFP. By the elections of 1999, the FLP again emerged victorious as the representative of Indo-Fijians as well as non-Indo-Fijian trade union supporters. The biggest challenge for the FLP's multi-ethnic trade union base has been government restructuring and the weakening of union powers through new labour laws. The FLP, however, remains a powerful force to be reckoned with in the 2006 elections.

Conclusion

For as long as it is adopted as a modern means of political representation, party politics in Fiji will continue to evolve according to the historical experiences of the different societies. For indigenous Fijians, the continuation of one mainstream Fijian political party and the consistent formation of many alternatives might yet be a long-term trend. Regional cleavages in the formation of political parties have continued throughout the more than four decades of party politics. In such circumstances, a coalition of parties that have similar platforms and ideologies, such as that between the ruling parties, the SDL and MV, becomes inevitable. The inclusion of the alternative-vote system with its multi-party cabinet provision in the 1997 Constitution appears to be a pragmatic provision, given such circumstances. To explain such development to its logical conclusion, this can also give rise to the long-term challenge of finding a common ground for the formation of multiracial political parties and hence a common ground for building a nation-state. There is a compartmentalisation of political views according to different *yavusa, vanua, matanitu* or regions. On a positive note, such development can also be a means of maintaining a 'balance of power' situation as each region checks the dominance of another.

A coalition of parties across the ethnic divide, however, remains a tough challenge in a country where ethnic politics is constitutionalised and accepted as a 'natural' state. The second overthrow of the FLP Coalition Government attests to this. In such a situation, the formation and evolution of an 'ethnically balanced' political party becomes critical as ethnicity is used constantly to marginalise the political rights of certain groups and political parties. In the long term, Fiji still has to achieve the ideal situation for any multi-ethnic and multicultural society, and that is to create multiracial political parties. This does not imply the old AP model of multiracialism, whereby people became members through their ethnic groups, but an open membership system in which there is equality for all. Political parties, after all, are social constructions; they turn out according to their intended structure and nature.

Footnotes

1   See Reid, R. K. 2003. 'Pacific's Oldest Man: Unearthed in Fiji Where He Lies Undisturbed for About Three Thousand Years.' In *Islands*, Vol. 2. Suva, Fiji: Island Business International. pp. 54–6.

2   See also Spate, O. H. K. 1959. *The Fijian People: Economic Problems and Prospects*. Suva, Fiji: Government Press. p. 31.

3   See also Lal, B. V. 1986. 'Politics Since Independence: Continuity and Change, 1970–1982.' In B. V. Lal (ed.), *Politics in Fiji*, Sydney: Allen & Unwin. pp. 74–106, at pp. 76–7.

4   See *Constitution of the Sovereign Democratic Republic of Fiji, 25 July 1990*. p. 49.

5   See *Constitution (Amendment) Act 1997 of the Republic of the Fiji Islands, 25 July 1997*. pp. 86–92.

6   In this paper, the words Fijian or indigenous Fijian or native Fijian refer to the indigenous people of the Fiji Islands. Under Fiji's electoral system, Fijians make up an ethnic category. All Fijians are registered in the '*Vola ni Kawa Bula*' (VKB) or the Fijian genealogy.

7   The first Indians in Fiji arrived from mainland India in 1879 to work as indentured labourers for the Australian-owned Colonial Sugar Refining (CSR) Company. The indenture system ended in 1920 and Indians were free to return to India or live permanently in Fiji. Other Indian immigrants, mainly from the state of Gujarat, arrived later in the early 20th century to establish their own businesses. Indo-Fijians make up an ethnic category in Fiji's electoral system.

8   Fijian general electors are composed of ethnic groups who are neither indigenous Fijians nor Indo-Fijians. These include Europeans, part-Europeans, Chinese, Pacific Islanders, etc.

9   Ali, A. 1986. 'Political Change: 1874–1960.' In B.V. Lal (ed.), op. cit. pp. 1–27, at p. 9.

10   Ibid, p. 10.

11   Ibid.

12   Ibid, p. 21.

13   Ibid.

14   *Vanua* and *matanitu* were political constructs that extended out of the kinship infrastructure of '*itokatoka*', '*mataqali*' and '*yavusa*'. The most basic Fijian social unit was the '*itokatoka*', '*bito*' or '*bati-ni-lovo*'. These are extended family units, traced patrilinealy in most parts of Fiji, and matrilineally in others. One or more '*itokatoka*' comprised a '*mataqali*' or sub-clan. A number of '*mataqali*' formed a '*yavusa*' or clan. Members of a yavusa descended from a common '*yavu*' or house foundation and a '*Kalou Vu*' or ancestral god. Above the *yavusa* were the political constructs of *vanua* and *matanitu*. The *vanua* was formed out of a unity of a number of *yavusa* by a *vanua* chief, usually through warfare. The *matanitu* was composed of the unity of a number of *vanua*. These were still being formed in some parts of Fiji when Europeans arrived in the 1800s. See also Derrick, R. A. 1946. *A History of Fiji*. Colony of Fiji: Government Printing Press. pp. 8–9. Traditional socio-political and economic relations evolve in these kinship and political constructs.

15   Butadroka was formerly a member of the Fijian Association arm of the Alliance Party. He came from the Province of Rewa in south-eastern Fiji. In 1972, he won a parliamentary seat on an AP ticket and served as Cabinet Minister for Cooperatives in Ratu Sir Kamisese Mara's Alliance Party. His conflict with the Fijian Association began in 1973, and eventually led to his dismissal from the AP and the formation of the Fijian Nationalist Party (FNP).

16   See Norton, R. 1990 (2nd ed.) *Race and Politics in Fiji*. St Lucia, Queensland: University of Queensland Press. pp. 111–18.

17   The VLV was formed before the elections of 1999 by a group in the Methodist Church. These members were mainly from the Provinces of Cakaudrove and Lau. The VLV was formed as an alternative to the SVT in an attempt to unite all indigenous Fijians under one political party. Interview with Ratu Inoke Tabualevu, a founding member of the VLV from the Province of Cakaudrove, 2002, Suva, Fiji.

18   Norton, op. cit p. 53.

19   See Ali, A. op. cit. pp. 9–15.

20   See also Norton, op. cit. p. 61.

21   See also Alley, R. 1986. 'The Emergence of Party Politics.' In B. V. Lal (ed.), op. cit. pp. 28–51, at p. 29.

22   All three Fijian constitutions since independence in 1970 have emphasised ethnic voting through the three major ethnic divisions: Fijians, Indio-Fijians and general electors.

23   Within Fijian society, hierarchy and protocol are '*vanua* specific' and, in regions where there are *matanitu*, also '*matanitu* specific'. This implies that there is a diversity of hierarchy and protocol given the diverse nature of Fijian society and culture. With the dominance of eastern Fijian chiefs in the Fijian Association arm of the Alliance Party, the dominant Fijian hierarchy and protocol were those found in eastern Fiji — more so from the dominant *vanua* in the *matanitu* of Kubuna and Tovata.

24   Durutalo, A. 2000. 'Elections and the Dilemma of Indigenous Fijian Political Unity.' In B. V. Lal (ed.), *Fiji Before the Storm: Elections and the Politics of Development*, Canberra: Asia Pacific Press, ANU. pp. 73–92, at p. 75.

25   See *The Alliance Newsletter*, No. 8, April 1982. p. 58.

26   Ibid.

27   See Howard, M. C. 1991. *Fiji: Race and Politics in an Island State*. Vancouver: University of British Columbia Press. pp. 79–80.

28   Interview with Viliame Savu, 2002, Suva, Fiji. See also Howard, ibid. p. 80.

29   The formation of the Native (later Fijian) Administration in 1875 facilitated the system of indirect rule whereby indigenous Fijians were governed through their chiefs.

30   Interview with Ratu Osea Gavidi, 2004, Suva, Fiji. See also Howard, op. cit. pp. 87–9

31   See also Durutalo, A. 2000. op. cit. p. 77.

32   Lal, B. V., 1986. op. cit. p. 98.

33   See also Norton, op. cit. p. 189.

34   Durutalo, A., 2000. op. cit. pp. 76–7.

35   Ibid. p. 77.

36   Ibid. p. 81.

37   Eight of the 14 provincial councils, including Prime Minister Rabuka's Province of Cakaudrove, rejected the review of the 1990 Constitution. Interview with Ratu Inoke Tabualevu, a member of the Cakaudrove Provincial Council, 2002, Suva, Fiji.

38   See Part 3, Cabinet and Government, Subsection 99 (1)–(9), on the Appointment of Other Ministers, *Constitution of the Republic of the Fiji Islands, 27 July 1998*. pp. 60–61.

39   The People's Coalition Government, since 2000, has legally challenged its dismissal in court, however, nothing has been resolved yet.

40   Interview with Ratu Rakuita Vakalalabure, 2003, Parliament of Fiji, Suva, Fiji.

41   Interview with Filipe Bole, 2002. Suva, Fiji.

42   See *Epeli Ganilau: From Hierarchy Pedia* on http://www.hierarchypedia.com/~hierarch/wiki/index.php/Epeli_Ganilau

43   See *Fiji Times*, April 5–8, 13, 19, 2005.

THE ESTABLISHMENT AND OPERATION OF SĀMOA'S POLITICAL PARTY SYSTEM

Asofou So'o

Abstract

When Sämoa gained independence in 1962, it was expected to adopt the Westminster model of parliamentary democracy. Framers of Sämoa's Constitution had, therefore, always envisaged the formation of political parties in the nation, but it was 17 years after independence before this vision became a reality. The consensus politics that dominated the first two decades of independence were swiftly replaced by party politics after the establishment of the first post-independence political party. Immediately thereafter, more political parties were formed, giving rise to the party system Sämoa still has today, in which the party in government is able to pass laws for the development of the country that would have otherwise been impossible. The nature of Sämoan political parties — their structures and the strategies they have adopted to keep their members tied to their collective cause and to win support during election campaigns — is partly a reflection of the political environment within which they operate. As the party system becomes entrenched, however, it has become increasingly associated with a widespread feeling of powerlessness and political paralysis among parliamentarians and the public generally. Nevertheless, as this chapter argues, the Sämoan political parties are here to stay, albeit with continuing piecemeal adjustments that are intended to consolidate the system.

Introduction

Sämoa gained independence on January 1, 1962, and its constitution[1] provides for a parliamentary democracy of the Westminster model. Until the 1993 enactment of the 1991 constitutional amendment[2] that extended the parliamentary term from three to five years, general elections were held every three years to select representatives to occupy the 49 seats of Parliament. There are 41 territorial constituencies, six of which have two seats each because of their larger voter population. Upolu Island has four of these seats and the larger island of Savai'i has the other two. Thus, of the 49 seats in Parliament, 47 are occupied by representatives of the 41 territorial constituencies who must hold *matai* (chiefly) titles.[3] Representatives of individual voters fill the other two seats. These are Sämoan citizens who have decided not to exercise any rights to Sämoan customary land and *matai* titles, thereby opting out of the *matai* system and its associated privileges and rights.

After confirmation of general election results and, in accordance with Section 52 of the Constitution, the Head of State will convene Parliament to elect from their number a Speaker and Deputy Speaker of the House (*Constitution*, 4[1–2]). The Head of State will also appoint a Member of Parliament who commands the confidence of a majority of MPs as Prime Minister to preside over the Cabinet (*Constitution*, 32[2.a]). After the establishment of political parties, this provision of the Constitution in reality means that the leader of the political party with the majority of seats in Parliament becomes the Prime Minister after their official election by Parliament to that position.

The political path to the establishment of the first political party

Consensus politics dominated the first eight years of parliamentary proceedings.[4] Sämoa's first Prime Minister, Matä'afa Fiamë Faumuinä Mulinu'ü II, was elected unopposed in 1961 (before Sämoa gained its independence), and again in 1964 and 1967. Parliamentary politics reflected the conservative nature of traditional politics. The Matä'afa title that the first Prime Minister held was one of the four highest-ranking titles in the country.[5] To have one of the *Tama-a-aiga* (or Royal Sons) hold the office of Prime Minister was in line with the feeling of the general public of the time. Although parliamentary debates became increasingly critical and potentially divisive in those early years, the general inclination was not to rock the boat too much. In other words, even though there were opportune moments to move motions of no confidence against the Prime Minister and his Cabinet, this did not occur during Matä'afa's first eight years as Prime Minister.[6] The one attempt to move against Matä'afa and his government was later withdrawn after the PM made it clear he would resign if the proposed *Forest Bill* was passed. If passed that bill would have prevented the Government going ahead with its plans for the establishment of a timber industry on Savai'i Island.

To contain criticism of his leadership and of government policies, Matä'afa made a practice of appointing MPs who had been critical in previous Parliaments to his Cabinet. This strategy contributed to the general nature of consensus politics in the early years of Parliament after independence. But, from 1970 onwards, Matä'afa's faced increasing difficulties in his attempts to keep things under control.

The general election of 1970 and its immediate aftermath will go down as an important moment in Sämoa's political history. Before then, there had been only one *tama-a-aiga* in Parliament. That was Matä'afa, who had been Prime Minister since 1961. In 1970, another *tama-a-aiga* was elected. He was Tupua Tamasese Lealofi IV (hereafter Tamasese), who was younger than Matä'afa and was a medical doctor by profession. Tamasese was immediately identified by the newly elected MPs as an alternative to Matä'afa's conservative approach to politics. Thus, Tamasese became the representative of a new political force in Parliament, comprising members who wanted changes in leadership and government policies but who were still comfortable with a *tama-a-aiga* retaining the leadership.

In the contest for the Prime Ministership, yet another political force emerged. It was made up of younger, modern and educated MPs who did not mind doing away with the traditional idea of having only *tama-a-aiga* as Prime Ministers. One of this younger generation, Leota Itu'au, has described his involvement in the 1970 Prime Ministerial election as follows:

> In 1970, when I first entered Parliament, we young and new members in the like of Le Tagaloa Pita (Leota then), A'e'au Täulupo'o, Leilua Manuao, Le'aumoana Fereti, Tautï Fuatau and Tiatia Lokeni secretly met at the old Casino Hotel to back Tupuola Efi for the top post.[7]

Leota Itu'au was one of the Sämoan students who had been sent to New Zealand for a university education. Leota Pita, a university graduate also entering politics for the first time, had been acting principal of the Alafua Agricultural Campus (in Sämoa) of the University of the South Pacific (USP) before he entered politics.[8] The Tupuola faction therefore comprised mainly young *matai*, newly elected MPs and Sämoans with relatively high levels of education. Tupuola himself had undertaken law studies at Victoria University in Wellington, New Zealand, before returning to Sämoa on the death of his father and late Joint Head of State, Tupua Tamasese Mea'ole, in April 1963.[9] Tupuola Efi was also a first cousin of Tamasese.

The three-way division of political orientation among the newly elected MPs was reflected in the 1970 Prime Ministerial election. As expected, Matä'afa stood again for the Prime Ministership. He won 19 votes. The newly elected and younger *tama-a-aiga*, Tamasese, polled 17 votes. Tupuola Efi won 10 votes. A second ballot was therefore required at which the two first cousins joined forces under the *tama-a-aiga* titleholder to defeat Matä'afa. The result of the second ballot was a draw. Matä'afa and Tamasese each polled 23 votes. The Speaker then adjourned Parliament until the next day and Tamasese was eventually elected by 25 votes to Matä'afa's 20.[10] Tupua Tamasese Lealofi IV included Tupuola Efi in his Cabinet as Minster of Works.

Describing Tamasese's new-look Cabinet, Davidson noted:

> It is a relatively young government, a government of well-educated men, of men who have travelled and lived abroad. Several of its members, including Tofa Fuimaono,[11] have taken a leading part in the campaign to replace the restrictive matai suffrage by universal suffrage … it looks like a government of reform — a government that will accelerate the process of both political and economic modernization … [12]

But the Government's accelerated rate of economic and political development proved unacceptable to the majority of the public. The Tamasese Government's liberalism (if not radicalism) and its departure from consensus politics (in terms of no longer allocating portfolios on the basis of districts from which ministers came) cost it the 1973 general elections.[13]

The first meeting of Parliament after the 1973 elections saw Matä'afa back at the country's political helm. He polled 23 votes against Tamasese's nine and Tupuola Efi's 13.[14] As a gesture of traditional respect to the other *tama-a-aiga* MP, Tamasese (who had regained his seat) was appointed to the cabinet.

Matä'afa passed away unexpectedly nine months before the completion of his fourth Prime Ministerial term. Given that Parliament was back to having only one *tama-a-aiga* among its members, it was half-expected that Tamasese would succeed the late Prime Minister. What was controversial was the manner in which the appointment was made. Instead of Parliament making its choice on the basis of majority support (*Constitution*, 32[2.a]), the Head of State invited Tamasese to see through Matä'afa's term.[15] MPs who had rallied around Tupuola Efi as their informal leader were critical. They argued that the Head of State was out of line with the provisions of the Constitution. Outside Parliament, the scenario was interpreted as the *tama-a-aiga* making sure they remained in the forefront of political leadership. Despite public and parliamentary criticisms, however, the Head of State's appointment was accepted, although Parliament did become extra vigilant about preventing this sort of manoeuvre in the future.[16]

The aftermath of the 1976 general elections saw yet more changes in the country's parliamentary scene. Matä'afa and Tamasese's supporters now rallied around Tamasese, wanting him to continue on as Prime Minister in the next Parliament. Their efforts were in vain. The leader of the new political force in Parliament, Tupuola Efi, won the Prime Ministerial office by a majority of 30 votes to Tamasese's 16. This was the first time since independence that a non-*tama-a-aiga* had held the office of Prime Minister. It represented another phase in the country's transition from traditional politics to the democratic ideals espoused in the country's liberal democratic constitution. Understandably, conservative elements within and outside Parliament argued strenuously against the new development, convinced the world was suddenly being turned upside down by Tupuola Efi and his power-hungry supporters. Backed by this conservative resentment, the outgoing Prime Minister criticised the appointment. Speaking metaphorically, Tamasese referred to the camel, which, after many years of trying, had now finally succeeded in placing itself in its master's tent.[17] Although Tamasese never elaborated on his analogy, both MPs and the public knew that he was referring to his first cousin, a non-*tama-a-aiga* titleholder, eventually succeeding in placing himself in the tent (the office of Prime Minister), which, to him and his supporters, was appropriate only for the master (the *tama-a-aiga*).[18]

In response, the newly elected Prime Minister, Tupuola Efi, told Parliament that he would make sure that Tamasese was given a special place befitting his status. That place was on the Council of Deputies,[19] which had been created in the Constitution to accommodate the three *tama-a-aiga* other than the one holding the office of Head of State. At the time Tupuola Efi won the Prime Ministership, the Council of Deputies was vacant. The holders of the Tuimaleali'ifano and Matä'afa *tama-a-aiga* titles had passed away and their titles were therefore vacant. The new Prime Minister's gesture was culturally acceptable as the outgoing Prime Minister was a *tama-a-aiga* titleholder. Interestingly though, the outgoing Prime Minister had resigned the same position in late 1969 in order to contest a seat in Parliament. In reality, therefore, Tamasese was being made to take a step back to a position he had held before being involved in politics. In hindsight, perhaps, Tupuola Efi was sending out the message to Tamasese and the public that *tama-a-aiga* should confine themselves to ceremonial positions and not be involved in the politics of the day. Interestingly, no other *tama-a-aiga* has held the Prime Ministership since Tupuola Efi's victory over his first cousin and *tama-a-aiga* titleholder: Tupuola 'Efi was Prime Minister for two consecutive terms from 1976 to 1982; Va'ai Kolone from 1982 to late 1982; Tofilau Eti Alesana from 1983 to the defeat of his budget in his second term in late 1985;, Va'ai Kolone again from 1986 to 1988; Tofilau Eti Alesana again from 1988 until his resignation in 1998; and Tuila'epa Sailele Malielegaoi from 1998 until the present (2005).

In the time of Matä'afa's consensus politics, once he had appointed his Cabinet, the rest of Parliament effectively became the Opposition. By 1970, however, the tone of parliamentary politics had changed. Factional politics had taken over. The Prime Ministerial election of 1970 is proof of that. The three Prime Ministerial candidates represented the three parliamentary factions that had emerged. As already noted, the Tamasese and Tupuola Efi factions later joined forces against Matä'afa's faction. The same scenario was repeated in 1973 and 1976. In 1976, however, the number of visible parliamentary factions was reduced from three to two after the unexpected death of Matä'afa in May 1975. The events of 1979 were even more intense.

After the official confirmation of the general election results of 1979, the old rivals of Tupuola Efi and their supporters among the newly elected MPs started organising themselves against the declining but still powerful force of the incumbent Prime Minister Tupuola Efi, and his followers. The intensity of parliamentary factions had stepped up to another level. After a meeting at the place of one of their supporters, the anti-Tupuola faction finally agreed on Va'ai Kolone, a seasoned politician, to be their Prime Ministerial candidate when the new Parliament convened.[20] On the day of the Prime Ministerial election, Tupuola Efi snatched victory once again, only this time, his parliamentary majority had been greatly reduced from his 1976 margin of seven seats to just one.[21] Ironically, it was Va'ai Kolone's younger brother and one of the 'old hands' in the Tupuola camp that represented Tupuola's majority.

The new politics of democracy were being seen to have radical and unpleasant implications for a family-oriented society such as Sämoa. Referring to his Prime Ministerial defeat, Va'ai commented in Parliament: 'the injury is inflicted by my own brother.'[22] To consolidate support and win more votes with an eye to the next Prime Ministerial contest in three years, the anti-Tupuola faction established themselves as the Human Rights Protection Party (HRPP) in May of the same year.

Before turning to the establishment and growth of political parties in post-independence Sämoa, I shall first reflect on the political developments that gave rise to their establishment.

Political precursors to the establishment of political parties

As has been shown, the first Sämoan political party, HRPP, originated within Parliament. Its primary objective was to defeat Tupuola Efi, thereby winning government.[23] The origin of Sämoan political parties is therefore true to von Beyme's institutional theory that associates the origin of political parties with the prior existence of Parliament.[24] It is also in line with Duverger's claim that 'first there is the creation of parliamentary groups, then the appearance of electoral committees, and finally the establishment of a permanent connection between these two elements'.[25] Once Sämoan parties were formed, they would try to keep winning government. As Macridis has noted, political parties, once they are established, become the instrument to gain power and to govern.[26] Moreover, once in power, a political party will try to remain there.

Incentives are needed to maintain political support. People expect recognition for their efforts in drumming up support and for toeing the party line. For example, in the combined government of two factions under Tamasese's Prime Ministership, the leader of the coalition partner, Tupuola Efi, was rewarded by being appointed Minister of Public Works.[27] This is an important portfolio as it determines what public work will be undertaken, when the work starts and where. Decisions made in this portfolio can win or lose elections.

After his Prime Ministerial victory in 1970 but before he announced his Cabinet, Tamasese admitted: 'There are so many people who want to be ministers. This is a difficult task.'[28] Commenting on the day the Cabinet was announced, on March 6, 1970, the *Sämoa Times* said that the reading out of the names of ministers must be like the Day of Judgment when people would be told whether to proceed to Heaven or Hell. When Tamasese eventually announced his Cabinet, he told Parliament, 'I rise with respect to say that I cannot satisfy all Hon. Members of this House. However, I have made my selection and it was … a very hard one.'[29]

Arguably, Tamasese's appointment by Matä'afa to the latter's 1973 Cabinet was for a slightly different reason, that is, in order to strengthen Matä'afa's leadership and his grip on power within Parliament and nationally. Even though Tamasese was the leader of a rival faction, he was nevertheless a *tama-a-aiga* like Matä'afa. In appointing his political rival to his Cabinet, Matä'afa was making public his support and respect for the only other *tama-a-aiga* MP. His gesture earned him approval from Tamasese's traditional families, the general public and other parliamentarians. Matä'afa was seen as a leader who had great respect for custom and tradition. His gesture was probably also an attempt to neutralise any political influence Tamasese had within Parliament, or better still, win Tamasese supporters over to the Matä'afa camp.

Va'ai Kolone's brother, Lesatele Rapi, who supported Tupuola Efi in the 1979 Prime Ministerial contest, was later reappointed by Tupuola Efi to his Cabinet. Given that Rapi was one of the ministers in the previous government, it is possible that he was promised another cabinet portfolio if he stayed with the incumbent Prime Minister. It was no secret in the period leading up to the 1979 Prime Ministerial contest that Va'ai Kolone and his supporters campaigned strongly to win Rapi over to their side, using the family argument as their main trump card. In the end, it did not work. By then, Rapi had seen the writing on the wall: were his brother at the helm, the chance of him getting a ministerial portfolio was probably nil. For, even though Sāmoa has a strong family-oriented culture, assuming that Va'ai Kolone defeated Tupuola Efi in the Prime Ministerial race, to appoint his brother to Cabinet would have been seen by the public as nepotism.

As Colin Aikman, one of the architects of Sāmoa's Constitution predicted, political parties emerged due to differences in opinions and policies.[30] The surfacing of these differences can be explained by the theory that associates the emergence of political parties with various aspects of modernisation.

LaPalombara and Weiner note at least two circumstances under which political parties emerge.[31] First, a change might already have taken place in the attitudes of subjects or citizens toward authority. That is, individuals in the society might believe that they have the right to influence the exercise of power. Tupuola Efi, the first non-*tama-a-aiga* to hold the office of Prime Minister, told Parliament in his victory speech:

> Please do not regard the result of the ballot this morning as an illustration of Sāmoa turning her back … [on] the the tama-a-aiga, neither is Sāmoa losing due allegiance to the apple of her eye. In simple terms actually Sāmoa is searching for remedies to her multi-problems while the dignity and sacredness of the tama-a-aiga have continued to be jealously guarded, and the position of tama-a-aiga has continued to be given precedence by the nation.[32]

Tupuola is clearly distiguishing between respect for tradition and the need to find solutions to problems of modern times. It implies that those solutions could be found in the talents of others, and not necessarily only with the *tama-a-aiga* leadership. Moreover, it is clear from the same speech that other citizens of Sāmoa besides the *tama-a-aiga* wanted to exert their influence on the exercise of power.

Secondly, a section of the dominant political elite or an aspiring elite might seek to gain public support so as to win or maintain power even though the public does not actively participate in political life. As has already been seen with the rise of parliamentary factions that eventually resulted in the establishment of political parties, the dominant elite, after the enactment of the Constitution and the establishment of Parliament, were the parliamentarians. They were the ones competing for power and using their parliamentary support to achieve their objectives. Eventually, political parties emerged as fully fledged organisations whose aim was to win the public's support even though the latter was not actively participating in political life. Thus, the process leading to the establishment of Sāmoan political parties accords with modernisation theory.

The change in the public attitudes whereby cultural and natural boundaries were transcended can also be attributed to factors that collectively comprise modernisation, among them the appearance of new social groups as a consequence of larger socioeconomic changes; increases in the flow of information; expansion of internal markets and transportation networks; growth in technology; and, above all, increases in spatial and social mobility. These aspects of modernisation seem to have profound effects on the individual's perception of himself in relation to authority. Access to a certain level of communication makes it possible for people to band together in political organisations. The secularising and individualistic effects of an educational system and the homogenising effects often associated with urbanisation might also be stimulants to the creation of political organisations, as is the shift from subsistence to a cash economy, which often involves the destruction of patterns of local authority, and greater individuality and independence in the marketplace.[33]

The establishment of the party system

The HRPP, established in 1979, tasted political success for the first time in the 1982 general elections, when Va'ai Kolone defeated the incumbent Prime Minister, Tupuola Efi, by one vote. Tupuola's faction became the parliamentary Opposition until Va'ai Kolone lost his parliamentary seat in an election petition five months later.[34] Exercising his discretion under the Constitution, the Head of State invited Tupuola Efi once more to form a government.[35] But in December 1982, a by-election gave the HRPP an extra seat[36] just in time for the Budget sitting of Parliament. That one-seat majority was sufficient for the HRRP to vote out Tupuola's Budget. On December 30, Tofilau Eti Alesana (who had taken over the HRPP leadership after his election to that position by his party on October 6) was sworn in by the Head of State as the country's next Prime Minister. On January 9, 1983, Va'ai Kolone was returned to Parliament when he regained his seat in a by-election. Va'ai Kolone, however, was confined to sitting out the present parliamentary term as a backbencher while Tupuola Efi and his supporters had to wait until the next elections for another chance to unseat the Government.

Two weeks before the general elections in February 1985, Tupuola Efi and his supporters formed the Christian Democratic Party (CDP) to help them get organised for the upcoming Prime Ministerial contest.[37] Unfortunately for them, the HRPP's success in the poll three years' earlier was improved further when it won 31 of the 47 seats in Parliament.[38] HRPP's landslide victory, however, was maintained only until the end of 1985. Up to this point, HRPP's unwritten policy had been that only after the general election results were confirmed would its caucus decide its next leader. In their leadership meeting after the general elections, four names were put forward.[39] Eventually, Tofilau Eti Alesana was given the nod to continue as leader although the vote resulting in that outcome was not as straightforward as it might seem. Supporters of Va'ai Kolone, Tofilau's main rival in this leadership meeting, were not happy with what they saw as manipulation in favour of Tofilau and his supporters. The events that unfolded after the leadership meeting were testimony to those feelings.

Before the first meeting of Parliament to decide the next government, rumours circulated that Va'ai Kolone and his supporters were breaking away from the HRPP.[40] Another prominent HRPP MP, Le Tagaloa Leota Pita, and his wife, Ai'ono Fanaafi Le Tagaloa Pita, who had won her constituency's seat for the first time, had already left the party.[41] Nevertheless, Tofilau was elected unopposed to continue as Prime Minister for another term.[42] Rumours that the HRPP situation was unstable continued to make media headlines.[43] These were reinforced when Tofilau's Budget, tabled in December 1985, was defeated because 11 former HRPP MPs crossed the floor to join forces with Tupuola Efi's CDP. Tofilau Eti Alesana resigned the Prime Ministership on December 27, 1985.[44] The combined political forces of Va'ai Kolone and Tupuola Efi, with the former as leader and Prime Minister, became known as the Coalition Government until the next general elections in 1988. They defeated the HRPP Government by 27 votes to 19.

In the period leading up to Parliament's April 6 meeting to elect a new government, the Coalition had a one-seat majority. On the night of April 4, however, Tanuvasa Livigisitone left the Coalition camp, having been there just six weeks, and joined the rival camp of the HRPP. His nomination of Tofilau as the HRPP's Prime Ministerial candidate was seconded by Sagapolutele Sipaia.[45] Having won the Prime Ministership, Tofilau appointed Tanuvasa to his new Cabinet as the Minister of Economic Affairs and Development, Tourism and Trade. Sagapolutele was appointed Chairman of the Pulenu'u (village mayors) Committee. In a speech to officially accept Tanuvasa into the HRPP camp, Tofilau made it clear to the HRPP caucus that Tanuvasa was a distant relative of his. Although Tanuvasa has stood as a parliamentary candidate for Tupua's old constituency of A'ana Alofa No. 2 against the HRPP-supported candidate, he had been a known HRPP-supporter. He had twice stood against Tupua (then Tupuola), in the 1979 and 1985 general elections.[46] The mood among the Coalition when Tanuvasa 'sneaked away' to the HRPP camp was conveyed by the spokesman of the Sämoa National Party (SNP), whose political party later sided with the Coalition:

> Another newcomer to politics, Tanuvasa Livigisitone hiked to Leufisa [Tofilau's residence where the HRPP MPs camped], thus betraying the trust Tupuola [or Tupua] had in supporting him during the general elections ahead of leading orator Alipia Siaosi of Leulumoega. Or was it a double job? Tanuvasa's political career is an interesting topic for discussion by political critics and students alike in years to come. Especially when this betrayal took place in a so-called Christian country 'Founded on God', and where its elders past and present, often referred to betrayal as — ia soloa i le vailalo ma ia soloa i le aufuefue [Author's note: a traditional curse which figuratively means, 'Let the betrayer be doomed underneath the ground indefinitely so that he should never be seen or heard of again'].[47]

To the HRPP, however, the turn of events regarding Tanuvasa's sudden defection to the HRPP camp seemed only fair, given that their 1985 victory had been snatched from them when the forces of Va'ai Kolone and Tupuola Efi had combined to defeat their budget.

On April 8, 1988, two days after their Prime Ministerial defeat, the Coalition renamed itself the Sämoan National Development Party (SNDP).[48] By this time, the SNP, formed by three of the successful candidates in the 1988 general elections, had joined the Coalition because, the SNP leader, Leota Itü'au Ale, said the HRPP had not approached them for support.[49]

Five new political parties were established in 1993, the year in which the constitutional amendment to increase the parliamentary term was enforced. On June 4, 1993, the Western Sāmoa Labour Party (WSLP) was founded by To'alepai Toesulusulu Si'ueva, who had been an MP from the Ä'ana Alofi No. 3 constituency for two consecutive terms (1982–84, 1985–87). He was one of the 12 HRPP MPs who, in late 1985, defected to form the Coalition Government, in which he was appointed Minister of Health. He lost his seat in 1988. Had the WSLP won a seat, it aspired to become a more effective parliamentary opposition than the SNDP, which had been rather 'mute', resulting, the WSLP claimed, in the HRPP Government becoming dangerously powerful. Among the issues the WSLP stood for were the rejection of the HRPP Government's policies on a number of development programs, and opposition to the manner in which the HRPP Government amended the Constitution in 1991 by a two-third majority of Parliament rather than through a referendum.

Another political party, the Temokalasi Sāmoa Fa'amatai (TSFPP — the Sāmoan Democracy of *Matai*), lodged its application for registration with the Justice Department on January 26, 1993. According to the leader of the TSFPP, Le Tagaloa Pita, the party had passed four main resolutions: that only the *matai* should have the vote; that only the *matai* who respected and had unwavering faith in the merits of the *matai* system should join the party; that the Value Added Goods and Services Tax (VAGST) was excessively burdensome on the substantial majority of the population; that the introduction of universal suffrage had duped the children of *matai* who had been granted the right to vote once they reached 21 years of age but not the right to stand for Parliament, as was the case with individual voters. In June 1993, the TSFPP organised a march on Parliament to present a petition registering its objections to the extension of the parliamentary term from three to five years and to the introduction of the 10 per cent VAGST.

Yet another political party, the Sāmoa Liberal Party (SLP), was formed in late June 1993[50] by three HRPP MPs who had been expelled from the party after they voted with the chairman and vice-chairman of the Public Accounts Committee and the Opposition to cut $WST106,522 from the Foreign Affairs budget for the financial year 1993-94. The Prime Minister told parliament, 'If the cuts are passed by the House then I will tender my resignation to the Head of State.' The Government survived the motion by 26 votes to 19. One of the three expelled HRPP MPs was Nonumalo Leulumoega Sofara.[51] He became the leader of the SLP.

Leota Itü'au Ale, deputy leader of the SNDP since September 1992, announced in Parliament on June 26, 1995, that he was leaving the SNDP to form his own political party, to be called the Sāmoa Conservative Progressive Party (SCPP).[52] In the same announcement, Leota said that his party supported the incumbent HRPP Government. Subsequently, as the first MP to speak on the Budget, Leota told the House that it was a 'responsible budget' and moved that it be passed. He also thanked the Prime Minister for all he had done for the country. Leota told the *Savali* newspaper that in February 1995 a member of the SNDP had suggested it might be time for the current leader of the SNDP, Tupua Tamasese Efi (formerly Tupuola Efi), to step down from the leadership. Tupua had refused to give up the party leadership, hence Leota's decision to form his own party.

Another political party, the Sāmoa All People Party (SAPP), was formed on March 24, 1996.[53] It was a landmark in Sāmoa's democratic development because the party's leader and co-founder, Matatumua Maimoaga, became the first female party leader. Matatumua had been an HRPP MP who had tendered her resignation the day before the SAPP was created. She told people at the party launch: 'We are a legal entity, duly constituted and registered as an incorporated society with the Department of Justice … [The party] is founded on principles and truth. It is not concentrated around individual politicians or personalities. It is truly a Party of the People.'[54] Matatumua on a different occasion said:

> Our party has had to reject candidates that want to be members of SAPP but run as independent candidates. It is not right. It is an attempt to deceive voters, we will not tolerate deception. People must be made aware of this so that they can make an informed decision when they vote.[55]

Although the party does not depart from the tradition of having only *matai* as parliamentary candidates, it allows people as young as 16, regardless of sex and whether or not they are *matai*, to be officers of its organisational structure, which includes village branches.[56]

Even though more political parties were formed in the period between the 1991 and the 1996 general elections, most have not been able to survive. The most important reason for this is that once the leaders lost their parliamentary seats or were unable to win a seat, that was also the end of the party. It thus left the HRPP and the SNDP as the main political parties to contest the next general election in 2001. As in 1982, 1985, 1988, 1991 and 1996, the HRPP became the Government after the 2001 general election.

The establishment of political parties saw another important development in Sämoa's political scene: the emergence of independent candidates without any party affiliation contesting general elections. Three independents won seats in the 1988 general election,[57] five in 1991,[58] 13 in 1996[59] and 12 in 2001.[60] The usual pattern for most, if not all, of these independents was to join one of the established political parties either immediately before the first meeting of Parliament or during the parliamentary term. After the Prime Ministerial election in 2001, however, the independents formed themselves into the Sämoa United Independents Political Party (SUIPP). Recently, though yet to be declared official by the Speaker of the House under the relevant Standing Orders, SUIPP has combined with the SNDP to form the Sämoa Democratic United Party (SDUP).

The issues of party-switching and independents later joining established parties prompted the Commission of Inquiry into Sämoa's Electoral System to make the following recommendations in its October 2001 report: (a) a candidate must remain affiliated to his party; (b) if he defects to another party, then a by-election should be called; (c) if he runs as an individual, or if he leaves the party to become an independent member, he cannot join another party in coalition, nor should he be allowed to hold a ministerial post in the ruling party for the duration of his parliamentary term; and (d) political parties must comply with the law and should be formed by election time, if they are to be accorded legal recognition.[61] The Parliamentary

Electoral Review on the Commission of Inquiry's Report 2001 accepted recommendation (a) subject to the following:

> [i] A Member of Parliament elected under a Political Party which is not recognized as a Party in Parliament pursuant to Standing Orders of Parliament may become a member of a Parliamentary Party on the Leader of that Party notifying the Speaker before the member takes the Oath of Allegiance; and

> [ii] A Member of Parliament ceasing to be a member of a Parliamentary Party through expulsion from that Party shall have his name omitted from that Parliamentary Party list and thereafter to become an Independent member.[62]

The Parliamentary Committee report also states that:

> A Member of Parliament who was elected as an Independent member may join a Parliamentary Party if the leader of that Parliamentary Party gives notice of his membership required under Standing Orders before that member takes the Oath of Allegiance.[63]

The Parliamentary Electoral Committee goes on to argue that the provisions already quoted provide the opportunity:

1. To a Member of Parliament who was elected under a political party which can not form a parliamentary party in pursuance to Standing Orders of Parliament to join a recognized parliamentary party.

2. [To] A member elected as an independent member to join a parliamentary party of his choice by giving notice pursuant to the Standing Orders of Parliament before he takes the Oath of Allegiance.

3. [To] A Member ceasing to be a member of a parliamentary party through expulsion to become an independent member.[64]

Section 15F of the *Electoral Amendment Act 2005* has incorporated the recommendations of the Parliamentary Electoral Committee as follows. A candidate elected as a member of a recognised political party 'shall sit in the Legislative Assembly as a member of that political party during the term for which the Candidate was so elected'. On the other hand, a candidate who is elected as an independent or under a party that does not have the number of members for it to be recognised in Parliament as a party can join another party as long as this is done in the period between the general elections and taking the oath of allegiance in Parliament, and as long as the Speaker of Parliament is notified about this by the leader of the candidate's new party. Failure to abide by these provisions would result in the loss of the parliamentary seat, resulting ultimately in a by-election to elect a new MP for that seat. The bottom line of section 15F is to prevent party-switching during the parliamentary term.

Even though the party system has governed the political affairs of the country since 1982, political parties as such were legally recognised only after the enactment of the

Electoral Amendment Act 1997. This amendment specifies the criteria for the registration of a political party, including that the party must have at least 100 financial members who are eligible to enrol as electors. The act also stipulates that: 'No application for registration [of a party] will be accepted after the day on which the writs for an election or by-election are issued.'

The growing importance of political parties prompted their inclusion in the Standing Orders of Parliament when the first major revision of that document since 1972 was carried out in 1997. As well as providing for the recognition of political parties in general and the Leader of the Opposition's party, the 1997 Standing Orders also stipulate that there have to be at least eight MPs in a political party before it can be recognised by the Speaker of Parliament.

The Parliamentary Electoral Review Committee (chaired by the Speaker of the House and including the Deputy Speaker as Deputy Chairperson, the Leader of the Opposition, the Leader of Government and five other MPs) sat on August 9, 2004, to discuss and refine issues relating to political parties. Recommendations of the committee have since been enacted in the *Electoral Amendment Act 2005* already referred to. Previously, issues that arose relating to political parties were dealt with by a ruling of the Speaker. One such ruling is that once an MP leaves his political party, he will remain an independent for the rest of the parliamentary term. He cannot join another political party.[65] Moreover, the recent announcement by the leaders of the SNDP, Mamea Ropati, and the Sämoa United Independents Political Party (SUIPP), Asiata Säle'imoa Va'ai, that they had formed a combined political party called the SDUP seemed to be invalid because they had not satisfied provision 7(1–4) of the Standing Orders of Parliament, which stipulated that:

(2) A party must inform the Speaker of:
   (a) The name by which it wishes to be known in parliamentary proceedings;
   (b) The identity of its leader and deputy leaders;
   (c) Its parliamentary membership.

The Speaker must be informed of any change [to] these matters.[66]

(3) A coalition between two or more parties must be notified to the Speaker but each party to the coalition remains a separate party for the purposes of the Standing Orders.

(4) In the period between the general election and the House electing a Speaker, the matters specified in this Standing Order may be notified to the Clerk.

According to the Clerk of Parliament, the announcement concerning the establishment of the SDUP is out of line because the Speaker of Parliament has not been informed of these developments as stipulated in the quoted provision of the Standing Orders. According to the Clerk of Parliament, as far as the Speaker of Parliament and Parliament are concerned, no new political party has been formed. Information given to the author on April 11, 2005, by the Ministry of Commerce, Industry and Labour at which political

parties are officially registered confirmed that the SUIPP and SDUP have not been registered. Eventually, the Speaker informed Parliament on April 6, 2005, that the SDUP
could not be recognised as a political party. Instead, what existed were the SNDP and
independents, in accordance with the provisions of the Standing Orders of Parliament
and the *Electoral Amendment Act 2005* already cited.

Effects of the party system

The year 1991 will go down as a watershed in Sämoa's political history. For the first time,
Sämoan citizens without *matai* titles could exercise their democratic right to elect
Members of Parliament to represent the country's 41 territorial constituencies.[67]

The introduction of universal suffrage in the 1991 general election would not have
been possible without the party system that became the main vehicle for rallying and
consolidating support for the change in voting rights. More specifically, the HRPP wisely
used its influence to push for the introduction of universal suffrage, arguing that there
had been a proliferation of *matai* titles in order to give parliamentary candidates an
improved chance of winning parliamentary seats. Giving all adults over 21 years of age
the right to vote in parliamentary elections would help minimise the political need to
confer titles indiscriminately, thereby upholding the dignity of the *matai* system. The
introduction of universal suffrage would also give educated Sämoans who might never
have the chance to hold *matai* titles the right to influence political decisions, thereby
making use of their education to influence national developments.

Opinion in the HRPP Cabinet and caucus was divided on the question of whether
or not universal suffrage should be introduced. In the end, Sämoan respect drowned
these dissenting views in favour of the Prime Minister, their party leader and father of
the country, as the local population prefer to call him, whose political conviction was
that the introduction of universal suffrage would uphold the dignity of the *matai* system
even if it had no other value. The political appeal of giving mothers and old women (the
substantial majority of whom did not have *matai* titles and were therefore not able to
vote in parliamentary elections) the right to vote in elections for the first time became a
political magnet that drew in support behind the HRPP's cause. Even culturally conservative supporters of the HRPP who preferred that voting rights remain restricted to
matai titleholders did not want to jeopardise their political support of that party by
voting against universal suffrage in the referendum. Once the public gave its positive
verdict on universal suffrage, the HRPP was also guaranteed another term in office. The
1991 general elections easily returned the HRPP with Tofilau Eti Alesana continuing as
Prime Minister.

Looking back to Matä'afa's Prime Ministership, which has been criticised for being
so cautious that it did not achieve a great deal, it can be seen that Matä'afa and his
Cabinet were constantly frustrated by a lack of political support for their development
policies from a party bloc in Parliament. As already mentioned, in those days, all MPs
who were not appointed to the Cabinet in effect became the Opposition, making it
extremely difficult for the Government to get things through the House even if, out of
respect for the Prime Minister's status as a *tama-a-aiga*, Parliament never went so far as to

move a motion of no confidence against Matä'afa. As one of the members in the Working Committee of the Constitution in 1960 said: '[*tama-a-aiga* should] be paid the respect due to them as *Tama-a-aiga* and would thus ... be appointed to some office such as PM and would undoubtedly hold these positions for life.'[68]

With the operation of the party system since the 1980s, the pace of development picked up significantly as can be seen in the discussion about whether to establish a national university; this had become a hotly debated parliamentary issue by the early 1980s. As the HRPP was committed to that cause, the strongly critical but minority voice of Tupuola Efi's opposition faction was drowned out, and the National University of Sämoa (NUS) was duly established by an act of Parliament in 1984 with a budget of only $WST5. Today (2005), NUS has 1,700 students, about 80 academic staff and a budget of more than $WST5 million.

Besides the NUS project, other initiatives delivered thanks to the operation of a party system include: the electrification program, which took electricity to all homes in the country; the road improvement program, which for the first time saw all roads around the country sealed; the introduction of television in the early 1990s; the establishment of a Ministry of Women's Affairs and a national Mothers of Sämoa Day in the period leading up to the introduction of universal suffrage in 1991; and the introduction of the Old Age Pension Scheme.

The parliamentary majority of the HRPP not only gave it the mandate to formulate policies but to implement them. The HRPP could also pass laws, including amendments to the Constitution, to suit its own political agenda. Until the enactment of the *Special Posts Act 1989*,[69] Cabinet found it a constant headache that some heads of departments (HoDs), all of whom were appointed by the Public Service Commission, would not heed their instructions in terms of implementing government policies. The passing of the *Special Posts Act 1989* gave Cabinet the right to hire and fire HoDs by means of a two-year contract system. The attitudes of senior government officials quickly changed in the Government's favour.

The establishment of the party system is one thing. Keeping supporters in the party organisation is quite another and examples of party-switching are commonplace. The 11 HRPP MPs who crossed the floor in late 1985 to form a coalition with Tupuola Efi's supporters did so when it became clear that they had not been considered by Tofilau Eti Alesana for Cabinet portfolios. In 1988, another MP left the party on whose ticket he had contested the election to join another that rewarded him with a Cabinet portfolio. Va'ai Kolone's brother, whom Va'ai Kolone expected to join his faction in the Prime Ministerial election of 1979, opted instead to remain with his old political clique. He was appointed by Tupuola Efi to his new Cabinet. The SNDP candidate who switched allegiance in 1991 when it became clear that the SNDP did not have the numbers to form a government was elected Speaker of Parliament by the HRPP, his new party.

To minimise such party-switching, new ways to reward political support had to be created, hence the passing of the *Parliamentary Under-Secretary Act 1988* (although there were other arguments put forward by the Government in its support) and the successful amendment of the Constitution in 1991 to increase from eight to 12 the number of ministers in Cabinet. Besides creating opportunities for loyal party members, the strategy of offering political rewards also strengthened the HRPP's overall position in Parliament. Another constitutional amendment passed in the same parliamentary session in 1991 increased the number of parliamentary seats from 47 to 49. With the Prime Minister and his 12 cabinet ministers each entitled to one parliamentary undersecretary, the HRPP now had guaranteed support in Parliament from 26 of the 49 seats, giving it the numbers to continue its hold on government at least until the next general elections.

The conservative politics of the 1960s and 1970s were a great contrast with the vibrant and effective manner in which the HRPP had passed laws and introduced policy changes since the 1980s. Interestingly, the HRPP's increased power and its unbroken success in the polls has been accompanied by a sense of political paralysis not only within Parliament but within the HRPP. Le Tagaloa Pita, one of the founding members of the HRPP, told the media that the main reason he left the HRPP in late 1985 and joined forces with the CDP was because his HRPP Cabinet would not heed any advice from caucus.[70] Le Tagaloa was making the point that non-Cabinet members of the HRPP caucus and the rest of Parliament felt that they were merely rubber-stamping decisions already made by Cabinet. Parliament was no longer doing its role of debating issues brought before it and making decisions accordingly. There was (and still is) a growing belief that Cabinet was no longer responsible to Parliament. If anything, it seemed to be the other way around. Thus, while the party system has achieved the intention of the framers of the Constitution for a strong Cabinet government to develop in Sämoa, it is coming to be disliked by the majority of parliamentarians, except, of course, those in Cabinet.

It took a controversial government policy for these anti-HRPP and anti-party system political sentiments to surface. In the early 1990s, the HRPP Government introduced the VAGST. Given the secure HRPP majority in Parliament at the time, the Opposition SNDP felt powerless to use Parliament to prevent the Government from implementing its VAGST policy. But with the public rallying behind the SNDP to get the Government to reverse its decision, the anti-HRPP forces wisely turned to other, traditional power bases in their fight against the Government. Thus, the Tumua ma Pule ma 'Äiga (TPA) protest movement was born. The inclusion of traditional institutions in the movement introduced an added dimension and intensified the magnitude of the protest. The general talk around the country and within the traditional political elite was that Parliament had no legitimacy in the country as it was a foreign and relatively new institution. Symbolically undermining the Prime Minister and his Cabinet, the protestors bypassed them and handed their petition instead to the Head of State because of his traditional status as one of the four *tama-a-aiga* titleholders. The Head of State's response was a delaying tactic that eventually resulted in the petition being handed back to the Government to consider. Although the VAGST on some goods was reduced and on others eliminated, the general policy remains unaffected.

There was also a general public feeling that the party system could easily act in the interest of no one but the party in government. That sentiment had some justification. One of the controversial issues in the TPA's petition related to the report of the Controller and Chief Auditor (CCA) in which he pointed to corruption in high places.

After several heated debates in Parliament and repeated court actions involving law suits against the Government by the CCA, the issue was put to rest through constitutional means. Taking advantage of its two-thirds majority in Parliament, the HRPP easily passed a constitutional amendment in which the CCA's term of office was reduced to a three-year contract in line with the rest of the heads of departments under the *Special Posts Act 1989*. The CCA, who had been suspended from his job by that time, was given the right to reapply. He did not.

Another complaint in the TPA petition related to the extension of the parliamentary term from three to five years. What was controversial about this extension was that rather than introducing that amendment in the next Parliament, as the majority of the voting public had expected, the HRPP enforced the extension in the current Parliament.

Thus, although the establishment of the party system brought about positive policy changes that benefited the majority of the public, it also introduced elements that made the public sceptical of not only the party system but democracy generally. The passing of a number of laws (such as those discussed above; namely, the increase in Cabinet positions, *the Parliamentary Under-Secretary Act 1988*, the *Special Posts Act 1989*, the reduction of the CCA's contract period and the extension of the parliamentary term) that seemed engineered by the HRPP for its own benefit contributed to that scepticism. Negative aspects of the HRPP regime aside, its ability to consolidate and win support can be attributed to its organisation and campaign strategies. I shall discuss its organisation first.

Party organisation

Because of its long record of success at the polls, the HRPP seems to be the most organised of all the existing political parties. Therefore, I shall discuss that party here as an example of a Sämoan political party structure. The party was founded in May 1979. It's name, Human Rights Protection Party reflects the international ideologies of the time; however, when asked how the name was derived, one senior HRPP MP said that it was a catchphrase in Sämoa arising out of the Tupuola Government's undermining of people's rights.[71] Moreover, the late Prime Minister, Tofilau Eti Alesana, said that the establishment of the HRPP was directly related to the Tupuola Government's 'infringement of the right of the people, especially the rights of the public servants'.[72] The immediate aim of the party was to overthrow the Tupuola Government.[73] Its long-term aim, according to one former prominent HRPP MP, was to prevent Tupuola from ever again becoming the Prime Minister of Sämoa.[74]

The official objectives of the party are very general:

1. To foster political education and provide leadership necessary to safeguard the rights, liberties, privileges and freedoms of the Sämoan people and individuals; to protect their interests and to secure ... [for] them peace, security and prosperity in their native land; and to provide institutions which promote and guarantee ... [for] them economic, social and political welfare.

2. To uphold the constitution of Western Sämoa.

3.   To encourage and foster amongst the Sämoans collectively and individually the spirit of independence, self-reliance, industry, assertiveness and acquisitiveness.

4.   To demand and guarantee the protection of the vital Sämoan interests by means of appropriate constitutional safeguards in the constitution of Western Sämoa or any future constitution of any government to be established in Western Sämoa.

5.   To devise the means of informing the … [Sämoan] people by means of political education or otherwise about the international or local body politics, and finer and worthy aspects of other cultures, arts, music, philosophy, economics and other disciplines.

6.   To promote and encourage the means of improving the living standards of the people of Sämoa.

7.   To do all such other lawful things as are incidental or conducive to the attainment of the foregoing … [objectives].

Women also had an influence on shaping the party. The wife of one former MP said that having always accompanied her husband to the HRPP's caucus meetings at Vaivase, she became tired of waiting outside for her husband. She and the wives of the other MPs therefore decided to organise the women's section of the party. At the time, she was reading the book by PNG's Chief Minister, Michael Somare, *Sana: An Autobiography of Michael Somare*, on how he had organised the Pangu Party. Somare's book gave her and the other women ideas on how to strengthen the organisation of the HRPP. Not only did the women conduct numerous fundraising activities for the party, they helped win over to the party the support of elected MPs and intending candidates through their spouses.[75]

The HRPP's constitution established the party's organisational structures and their respective functions. Elected every year at the party's annual general meeting (AGM), the executive committee comprises the president (the leader of the parliamentary caucus), vice-president (caucus member), secretary (not a caucus member), treasurer (caucus member), six members appointed by caucus, one non-caucus member each from Upolu and Savaii Islands and one representative of women (*HRPP Constitution,* Art.7.a[i–vii]). All party policies are formulated by the executive committee but have to be approved at the AGM. They are made available to constituencies before by-elections and general elections (Art. 3). The constitution also provides for the establishment of committees such as those for fundraising, policy and planning, campaigning and education, women, youths and membership. The president and leader of the party can be present in meetings of all the committees (Art. 6). Membership of the party is open to all people aged 18 years and over, who have paid an initial $WST2 registration fee and $WST5 every year thereafter (Art. 4).

For a long time, Sämoan parties relied solely on their own members and donations for funding. Generally, all parties were reluctant to publicise the names of their donors as this was one of the conditions under which financial and other means of support were given to them. Recently, the Government budget has allocated a total of $WST100,000 for the support of party offices. That amount is divided between the parties on the basis of the number of parliamentary members each has. Given that in the present Parliament about two-thirds of its members are HRPP MPs, the bulk of present government funding for political parties goes to the Government party, the HRPP.

Party campaign strategies

Party campaigns can be divided into two general categories: the collective party campaign and the individual candidate's personal campaign. For an example of an individual's personal campaign, see So'o 1998a.[76] Examples of party campaign strategies, however, are given here.

In the 1982 general elections, the names and photographs of HRPP candidates were published in a party statement, thereby making it the first post-independence political party to utilise modern campaign tactics. For the first time, parliamentary candidates were made known to the public. The HRPP declared that its aim was to change the Government.[77] In 1985, the HRPP adopted the practice of including not only the photographs of its candidates in the party's official campaign statement, but the programs and projects the party intended to complete in the next term. For example, its 1991 election manifesto stated its policies on roads, water, the country's electrification program, wharves, communication, town beautification, agriculture, education, hospitals, environment, sports development, tourism and other revenue-earning industries, women, old-age pensions and reconstruction of houses damaged by Cyclone Ofa. Because copies of this document were distributed throughout most parts of the country by the HRPP candidates and their supporters, a substantial majority of the public had a good idea of who the candidates were and what the party intended to do.

Although the CDP and SNDP, in 1985 and 1988 respectively, adopted the practice of publicising the names of their parliamentary candidates and their programs, neither party included the photographs of its members in their party statements. The reasons for this are not clear. Perhaps, these parties were not as well organised (in terms of having a party constitution and other necessary party regulations with which to discipline party members) and did not have enough funds for such activities. Or perhaps they suspected that the HRPP was more popular among the people, hence identifying their candidates would not help the party's cause. Whatever the reasons, the fact that a substantial majority of voters did not know who the parties' candidates were probably contributed to their lack of success at the polls. In 1991, at the launch of its manifesto, the SNDP invited all its candidates who were present to line up at the front of the hall so that members of the public could see who they were. About 400 people were present and most of them were SNDP supporters. The party campaign strategies given above have generally remained unchanged.[78]

Conclusion

The nature of the party system and the manner in which Sāmoan political parties have developed are in part a reflection of the Sāmoan context. For example, the selection of candidates for elections, the campaign strategies adopted and some of the factors that contributed to the emergence of the party system, contain elements of Sämoa's traditional political culture. On the other hand, the emergence of the party system also lends credence to the *modernisation* theory of the origin of political parties espoused by Labalombara and Weiner. Duverger's thesis that political parties originate within Parliament is also proven in the case of Sämoa.

Despite some of the politically stinging criticisms against political parties and the party system, it seems clear that these institutions of democracy are here to stay. Ironically, some of the staunchest critics of political parties and the party system have in the end reversed their original positions and formed their own parties. Their change of view follows the realisation that to have any hope of winning government, they must form political parties. The Government, on the other hand, has found it politically useful that it has been able to utilise the party system to get some of its controversial policies through Parliament. The issue of the Executive becoming so powerful that Parliament feels powerless to control it remains a problem for which the constitutional experts will have to find solutions. Meanwhile, the party system and democracy in general are becoming entrenched in Sämoa even if they are still not fully endorsed by a substantial section of the local population.

Footnotes

1   *The Constitution of the Independent State of Sämoa* (Constitution). 1962.
2   Parliament passed this amendment on November 28, 1991.
3   *Sämoa Electoral Act.* 1963. 5[1].
4   So'o, A. 1996. 'O le fuata ma lona lou: Indigenous institutions and democracy in Western Sämoa.' PhD Thesis, The Australian National University. pp.158–65.
5   The other three of these titles are *Tupua Tamasese* (which at the time was held by Mea'ole, who was a Joint Head of State), *Mälietoa* (which is still held by Tanuamfili II, who was Joint Head of State with Tupua Tamasese Mea'ole before the latter died in April 1963), and *Tuimaleali'ifano* (who held the post of Deputy Head of State). These four titles are called *Tama-a-aiga*, literally, 'Sons of the Families'. *Tama-a-aiga* has been translated as 'Royal Sons' because they are the sons of Sämoa's royal lineages that have survived to modern times.
6   So'o, op. cit. p. 163.
7   Ale, L. L. I. 1990. 'The development of political parties in Western Sämoa.' An unpublished essay in the author's possession. p. 6.
8   *Sämoa Times,* February 13, 1970.
9   *Pacific Islands Monthly,* April 1970. p. 50; Davidson, J. W. 1967. *Sämoa mo Sämoa: The Emergence of the Independent State of Western Sämoa.* Melbourne: Oxford University Press. p. 428.
10   *Sämoa Hansard.* 1970. Vol. I. p. 7.
11   This was the same Fuimaono who had moved a motion of no confidence against Matä'afa in the previous Parliament.
12   *Pacific Islands Monthly,* April 1970. p. 51.
13   So'o, op. cit. pp. 1972–3.
14   *Sämoa Hansard.* 1973. Vol. I. pp. 5–6.
15   *Sämoa Hansard.* 1975. Vol. I. p. 11.
16   So'o, op. cit. pp. 180–1.
17   *Sämoa Hansard,* 1976, Vol. I. p.14.
18   So'o, op. cit. pp. 185–6.

19   *Sämoa Hansard.* 1976. Vol. I. p. 14.
20   *Sämoa Times*, February 16, 1979.
21   *Sämoa Hansard.* 1979. Vol. I. p. 7.
22   Ibid,.p. 10.
23   *Pacific Islands Monthly*, April 1980; *Savali*, November 13, 1979.
24   von Beyme, Klaus. 1985. *Political Parties in Western Democracies*. New York: St Martin's Press. p. 15.
25   Duverger, M. 1954. *Political Parties: Their Organization and Activity in the Modern State*. Cambridge: University Printing House. p. xxiv.
26   Macridis, R. C. 1967. 'Introduction: The history, functions, and typology of parties.' In R. C. Macridis (ed.), *Political Parties: Contemporary Trends and Ideas*. New York, Evanston, London: Harper & Row Publishers. p. 9.
27   Ale, op. cit. p. 4.
28   *Sämoa Times*, February 27, 1970.
29   *Sämoa Hansard.* 1970. Vol. I. p. 14.
30   *Minutes of the Working Committee on the Constitution.* February 3. 1959.
31   LaPalombara, J. and M. Weiner. 1966. 'The origin and development of political parties.' In J. LaPalombara and M. Weiner (eds), *Political Parties and Political Development,* Princeton: Princeton University Press. p. 19.
32   *Sämoa Hansard.* 1976. Vol. I. p. 11.
33   LaPalombara and Weiner, op. cit. pp. 19–21.
34   *Sämoa Times*, October 11, 1982.
35   Ibid. September 24, 1982.
36   Ibid. December 3, 1982.
37   Ibid. February 8, 1985.
38   *Western Sämoa Gazette*, 14 [3], March 2, 1985.
39   So'o, op. cit. p. 205.
40   *Sämoa Times*, March 22, 1985.
41   Ibid. March 15, 1985.
42   *Sämoa Hansard,* 1985. Vol. I. pp. 2–3.
43   So'o, op. cit. pp. 416–17.
44   *Sämoa Hansard.* 1985. Vol. I. p. 363.
45   *Observer*, March 13, 1988; *Sämoa Times*, April 8, 1988.
46   *Western Sämoa Gazette*, 9 [3], March 9, 1979; 14 [2], February 7, 1985.
47   Ale, op. cit. p. 18.
48   *Observer*, April 3, 1988.
49   Ale, op. cit. p. 18; *Sämoa Times*, March 4, 1988; *Observer*, March 2, 1988.
50   *Observer*, March 16, 1994.
51   Ibid. March 16, 1994.
52   *Savali*, June 28, 1995.
53   *Sämoa Newsline*, March 23, 1996.
54   Ibid.
55   Quoted in *Observer*, April 10, 1996.
56   *Sämoa Newsline,* March 24, 1996.
57   *Observer*, March 23, 1988.
58   Ibid. April 10, 1991.
59   So'o, A. 1998. 'Sämoa political review.' *The Contemporary Pacific: A Journal of Island Affairs*, Vol. 10, No. 1. pp. 222–30, at p. 223.
60   So'o, A. 2002. 'Sämoa political review.' *The Contemporary Pacific: A Journal of Island Affairs*, Vol. 14, No. 1. pp. 224–36, at p. 224.
61   Muli'aumaseali'i, S. 2001. *Report of the Commission of Inquiry on Sämoa's Electoral Act 1963 and Its Amendments*. Apia: Government Printing Press.
62   'Report of the Parliamentary Electoral Review Committee.' *Parliamentary Paper 2002/2003*, No. 52. p. 7.
63   Ibid.

64   Ibid. pp. 7–8.
65   Author's personal communication with Mase To'ia Alama [Clerk of Parliament], August 3, 2004.
66   *Standing Orders of Parliament*, 1997, 19.2.
67   Members occupying the other two seats of Parliament are an exception to the rule as they represent those who have opted out of Sämoan customary rights to ownership of land and *matai* titles. MPs occupying those seats and those who vote them into Parliament do not hold *matai* titles. They are registered on the Individual Voters Roll.
68   *Minutes of the Working Committee on the Constitution*, March 21, 1960.
69   This act was repealed in 2003 to increase from two to three years per term of the Head of the Corporation/Ministry.
70   *Sämoa Times*, March 15, 1985.
71   So'o, 1996, op. cit. p. 194.
72   Quoted in *Pacific Islands Monthly*, September 1988. p. 46.
73   *Pacific Islands Monthly*, April 1980. p. 19; *Savali*, November 13, 1979.
74   So'o, 1996, op. cit. p. 193.
75   So'o, 1996, op. cit. p. 197.
76   So'o, A. 1998. 'The price of political campaigning in Sämoa.' In P. Larmour (ed.), *Governance in the Pacific*, Canberra: Asia Pacific Press. pp. 289–304.
77   *Observer*, February 25, 1982.
78   See also So'o, 1996, op. cit. pp. 224–52.

GLOSSARY

ABC	Australian Broadcasting Corporation
ADB	Asian Development Bank
ADV	Alliance for the Development of Vanuatu
ANC	All National Congress (Fiji)
ANU	The Australian National University
ANZUS	Australia, New Zealand and the United States of America (Security Treaty)
AP	Alliance Party (Fiji)
APODETI	Associacao Popular Democratica de Timor
ASDT	Associacao Democratica de Timor
AusAID	Australian Agency for International Development
AV	Alternative-vote System (Fiji)
BBC	British Broadcasting Corporation
CAMV	Conservative Alliance-Matanitu Vanua (Fiji)
CCA	Controller and Chief Auditor (Sämoa)
CDI	Centre for Democratic Institutions
CDP	Christian Democratic Party (Papua New Guinea)
CIP	Cook Islands Party
CNRM	Concelho Nacional da Resistencia Maubere (Timor-Leste)
CNRT	Concelho Nacional da Resistencia de Timor
COIN	Coalition of Independent Nationals (Fiji)
CRP	Comprehensive Reform Programme (Vanuatu)
CSR	Colonial Sugar Refining
DP	Democratic Party (Solomon Islands)
DPSC	Department of Political and Social Change (The Australian National University)
FALINTIL	Forcas Armadas da Libertacao Nacional de Timor Leste
FAP	Fijian Association Party
FC	Front Calédonien (New Caledonia)
FCCI	Fédération des Comités de Co-ordination des Indépendantistes (New Caledonia)
FDP	Fiji Democratic Party
FI	Front Independentiste (New Caledonia)
FIP	Fiji Independent Party
FLNKS	Front de Liberation National Kanak et Socialiste (New Caledonia)

FLP	Fiji Labour Party
FMP	Fren Melanesia Pati (Vanuatu)
FN(NC)	Front National — New Caledonian Chapter
FNP	Fijian National Party
FPI	Frente Politica Interna (Timor-Leste)
Fretilin	Frente Revolucionaria Timor-Leste Independente
FSM	Federated States of Micronesia
FULK	Front Uni de Liberation Kanak (New Caledonia)
GNUR	Government of National Unity and Reconciliation (Solomon Islands)
GP	Grin Pati (Vanuatu)
HoD(s)	Head(s) of Department(s)
HRPP	Human Rights Protection Party (Sämoa)
IDS	International Development Studies (University of Sussex)
IMG	Independent Members' Group (Papua New Guinea)
IPS	Institute of Pacific Studies (University of the South Pacific)
IRI	International Republican Institute
JF	Jon Frum (Party) (Vanuatu)
K	Kina (Papua New Guinea) (currency)
KOTA	Klibur Oan Timor Aswain (Timor-Leste)
LKS	Liberation Kanak Socialiste (New Caledonia)
LPV	Limited Preferential Voting (Papua New Guinea)
MA	Melanesian Alliance (Papua New Guinea)
MANH	Mouvement Autonomiste des Nouvelles-Hebrides (New Caledonia)
MGA	Movement for Greater Autonomy (Papua New Guinea)
MIG	Morobe Independent Group (Papua New Guinea)
MODIPE	Morobe District People's Association (Papua New Guinea)
MP	Member of Parliament
MPP	Melanesian Progressive Party (Vanuatu)
MUF	Melanesian United Front (Papua New Guinea)
MV	Matanitu Vanua (Fiji)
NA	Namangki Aute (Vanuatu)
NADEPA	National Democratic Party (Solomon Islands)
NAL	National Alliance (Papua New Guinea)
NAM	Non-Aligned Movement (Vanuatu)
NAPSI	National Action Party of Solomon Islands
NCA	National Community Association (Vanuatu)
NCDS	National Centre for Development Studies (The Australian National University)
NCP	National Coalition Partnership (Solomon Islands)
NFP	National Federation Party (Fiji)
NFP	Nationalist Front for Progress (Solomon Islands)
NGM	Nagriamel (Vanuatu)

NHNP	New Hebrides National Party
NLUP	New Labour Unity Party (Fiji)
NP	New Guinea National Party
NPG	Nationalist Pressure Group (Papua New Guinea)
NRA	National Representative Assembly (Vanuatu)
NUP	National United Party (Vanuatu)
NUS	National University of Sämoa
NVTLP	Vanua Tako-Lavo Party (Fiji)
OLIPPC	Organic Law on the Integrity of Political Parties and Candidates (Papua New Guinea)
Palika	Parti de Liberation Kanak (New Caledonia)
PAP	People's Action Party (Papua New Guinea)
PAP	People's Action Party (Singapore)
PAP	People's Action Party (Vanuatu)
PAP	People's Alliance Party (Solomon Islands)
PD	Partido Democratico (Timor-Leste)
PDC	Partido Democratico Crista (Timor-Leste)
PDI	Indonesian Democratic Party
PDM	People's Democratic Movement (Papua New Guinea)
PDP	People's Democratic Party (Vanuatu)
PIG	Pangu Independent Group (Papua New Guinea)
PNC	People's National Congress (Papua New Guinea)
PNG	Papua New Guinea
PNGFP	Papua New Guinea First Party
PNGP	Papua New Guinea Party
PNT	Partido Nacionalsta Timorense
PPP	United Development Party (Indonesia)
PPP	People's Progress Party (Papua New Guinea)
PPP	People's Progressive Party (Solomon Islands)
PPP	People's Progressive Party (Vanuatu)
PPT	Partido Povu Timor
PR	Proportional representation
PSC	Parti Socialiste Calédonien (New Caledonia)
PSD	Partido Social Democrata (Timor-Leste)
PSP	People's Solidarity Party (Papua New Guinea)
PST	Partido Socialista de Timor
RAMSI	Regional Assistance Mission to Solomon Islands
RDO	Rassemblement Démocratique Océanien (New Caledonia)
RENETIL	Resistencia Nacional de Estudantes de Timor Leste
RPCR	Rassemblement pour la Calédonie dans la République (New Caledonia)
RPR	Rassemblement pour la Republique (New Caledonia)
RSPAS	Research School of Pacific and Asian Studies (The Australian

	National University)
SAPP	Sämoa All People Party
SAS	Solomone Ago Sagefenua (Solomon Islands)
SCPP	Sämoa Conservative Progressive Party
SDL	Soqosoqo Duavata ni Lewenivanua (Fiji)
SDP	Sämoa Democratic Party
SDUP	Sämoa Democratic United Party
SIAC	Solomon Islands Alliance for Change
SIBC	The Solomon Island Broadcasting Corporation
SIG	Solomon Islands Government
SIUNP	Solomon Islands United National Party
SIUP	Solomon Islands United Party
SLP	Sämoa Liberal Party
SNDP	Sämoan National Development Party
SNP	Sämoan National Party
SNTV	Single non-transferable vote (Vanuatu)
SSGM	State, Society and Governance in Melanesia Project (The Australian National University)
SUIPP	Sämoa United Independents Political Party
SVT	Soqosoqo ni Vakavulewa ni Taukei (Fiji)
TPA	Tumua ma Pule ma 'Äiga (Sämoa)
TSFPP	Temokalasi Sämoa Fa'amatai — the Sämoan Democracy of *Matai*
UC	Union Calédonien (New Caledonia)
UCNH	Union Communautes des Nouvelles Hebrides
UDC	Uniao Democratica Crista (Timor-Leste)
UDP	United Democratic Party (Papua New Guinea)
UDT	Uniao Democratica Timorense
UMNC	Union Multiraciale de Nouvelle-Calédonie (New Caledonia)
UMNO	United Malays National Organisation (Malaysia)
UMP	Union of Moderate Parties (Vanuatu)
UN	United Nations
UNCT	Une Nouvelle-Calédonie Pour Tous (New Caledonia)
UNIFEM	United Nations Fund for Women
UNMISET	United Nations Mission Support in East Timor
UNTAET	United Nations Transitional Administration in East Timor
UO	Union Oceanien (New Caledonia)
UP	United Party (Papua New Guinea)
UP	United Party (Solomon Islands)
UPM	Union Progressiste Melanesien (New Caledonia)
UPP	United People's Party (Fiji)
UPNG	University of Papua New Guinea
USIPA	United Solomon Islands Party
USP	University of the South Pacific

USTKE	Union Syndicalist des Travailleurs Kanak et Exploité (New Caledonia)
VAGST	Value Added Goods and Services Tax (Sämoa)
VANWIP	Vanuatu Women in Politics
VAT	Value Added Tax (Vanuatu)
VCC	Vanuatu Cultural Centre
VKB	Vola ni Kawa Bula (Fijian genealogy)
VLV	Veitokani ni Lewenivanua Vakarisito (Fiji)
VMF	Vanuatu Mobile Force
VP	Vanua'aku Pati (Vanuatu)
VRP	Vanuatu Republican Party
VULCAN	Luganville Land Corporation and Vila Urban Land Corporation (Vanuatu)
WDP	Western Democratic Party (Fiji)
WSLP	Western Sämoa Labour Party
WUF	Western United Front (Fiji)
$WST	Western Sämoa Tala (currency)

BIOGRAPHIES

Alaine Chanter is the Chair of Divisional Research Degrees in the Division of Communication and Education at the University of Canberra. She is also Program Convenor of the University's Bachelor of Arts degree. She teaches in a diverse range of subjects in the core communication program at the School of Creative Communication. Her research focus is the politics of cultural identity. She has published in this area in several international journals. More recently, this focus has developed into research on the manner in which progressive politics is being infused by postmodern culture.

Alumita L. Durutalo is a PhD candidate in the Pacific and Asian History Division of the Research School of Pacific and Asian Studies at The Australian National University. She is writing a thesis on 'Fijian Political Thinking: Dissent and the Formation of Political Parties (1960–1999)'. Alumita teaches in the Department of History and Politics at the University of the South Pacific, Laucala Campus, Suva, Fiji.

Jon Fraenkel is a Senior Research Fellow in Governance at the Pacific Institute of Advanced Studies in Development and Governance at the University of the South Pacific. He is author of *The Manipulation of Custom: From uprising to intervention in the Solomon Islands* (Victoria University Press and Pandanus Books, 2004). His research and publications focus on the economic history of Oceania, electoral systems and contemporary Pacific politics.

Tarcisius Tara Kabutaulaka is a Fellow at the Pacific Islands Development Program, East-West Center, Honolulu, Hawai'i. Prior to this, he was a lecturer in history and politics at the University of the South Pacific in Suva, Fiji. He has a PhD in political science and international relations from The Australian National University in Canberra. Dr Kabutaulaka comes from the Tasimauri area of Guadalcanal in Solomon Islands.

R. J. May is Emeritus Fellow of The Australian National University and is attached to the State, Society and Governance in Melanesia Project in the Research School of Pacific and Asian Studies. He was formerly a senior economist with the Reserve Bank of Australia and later foundation director of IASER (now the National Research Institute) in Papua New Guinea. In 1976, he was awarded the Independence Medal for services to banking and research in Papua New Guinea.

Michael G. Morgan earned a BA (Hons 1st Class) from the University of Sydney, and a PhD from The Australian National University. At the time of compiling this volume he was the Acting Director of the Centre for Democratic Institutions and a Research Fellow of the Research School of Pacific and Asian Studies at the Australian National University. His current research interests are political culture, governance and representation in Melanesia, with a special interest in cabinet and coalition politics. He has undertaken several consultancies on politics and development policy in Melanesia.

Steven Ratuva is a Fijian political sociologist who gained his PhD from the Institute of Development Studies at the University of Sussex. He was a Fellow at The Australian National University and has been a consultant for a number of international institutions, such as the United Nations Development Program, the International Labour Organisation and the Asian Development Bank. His academic and research interests include affirmative action, peace studies, development, governance and sociopolitical change.

Roland Rich is a Reagan-Fascell Democracy Fellow with the International Forum for Democratic Studies at the National Endowment for Democracy, Washington DC. At the time of compiling and editing this book, he was the Foundation Director of the Centre for Democratic Institutions at The Australian National University. He received his Arts and Law degrees from the University of Sydney and his Masters degree in International Law from The Australian National University. He has served in a number of capacities in the Australian Department of Foreign Affairs and Trade, including positions as Ambassador to Laos, Legal Advisor and Assistant Secretary for International Organisations.

Joao M. Saldanha is Executive Director of the Timor Institute of Development Studies, Dili, Timor-Leste. He lectures at the National University of East Timor, holds a PhD in economics from the Graduate School of International Relations and Pacific Studies at the University of California in San Diego. As a Fulbright Scholar, he has spent time as a visiting scholar at many institutions, including the Harvard Institute for International Development in the US, and The Australian National University. His research interests include economic growth and income distribution, property rights, fiscal and monetary policies, and political institutions.

Asofou So'o is Professor of Samoan Studies and Director of the Centre for Samoan Studies at the National University of Samoa. He graduated with a PhD from the Research School of Pacific and Asian Studies at The Australian National University in 1997. He has published widely on Samoan politics, culture and history and is currently the president of the International Council for the Study of the Pacific Islands.

INDEX